CURRICULUM RESEARCH

IN THE BACKGROUND OF CURRICULUM REFORM

By Lv Lijie

Translated by Cheng Shuang, Zhang Yushuang

This publication was supported by the Shanghai Educational Science Research Project. (Project Number:C2025296)

CURRICULUM RESEARCH

IN THE BACKGROUND OF CURRICULUM REFORM

By Lv Lijie

Translated by Cheng Shuang, Zhang Yushuang

Curriculum Research In the Background of Curriculum Reform

By Lv Lijie

Translation Copyright: © 2025, 2025 by Cheng Shuang, Zhang Yushuang

A Publication by Cosmos Publishing Group

Address: 1312 17th Street Unit #2023, Denver, CO 80202, US

Word Count (for Space of all Pages): 312 Thousand words

First Edition: September, 2025

ISBN: 978-1-967277-40-7

Translator Profile

Cheng Shuang (成爽), the lecturer at the School of Foreign Languages, Shanghai Dianji University. She holds a Master's degree, with research interests in translation teaching and translation technology studies. She has been awarded "March 8th Red Banner Holder" and "May 4th Youth Medal" by Shanghai Dianji University, and has won the Third Prize in the Humanities Category of the 4th Shanghai Young College Teachers Teaching Competition and the First Prize in the Shanghai Dianji University Teaching Methodology Competition.

She has presided over two Shanghai municipal-level research projects, one Education Ministry's Collaborative Education Program with Industry, multiple university-level research projects, with cumulative industry-sponsored funding exceeding 250,000 RMB. Her research has been published in several domestic and international core-indexed journals, including *Contemporary Foreign Language Studies* and *Studies in Educational Evaluation*.

She has participated in the translation of two books, including *Shanghai Through our Eyes*, for which she received a letter of appreciation from the Information Office of Shanghai Municipality. Additionally, she has co-authored one textbook.

Zhang Yushuang（张玉双）, Professor, Ph.D., is a provincial-level Distinguished Teacher and a representative of the Fifth People's Congress of Fengxian District, Shanghai. She currently serves as the Dean of the School of Foreign Languages at Shanghai Dianji University and is an Adjunct Master's Supervisor at the School of Foreign Languages of Shanghai University. Additionally, she holds concurrent positions as Executive Council Member of both the Shanghai International Studies Association and the Shanghai Science and Technology Translation Society. Her primary research focus lies in Foreign Linguistics and Applied Linguistics.

As the lead instructor of a Shanghai Municipal First-Class Undergraduate Course, she has edited over ten textbooks, completed more than twenty provincial and ministerial-level research projects, published over thirty academic papers, and received more than ten provincial and ministerial-level awards.

Contents

Topic One: Curriculum Design and Decision-making

1. The Process and Essence of National Curriculum Policy Formulation

The study of national curriculum design can be viewed from a variety of perspectives. We can see it as the first phase of curriculum development, a large-scale curriculum research process, and also a process of formulating national public policy. After the 1980s, countries with traditionally decentralized curriculum management system, such as the United Kingdom and the United States, successively introduced their national unified curriculum planning and standards to effectively control and guide the education efficiency and quality. Meanwhile, some countries with highly centralized curriculum policy, such as China, France and Russia, adjusted the national curriculum policy function and limited the power of national curriculum policy to aspects such as the macro-planning of curriculum program, value definition and core content selection of subjects. It can be seen that contemporary countries have new understanding and positioning of the national curriculum and different directions of reforms have been adopted in response to respective histories because of the global convergence of the positioning. As a specific type of public policy in modern society, the formulation of national curriculum policy has processes and attributes that are both common and unique to other policies.

Ⅰ. Policy, Educational Policy and Curriculum Policy

What is policy? The American scholar David Easton (1953) has ever defined it as the authoritative allocation of values for a society. In other words, as a behavioral process with the government being the main body, policy readjusts and distributes the social values in response to some of the public problems in society to achieve the purpose of interest coordination and social development. Since the allocation of policies in modern society is not limited to property and interests in the economic field but also includes rights, obligations, responsibilities, respect, order, etc. in public affairs, the research object is often referred to as public policy in policy research. The efficacy of public policy lies in the social distribution of values and there are bound to be situations where this distribution responds to the needs of some people while to the detriment of others. Therefore, the rationality of the authoritative allocation of public policy lies in achieving the balance of values among different interest groups that is most conducive to social stability and development and solving social problems caused by the imbalance of interests and values. In the 1950s, when policy science began to develop, Harold Lasswell, a founding figure of policy science in the US, defined it as a discipline that explains the process of policy formulation and implementation, and is concerned with collecting data and providing explanations for policy issues in specific periods. Research in this period focused on the integration of methods such as operations research, system analysis, linear programming, and cost-benefit analysis on the basis of quantitative research, regarding policy formulation as a rational process and exploring the optimal decision-making mode in it. In the 1960s, there was a paradigm revolution in sociological methodology, and the questioning of absolute rationality was also manifested in the interpretation of the policy formulation process. Herbert A. Simon was a representative of this period. He believed that absolutely rational policy decisions were impossible in reality and that a series of difficulties would be encountered in policy formulation. Whose values and goals are decision-making seeking to realize? An organization is not a homogeneous entity, so the value of the organization as a whole may differ from the values of individual members in the organization. In addition, decision-makers cannot possess all information about the decision-making situation, their problem-solving capacity is limited, and the decision-making process is one of bounded rationality. Therefore, Simon put forward the focus of policy decision research. He believed that previous decision-making theories focused on the rationality of decision-making results and paid little attention to the process itself. In fact, decision-making is not just a matter of the last moment but the entire process.[1] This process is not necessarily standardized and orderly, but it is such a process that determines the final result of the policy. In David Easton's work, this decision-making process is regarded as an unobservable black box while in modern policy research, it is this invisible process that is an important link in policy formation and an object of policy research. The British scholar Michael Hill believes that: "Policy process research should be case studies with qualitative methods, while quantitative methods are mainly used to analyze the consequences of policies."[2] He sees the process of policy formation as a political process in which some political subjects always have more legitimate decision-making power than others. Therefore, there exit potential conflicts between the optimal decision-making approach and political subjects with specific powers. Who decides the policy? How is the policy determined? The research on the policy formulation process focuses on analyzing the subject of policy making, their interrelationships and their roles. It demonstrates the agenda of policy decisions, the process of "transaction", the process of administration, and the influence of systems and culture on decision-making, so as to help people understand and justify the policy.

Educational policy also aims to solve public problems of the society, and the target objects are quite extensive. The power subjects are the national political parties and the government, which macroscopically stipulate the development direction of education. Public educational problems will arise when the reality of educational development deviates from the will of the power holders of policy formulation, thus promoting the introduction of new educational policies. Each time a new educational policy is introduced, the development goal, quality standard and public values of education are reoriented

---

1 Piao Zhenzi & Jin Jionglie. *Theories of Policy Formulation*[M]. Jinan: Shandong People's Publishing House, 2005:101.

2 Hill, M. *The Policy Process in the Modern State*[M]. Translated by Zhao Chenggen. Beijing:China Youth Publishing Group, 2004:22.

and guided, and changes are triggered in educational practice, resulting in new orders, standards and behaviors in education. Some scholars in China believe that the connotation of educational policy should be recognized from four aspects, namely, the phenomenal form, the ontological form, the process characteristic and its special nature.[1] The phenomenal form refers to the sum of policy texts of political measures in education field, which implies the purposes and contents of the policy. People with different backgrounds may have different interpretations of the same policy text. The ontological form refers to the distribution of educational benefits. Through policies, educational resources are reallocated among different interest groups, indicating the state's and government's control over the development direction and functional significance of education. The process characteristic refers that educational policy is a dynamic and continuous process of active choice. From the perspective of policy outcomes, educational policy is the result of government choice while from the policy selection process perspective, it is a multi-cooperation game process in which individual and collective choices interact. The special nature of educational policy lies in its public welfare and non-profit nature and services provided are non-commodities. A reasonable educational policy must be premised on respect for the laws and rules of education itself.

Curriculum policy is a specific part of educational policy, which has its own professional content, carrier and operation mode besides sharing the power and meaning of general educational policy. Curriculum policy aims to adjust the deviations between the objectives of school training and the contents and methods of training. When the curriculum policy formulation is carried out by the relevant national authorities, such policy would be a part of general public policy. National curriculum policy can be of different levels and types. For example, macro curriculum policy need to establish the values and norms that

---

1 Liu Fuxing. *Value Analysis to Educational Policy*[M]. Beijing: Educational Science Publishing House, 2003:36.

prescribe and guide the development direction of national curriculum, plan the goals of curriculum arranged by the state, that is, the talent specifications to be achieved through curriculum, as well as the value tendencies and institutional requirements for cultivating talents of these specifications. It is meta-policy related to the curriculum. Specialized curriculum policy is concrete and reflects the particularity of curriculum policy. It stipulates the functional significance of each subject, as well as the content and implementation methods of knowledge. Supporting curriculum policy refers to a series of administrative measures formulated to ensure the effective implementation of macro curriculum policy and specialized curriculum policy. The above three types of policies constitute the system of curriculum policy. Generally speaking, textual or static curriculum policy includes curriculum program, curriculum plan, curriculum standard, curriculum syllabuse, textbook and related supporting or explanatory documents.

II. The Formulation Process of Curriculum Policy

Policy formulation can be understood from two aspects. One holds that it should cover the entire policy process, that is, the implementation, evaluation and revision of policy should all be regarded as a dynamic formulation process. The other believes that policy formulation is the stage of policy formation and planning, relatively independent of policy implementation, feedback and improvement. This paper integrates these two views and sees the formulation of curriculum policy as a continuous process of adjustment. The formation and planning of curriculum policy is a stage in this process with relative independence and is also a process itself with stages and links. In policy research, the policy formulation process is usually divided into three stages: setting the policy agenda, planning the program and legalizing the program.[1]

Stage One: Setting the policy agenda. During this stage, curriculum

---

1 Chen Zhenming. *Policy Science*[M]. Beijing: China Renmin University Press, 1998:212.

problems are investigated and researched and curriculum policies are ensured to target real problems. There are many problems in society that need to be addressed by the government and only some of them are concerned by the government and put on the agenda to be included in the decision-making area. The process of establishing such problems is the process of setting the policy agenda and the process of forming the policy agenda is also the process in which problems are expected to be solved. When curriculum problem enter the policy agenda, there must be significant deviations between the actual state of the curriculum and the development of social life, the needs of people, and the ideals of politicians. Political leaders, by virtue of their position and knowledge, wisdom, theoretical competencies, authority, and practical experience, etc. discover, predict and confirm certain curriculum policy problems and put them on the policy agenda. It can also be educational researchers or subject experts and scholars who discover important problems in their respective studies and, relying on their social influence, make social problems enter the agenda through decision-makers or with the help of the media. Curriculum problems listed on the agenda, regardless of their sources, need empirical research to prove that they are real problems.

Stage Two: Curriculum program planning and formation. Program planning is the process of proposing corresponding solutions or programs based on an analysis and research of curriculum policy problems, which is a period of time and also a process of combining work in different links. This process can be further divided into specific stages. First, clarify the main problems to be adjusted by the curriculum policy, find the gap between the actual state and the expected state and set educational goals formulated by the curriculum policy. Second, collect data and information and formulate policy based on existing research. Third, predict the environment for implementing the program and the possible results. Finally, determine the best program among many alternatives.

Stage Three: Legalizing the curriculum policy. This is a behavioral process in which policy makers implement a series of actions such as consultation, argumentation, review, adoption, approval, signing and promulgation in accordance with legal authorities and procedures to give the policy a legal status. The legalization of curriculum policy comes from a variety of sources. It obtains the support and affirmation from educational experts, scientists and sociologists through argumentation. It can absorb more relevant stakeholders to participate in curriculum policy evaluation and decision-making, strengthen communication and coordination and make decisions understood by a wider range of curriculum users through consultation. Most importantly, curriculum policy acquires binding force with authority and legal effect through direct review and approval by power institution. This link is therefore a prerequisite for policy implementation and is necessary for improving the legalization process of policy formulation.

III. The Essence of the Curriculum Policy Formulation Process

House and Corbett *et al.* believe that in terms of curriculum decision-making, the curriculum policy reform can be analyzed from three aspects: the technical approach, the political approach and the cultural approach of curriculum policy decision-making.[1] The technical approach is a simplified view of curriculum reform that sees the pathway of curriculum policy reform as a replicable and transferable technique that can be completed by professional planners using professional techniques, methods and materials. The political approach of curriculum policy decision-making takes into account various interests involved in curriculum policy reform, such as governments at all levels, teachers, educational administrators and parents of students. Those who view curriculum decision-making as a political approach manage to mobilize and coordinate various conflicting interest groups to make them compromise and

---

1 Tsai Ching-Tien. *Curriculum Policy Decision:Educational Policy Based on National Educational Reform Act*[M]. Taipei: Wu-Nan Book Inc., 2003:34.

accept each other. The cultural approach of curriculum policy decision-making emphasizes that different participants in curriculum policy reform represent different cultural backgrounds and values. These different perspectives of exploration precisely show the complexity of curriculum policy in the formulation process, that is, its formulation is not a simple technical process or a pure technical problem but an issue related to politics and social culture. These complex attributes can be specifically described as follows:

(1) The Formulation of Curriculum Policy Is a Political Process

The fact that curriculum policy has a discourse system different from ideology is a manifestation of the professionalization of modern curriculum policy development. However, curriculum policy, especially national curriculum policy, as a part of national public policy, is inevitably driven, supported and controlled by ideology, which is determined by the ideological function condensed in curriculum and education themselves. In this way, in all stages of curriculum policy formulation, political forces will keep the consistency between curriculum policy and ideology in the forms of instructions, guidance, hints, consultations and approvals. As the most typical representative of the determination of the national curriculum, the United Kingdom, originally lacking a unified national curriculum, carried out large-scale adjustments to its educational policy to clearly serve political purposes and national policy guidelines after the 1980s. After World War II, the United Kingdom experienced sluggish economic growth, a phenomenon known as the British Disease in the world economy. Besides aging industrial structure, large proportion of the state-owned sector and heavy welfare burden, the slow increase of labor productivity was also an important factor. Politicians attributed these problems to the low quality of education. Kenneth Baker, former Secretary of State for Education once said in a speech that the British education system was a monstrosity, lacking centralization and unity compared with France and Germany. He believed that the British curriculum standards were not high enough, particularly demonstrating a lack of curriculum consistency in the 14 - 16 age group. In 1979, the Thatcher government began to reform the British economy and adopted a series of measures to promote economic growth, abandoning the Keynesian economics of expanding government spending and stimulating consumption, which had been practiced since the war to drive economic growth. The core principles of Thatcherism were the free market and state authority. That is, the government on the one hand, enhanced individual freedom of choice, thus creating a society dominated by market forces and on the other hand, carried out large-scale state intervention in the social field, increasingly showing the trend of having authority and centralization. In education, the market economy component was manifested in encouraging school autonomy, treating parents as consumers of education and meeting parents needs for choosing schools. A unified curriculum and unified test measurements not only provided a basis for parental choices but also created the possibility for parents to choose and change schools. After 1997, under the influence of Anthony Giddens, the Blair Labour government took the Third Way between laissez-faire capitalism and the welfare state. Although it began to emphasize equal educational opportunities and the success of all students in all schools in its educational policy, it was in line with the principles of the right-wing Conservative Party in pursuing educational quality and diversity, so problems such as the national curriculum and national test ability grouping still persisted. Promoting educational reform to save the British international status was a common aspiration of both politicians and the public.

(2) Seek Rationality between Democracy and Authority

The public policy in any country has either obvious or potential authority because their main body is the country authoritative institutions. Public policy is legal and need to be enforced. At the same time, since policy is the process of publicizing and legalizing personal interests and values, democracy has become an important value orientation in the formulation of modern public policy. Harold Lasswell believes that policy science is the knowledge about democracy. It involves personal choices and must take the democratic system as a prerequisite[1]. If democracy is abandoned, a policy will no longer be a modern public policy but an imperial edict, the legitimacy of which is maintained from people unconditional worship of the earthly representatives of God. However, what modern society pursues is precisely an order life free from divinity. Order exists on the basis of rules that express the will of different interest subjects and when rules reach a consensus, they become the order that these interest subjects observe and maintain on their own initiative. The formulation of curriculum policy is to formulate common rules about how knowledge is chosen and used, and these rules are expected to become an order. Allowing knowledge holders and users to express their wishes in the policy formulation process is a requirement for the legitimacy of curriculum policy and also a guarantee and prerequisite for its enforceability. In this way, the will of different value stakeholders can be expressed from different perspectives and in different ways. The rationality and legitimacy of policy formulation lie in establishing a mechanism that enables multiple subjects to express themselves. In the process of curriculum policy formulation, policy authority is reduced in the democratic consultations among different value subjects and more autonomous decision-making and disposal powers are given to various professional institutions. However, in the process of attracting different professional groups and personnel to participate in decision-making, the government demonstrates constantly its own authoritative power. As a result, the guidance of government authority to the counter-authority and the authority itself constitute a pair of irreconcilable contradiction, in which curriculum policy is formulated to seek a balance.

(3) The Formation of Curriculum Policy Requires a Procedural Decision-making Mechanism

Public policy is the rule observed by all and once implemented, interests of policy recipients are authoritatively distributed. Therefore, the fairness and

---

1 Chen Zhenming. *Policy Science*[M]. Beijing: China Renmin University Press, 1998:5.

rationality of policy content must rely on the legitimacy of the policy decision-making process. Modern policy science emphasizes that the policy formulation process must be a very important normative behavior with a strict and standardized procedural system. Curriculum policy is also a matter of individuals making authoritative allocations of their own curriculum values and making legal and operable expressions. The formulation of curriculum policy also requires scientific and normative procedures and decision-making bases. Information collection on curriculum policy problems, data processing and analysis and standardized decision-making links and procedures are also guarantees for the fairness and rationality of curriculum policy.

(4) The Formulation of Curriculum Policy Is a Bounded Rational Process of Authoritative Allocation of Values

The formulation of curriculum policy requires a rational procedure, but the results cannot be completely rational. Curriculum policy makers represent political, professional and multiple value subjects, influencing policy formulation through different channels and with different levels of impact, so policy is logically inseparable from interests, conflicts, autocracy or justice. The subjects of curriculum policy are also pluralistic. The difference between the value subject characteristics of curriculum policy and those of general public policy lies in that its value subjects include a considerable number of professionals and its value significance is firstly manifested as a spiritual value, the recognition of professional schools of thoughts and the pursuit of professional interests. Therefore, whether the different value needs of various value subjects are reasonable is even more uncertain in identification. Even facing the same information basis and being in a standardized decision-making agenda, perceptions about curriculum policy will also vary from person to person. Policy is the product of continuous concessions by various value subjects at different stages, so it is the product of the reassembly of various influences and agendas. Inside the government, the policy formulation process is full of temporariness, contingency and bargaining.[1] As a result, the curriculum policy text that people finally see may be unclear and not belong to any of the competing theoretical schools because it is a product of continuous compromises and reconciliations among various interests and can only strive to make relevant interest parties accept, or at least tolerate, both benefits and costs.

(5) The Formulation of Curriculum Policy Is a Closed and Professional Process of Theoretical Materialization

The unique professionalism of curriculum policy is different from that of other public policy and educational policy. That is to say, curriculum policy should not only conform to the national ideology and the laws of education but also integrate the logical relationships of knowledge in each subject with the characteristics of children development and the changes and needs of social culture and social life. Meanwhile, the comprehensive understanding of subjects, children, life, and national development should be transformed into mandatory and authoritative guidance documents for operation and implementation in the education system. Therefore, the formulation of curriculum policy requires long-term, large-scale and multi-dimensional theoretical accumulation as a foundation. Such accumulation is specialized or professional and is impossible to widely absorb public opinions and involve all people in the curriculum planning process like other public policy or educational policy. Due to the professionalism of the problems involved, "it is mainly controlled by experts and seldom interfered by laymen". Therefore, "curriculum decision-making is a matter with strong specialization, closure and professionalism"[2].

---

1 Ball, S. J. *Educational Reform: A Critical and Post-structural Approach*[M]. Translated by Hou Dingkai. Shanghai: East China Normal University Press, 2002:31.

2 Brian, H. *The Curriculum:A Comparative Perspective*[M]. Translated by Zhang Wenjun. Beijing: Educational Science Publishing House, 2001:83.

(6) The Formulation of Curriculum Policy Is a Text, as Well as a System and a Process

The policy will inevitably encounter other realities and other situations during the implementation process, such as constantly disrupted classrooms, shortage of textbooks and classes with multilingual teaching. Some policies can partially change the environment in which we work, but not all aspects. Therefore, a good curriculum policy can only be an accident if it is not supported by a good curriculum policy system.[1] It requires the successive introduction of relevant supporting policies, such as funding supply system, evaluation system, teacher training and management method. Curriculum policy is also a constituent part of the pyramid of larger educational policy and even social public policy, rather than a separate piece or a pile of stone, involving the consistency with other policies. The internal and external correlations of the policy system requires that the formulation of curriculum policy should consider the goal coordination, function coordination and time coordination of curriculum policy in the policy system. Thus, the formulation of curriculum policy does not end with the introduction of the text, but the comprehensive solution of curriculum problems with no contradiction between needs and reality any more. Therefore, after the text is introduced and implemented, feedback on information, and modification, supplementation and adjustment of the policy are necessary links in the formulation of curriculum policy.

[Originally published in *The Process of National Curriculum Design: A Case Study on "New Curriculum" Design of Chinese Basic Education* 2008 (Lv Lijie)]

---

1 Ball, S. J. *Educational Reform: A Critical and Post-structural Approach*[M]. Translated by Hou Dingkai. Shanghai: East China Normal University Press, 2002:35.

2. Procedures and Characteristics of Large-scale Curriculum Design

—A Comparison and Analysis Between China's New Curriculum Design Process and Western Curriculum Design Models

Part One

The new curriculum reform of basic education in China was first planned in 1996. It took five years until the release of the *Outline of Basic Education Curriculum Reform (for Trial Implementation)* and the curriculum standards for all subjects in compulsory education in 2001. The curriculum design process during these five years has formed a history of curriculum research and curriculum design in China.

In 1996, the Department of Basic Education of the State Education Commission signed an international cooperation education project with the United Nations International Children's Emergency Fund, which aimed at understanding the development status of compulsory education in developing countries. With the support of this project, the Department of Basic Education organized a large-scale Investigation on the Implementation Status of the Nine-year Compulsory Education Curriculum Program. In July 1996, the Department of Basic Education organized a project team composed of experts and scholars from six normal universities and China National Academy of Education Sciences to discuss and formulate a plan for a comprehensive investigation on the curriculum implementation in the compulsory education stage across the country, and officially began the investigation in May 1997. This large-scale curriculum investigation involved primary and secondary school students, teachers, principals, parents and other public figures (mainly members of the National Committee of the Chinese People's Political Consultative Conference) in nine provinces across the country and samples were randomly selected from

72 districts (prefecture-level cities) in these nine provinces. The questionnaire was designed around four aspects: the implementation status of curriculum objectives, current status of the educational process, current status and impact of examinations and students academic burden and their experience in school. Principals, teachers, students and parents were asked to view these four aspects from their own perspectives. After the investigation, the project team processed and analyzed the results and formed a report in which a preliminary outline was drawn of the trend of the upcoming basic education curriculum reform in China. On the basis of this report, relevant departments began to draft the guiding documents for a new round of basic education curriculum reform in 1998 and after nearly two years of revisions, the *Outline of Basic Education Curriculum Reform (for Trial Implementation)* was formed, which became the general guiding ideology and the soul of the new curriculum design.

In 1999, the Ministry of Education identified curriculum reform as a key project in the national educational reform and concurrently initiated preparations for the new curriculum design. During this period, anonymous project bidding was a core task which refers to the confirmation of subject standard and the design of each project team as well as the bidding methods for researchers. The development of curriculum standard and related research projects were open for bidding to national education researchers, experts and scholars in relevant fields, teaching and research personnel and teachers. In order to ensure fairness and rationality in project review, the bidding application form was designed into two parts, one for the introduction of the bidder and the other for the argumentation of the project. In the expert review, the part of the researcher's introduction was not provided to the experts, who can only have access to the argumentation part without seeing the applicant's identity. The project leader, identified through the anonymous review, was the main undertaker and the "leading unit" of the project. Members of other units applying for the same project could voluntarily join this project team and the excellent and feasible parts in other projects were also adopted into the formal project team. After extensive argumentation by experts, 18 working groups for curriculum standard development and project teams for new curriculum research were officially established with the participation of hundreds of experts in May and June 2000.

In October 1999, on the basis of these preliminary studies, the development of curriculum standard entered the drafting stage, with the primary link being the preliminary study which means that all curriculum standard project teams had to conduct five special studies. Taking the mathematics group as an example, the following five studies should be included. Study One: Research on the Latest Progress of International Mathematics Curriculum Reform; Study Two: Evaluation of the Current Implementation Status of Domestic Mathematics Curriculum; Study Three: Research on the Psychological Development Laws of Primary and Secondary School Students and Its Interrelation with the Mathematics Curriculum; Study Four: Social Development and the Prediction and Analysis of Its Needs for Mathematics; Study Five: Development of Modern Mathematics and Its Impact on the Mathematics Curriculum in Primary and Secondary Schools. The curriculum standard for each subject was formulated on the basis of the preliminary study.

Members of each group and team came from all over the country so they needed to gather once a month, each time for about one week. During the week, more than 200 experts participating in the new curriculum development needed to follow the unified deployment of the Ministry of Education, receive the feedback on the standard writing, spend more time on exchanges and discussions within the project research team, and at the same time, report the progress of the project to the Ministry of Education. Members of the development team had different professional backgrounds and the curriculum designers from universities were divided into subject experts and curriculum experts. Among them, curriculum experts generally came from normal universities and educational research institutes with pedagogical, psychological or curriculum theory background. Subject experts were generally researchers specializing in subjects and majors in normal and ordinary universities. Teaching and research staff and primary and secondary school teachers among the expert members were also backbones in their respective positions, and some were nationally renowned special-grade senior teachers. Researchers from publishing houses were also included in many curriculum standard groups for their familiarity with China past and current curriculum and textbook.

After the drafts for each subject were formed, large-scale social consultation activities were organized to three types of target audience. First, people from the educational field and all walks of life, including 67 senior leaders (chairpersons, general managers, chief engineers, chief economists) from large state-owned enterprises, Sino-foreign joint ventures, wholly foreign-owned enterprises and private technology enterprises. Second, front-line teachers. For example, after the draft of the mathematics curriculum standard was formed, opinions were sought in some provinces, and 138 front-line teachers were recorded as participating in the discussion. Third, academicians of the Chinese Academy of Sciences, academicians of the Chinese Academy of Engineering, literary and historical scholars, artists and education experts who reviewed the curriculum standard for each subject. The experimental draft of the curriculum standard for full-time compulsory education and that for ordinary senior high school were officially announced in 2001 and 2003 respectively.

The aim of the new curriculum design is to establish an ideal curriculum system to influence and promote the curriculum culture of China's basic education and even the development of education. The curriculum design is a process of selecting, arranging and optimizing all relevant factors with the curriculum ideal as the goal. For the design of the new curriculum, these factors include: objective factors, namely curriculum concepts, objectives, contents, implementation methods, evaluation methods, curriculum resources, teaching materials, etc.; instrumental factors, namely designers, time, space, funds, etc.; procedural factors, namely text production, promotion and implementation, social publicity, text revision, teacher training, etc. The process of designing the new curriculum has always been accompanied by the overall planning of these factors and directed towards the established ideal, so it is a process of action centered around the goal. Meanwhile, the new curriculum design is not a mechanical or dehumanized but a generative process full of uncertainties.

Changes in personnel, conflicts of views and changes in time and funds often occur, so the design for the project design has also to be constantly adjusted. The description of this process forms a research process description diagram:

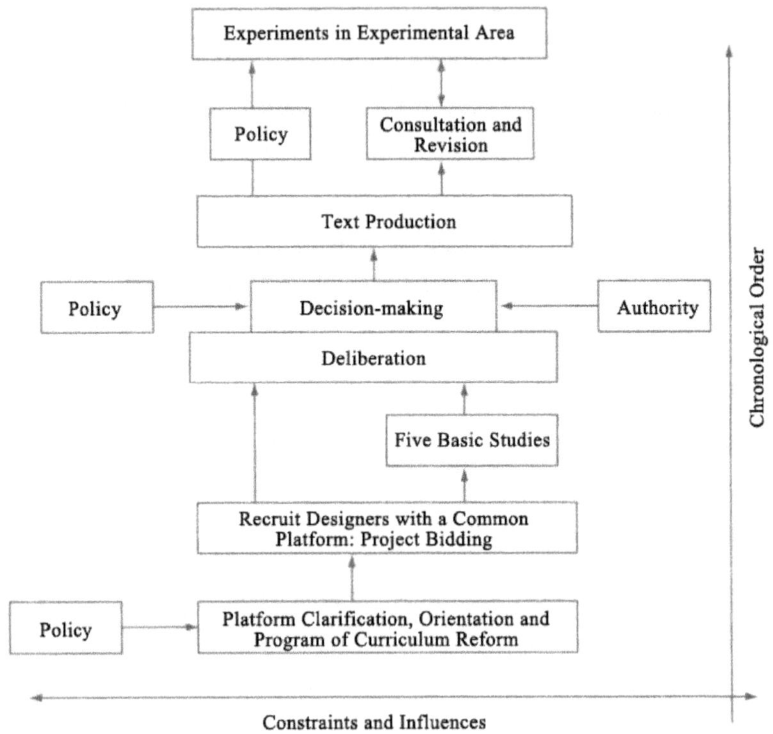

Figure 1-1 Process Description Diagram of New Curriculum Design

Part Two

In the 1960s and 1970s of the 20th century, Decker F. Walker, an American curriculum scholar, extracted some valuable information about curriculum design by tracking and describing the process of large-scale curriculum design.

In the late 1960s, Walker participated in the supervision and evaluation of the Kettering Art Project. During the three years, he recorded in detail the actions, debates and decisions of the curriculum design team. By analyzing their meeting recordings and collecting materials, Walker isolated the important elements in the curriculum design process and described the natural process of curriculum design by comparing many important national curriculum designs in the United States in the 1960s and 1970s.

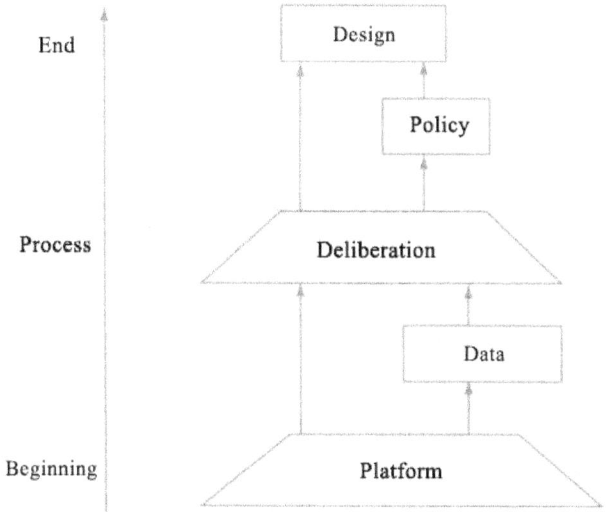

Figure 1-2 Walker's Curriculum Design Model

Walker explained several key concepts among them. *Platform* refers to beliefs, theories, aims and objectives procedures. He believed that each member of the team brought their own beliefs and values to curriculum development activities, so the most fundamental step was to let everyone participate, express, discuss or even argue about what the program was exactly. Walker used the term *platform* to provide a platform or foundation for future discussions. The process through which designers debated contentious issues, generated alternatives, weighed the pros and cons of these alternatives, and made a choice is known as *deliberation*. This was a confusing and time-consuming stage and the value of deliberation would be manifested if the issues could be clarified through deliberation. Deliberation did not come out of thin air but was based on consensus about beliefs, theories, aims and procedures. When it was impossible to make a choice based on platforms, some empirical *data* had to be used to illustrate one's own views. *Design* refers to decision-making process during the deliberation phase that leads to final action.

Part Three

By comparing Walker's description of the curriculum design model with the process of new curriculum design in China, it can be found that there are many consistencies in elements and links between the two research procedures:

1. Curriculum designers should have a basic common curriculum ideal and curriculum view, that is, a common curriculum philosophy and orientation of curriculum change. In the new curriculum, the grasp of the "platform" is achieved through the publicity of the guiding ideology of curriculum reform and the project bidding. When designers start to design the curriculum standard, there must already exit a curriculum philosophy concept, whose advancement serves as the driving force for promoting change. Curriculum change, as a controlled social activity, must and should be philosophically in the hands of the initiators and organizers of the change because curriculum design is not only the selection of learning content but also a social value orientation, a platform that all those involved in the reform project should hold or at least understand. This orientation is determined by the purpose of the change and serves as a necessary prerequisite for the conduct of curriculum design, a starting point both in time and logic.

2.There should be some accumulation of empirical research. Each development group that win the bids should have some foundation in empirical researches and all curriculum standard designers are required to participate in the Five Basic Studies, manifesting that this curriculum design is an emprical research. The five studies are a process of deeply understanding the curriculum orientation and curriculum view, or in other words, a process of purposefully guiding the standard designers to think about the direction of curriculum change at the subject level, thereby further generating consensus. Moreover, the empirical experience provided by these basic researches is the best basis for designers to argue when disagreements arise. Just as Walker said: when it is impossible to make a choice based on the platform, some empirical data should be used to illustrate one's own views. The platform and concepts are theoretical understandings and judgments, while curriculum design is precisely to make choices and considerations in quantity and degree for countless real curriculum situations. In addition, empirical research is to analyze and study the real structure and elemental characteristics of the object with intuitive judgement, providing a basis for value weighing and judgment in specific curriculum decisions.

The chart on this page only represents a thinking tendency rather than the logical steps of behavior. The five studies, as an intertwined and overall information base, are reflected in the designers' knowledge background either implicitly or explicitly when designers express their subject claims. There is not necessarily a significant one-to-one cause-and-effect relationship between the basic information and specific design views.

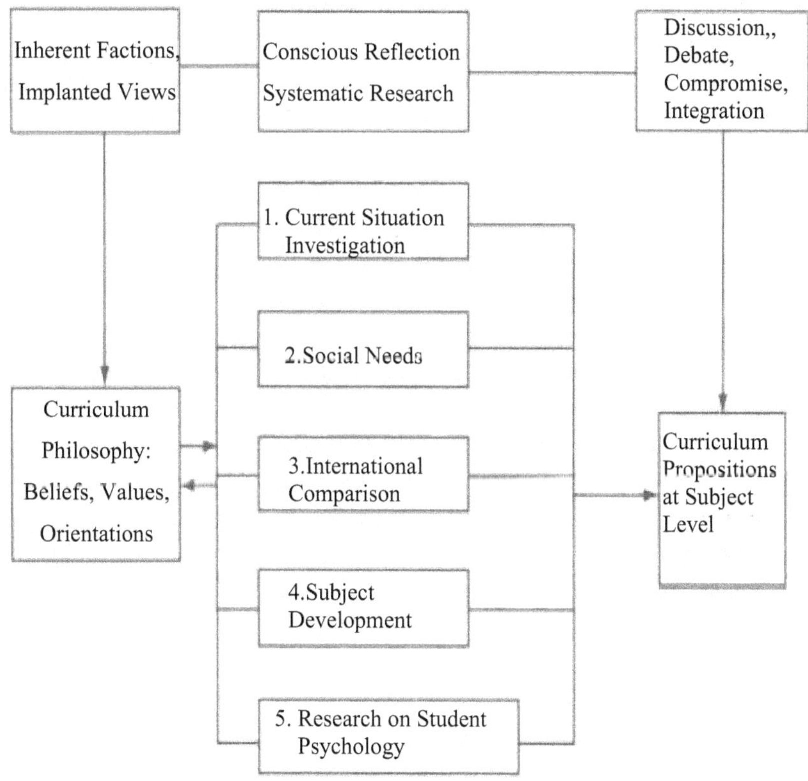

Figure 1-3 Five Basic Studies in New Curriculum Development

3. The discussion method of deliberation is essential. Curriculum design

requires multi-dimensional thinking on issues such as the knowledge system, social needs, student characteristics and curriculum conditions in different regions. Curriculum designers are faced with a heterogeneous and complex object and when we try to grasp such an object, the levels and angles of any viewpoints are relative and limited, and of course, uniquely effective. Limitations and effectiveness are prerequisites for each other and exist dialectically in people's cognitive abilities. That is to say, in communication and statement, while each person provides the directivity and uniqueness of his or her own understanding, he or she also gives the research object prejudices and limitations. Therefore, designers need to have dialogue and communication on a diversified basis, not only listen to viewpoints from different perspectives with an open mind but also call for heterogeneous perspectives and evaluation standards, and at the same time, maintain a positively complementary and dialogical relationship among heterogeneous perspectives.

4.The results of decision-making are modified by various factors such as policy. Curriculum decision-making is affected by many factors, especially for large-scale curriculum design, the differences arising from deliberation are ultimately influenced more by decision-makers. Walker has ever mentioned that when the deliberation group lacks the power of decision-making and implementation, the viewpoints obtained through deliberation can only influence curriculum implementers to a certain extent, and on the other hand, deliberation can be a waste of time if it ignores the wishes of curriculum decision-makers. China's new curriculum is a large-scale national curriculum design and the organizers are the national education authorities, so the regulation and control of the curriculum design process is more significant. There are many other factors that influence curriculum design and Clark has summarized ten kinds: the public, political leaders, textbook publishers, examination intermediaries, the media, personnel in colleges and universities, education professional groups, central government departments, teacher groups and individual teachers. Besides the personnel factors listed by Clark, social trends, social changes especially educational changes, international relations, national politics and the overall development level of social production are all direct or indirect forces affecting curriculum decision-making. Perhaps some forces do not subjectively intend to exert such influence, but the curriculum is indeed the product of the interaction among these forces which constrain each other to influence curriculum decision-making. As Clark said: "Each influencing force has to be restrained by other forces, decision-makers influence each other and the result is that the final decision deviates from everyone's original intention. Therefor, curriculum is a political issue rather than a technical issue."

Part Four

The Western scholar Marsh has analyzed and evaluated the characteristics of this large-scale curriculum design in his work:

This large-scale curriculum design has its own advantages and disadvantages in curriculum change and development. The advantages are as follows: (1) It provides a delivery system for unified curriculum standards, improves the uniformity of educational requirements, advocates curriculum standards and improves the fairness in the allocation of scarce resources; (2) It saves time, management costs, energy and money without detailed analysis of the need of each school; (3) It ensures continuity as policies can last for many years, ensuring that students and parents can enjoy the same policies when students transfer schools; (4) It concentrates professional advantages to create something valuable with effective funds under the guidance of expert groups; (5) It ensures a close connection between schools and the education system so that education departments can control each school and require schools to achieve certain goals. The disadvantages are as follows: (1) It hardly improves teachers' initiative and teachers just work like machines without being considered by the curriculum plan; (2) It lacks implementation strategies with insufficient attention given to providing school-level implementation strategies, and personnel at the education center do not participate in the implementation supervision; (3) It raises curriculum standards and easily leads to narrow curriculum goals by assuming that every school is the same; (4) It relies on rational models, assuming that school personnel all want to implement centralized development policies.

The national curriculum design has the ability and funds to organize large-scale and professional curriculum design teams. Marsh has already summarized the advantages and disadvantages of expert-designed curriculum very well and it is particularly important to enrich the roles and levels of team members and adopt the deliberation method. Through Marsh's reminder, we realize that the common challenge of this large-scale curriculum reform is to how to improve teachers' initiative, to provide curriculum implementation strategies at the school level, and to make school personnel implement real changes.

[Originally published in *New Curriculum Research (Educational Research and Experiment)* 2005(4) (Lv Lijie)]

3. Popularization of the Human Researches and the Chinese Curriculum Reform in Senior High Schools

In 2004, the Chinese curriculum reform in senior high school entered the experimental stage and to date, it has been implemented in 15 provinces and municipalities. Great attention from the state, local governments, schools, teachers and parents has been paid to this reform. How to better promote the curriculum reform and avoid it from becoming a mere formality is a problem that needs to be considered and solved. From the perspective of new curriculum promotion, this paper conducts a comparative analysis of the promotion of the American curriculum reform program "The Human Researches" in the United Kingdom and the promotion of China's new high school curriculum, hoping to draw some experiences and lessons from it, so as to reflect on the promotion of China's new high school curriculum and make it promoted and implemented better and more profoundly.

I. "The Human Researches" Curriculum Program

In 1957, after the Soviet Union successfully launched the first artificial satellite, Americans shifted their focus to education, believing that education was responsible for the backwardness of American science and technology. In 1958, the United States promulgated the *National Defense Education Act*, which affirmed the importance of school education and "The Human Researches" emerged under the trend of the pursuit of excellence. "The Human Researches" is a curriculum reform program in the field of primary school social learning developed by the Cambridge Education Development Center in Massachusetts, USA, under the guidance of top scholars such as Bruner and Barlex in the 1960s.

The promotion of "The Human Researches" in the United Kingdom originated from a seminar discussion in 1970 between Stenhouse and Daluch and Francis Lincoln, the person in charge of the promotion of "The Human Researches" in the United States. Coincidentally, "The Human Researches" also conformed to the values and principles of the United Kingdom at that time.

Stenhouse and others went to the United States to receive training and started the promotion of "The Human Researches" in the United Kingdom from 1970 to 1987. Its promotion in the United Kingdom can be regarded as a model of the curriculum promotion, leaving us with a lot of experiences and also many points worthy of thinking.

(1) The Curriculum Aims of "The Human Researches"

"The Human Researches" transformed Bruner's educational concepts into curriculum aims, with a key emphasis on the idea that education is a process. It used the subject structure as a tool to assist students in exploring important issues during the learning process, advocates the inquiry-based learning method, encourages students to have discussions, and establishes an innovative role for teachers to serve as resources for student learning.

(2) The Contents of "The Human Researches" Curriculum Reform

"The Human Researches" curriculum program challenged the traditional wisdom regarding previous subjects and knowledge, bringing about fundamental changes in textbooks, knowledge, learning methods and teaching methods.

"The Human Researches" curriculum program has updated textbooks and produced many supporting resources. The teaching materials used were rich in content, film-based curriculum learning subjects were mainly used and curriculum resources were organized in units. Film equipment and documentary files were based on Bruner's cognitive theory.

In terms of learning methods, "The Human Researches" curriculum program emphasized the knowledge structure and its transfer. Bruner's theory of cognitive development emphasized the process of cognition, the order and sequence of learning materials, and the importance of experience in promoting human development. The program advocated that learning is a process rather than a result, attached importance to the connection between students' existing experiences and external information, promoted discovery learning and emphasized that learning is a dynamic process in which students are active participants. The program put forward higher requirements for teachers. For example, teachers are the guides for students to raise new questions and the providers of learning resources, teaching methods should adapt to students' cognitive development, and "teachers are researchers in classroom teaching".[1]

II. The Promotion Strategies and Reflections on "The Human Researches" Curriculum Program

Center for Applied Research in Education at the University of East Anglia was responsible for the training of the promotion of "The Human Researches" in the United Kingdom. In particular, Stenhouse and Daluch had already participated in the promotion of the "Humanities Project" and based on their practical participation experience, they started the 17-year promotion of "The Human Researches" in the United Kingdom.

(1) Basic Concepts of "The Human Researches" Promotion

1. Teachers play an important role in curriculum promotion.

2. New curriculum concepts are learned through inquiry-based training which is non-didactic and enables trainees to obtain their own understanding and recognition of the new curriculum during the training process.

3. Extension workers and teachers adopt a critical attitude. The promotion of "The Human Researches" in the United Kingdom was different from the unquestionable way in its promotion in the United States. Instead, it was regarded as "a hypothesis to be tested" and was adjusted according to the professional literacy level of school teachers in the United Kingdom at that time.

4. Its textbooks were sold only to schools and organizations that received training, in the hope of preserving the integrity of the curriculum.

---

1 Tsai Ching-Tien. *Curriculum Innovation*[M]. Taipei: Wu-Nan Book Inc., 2006.

(2) The Promotion Strategy of "The Human Researches" - A Teacher-centered, Phased, Top-down Approach

The promotion of "The Human Researches" in the Unite Kingdom adopted a teacher-centered model of research, development and diffusion with phased and top-down model to train seed teachers and carry out specific promotion from the center to the periphery[1], spreading its concepts to local schools in the United Kingdom.

1. Give Full Play to the Role of Seed Teachers

Seed teachers were trained firstly, through whom more teachers were helped to identify with and understand the concepts and measures of curriculum reform. Through demonstration and training, more seed teachers were cultivated, forming an inquiry-based training method. In the promotion process, trainees obtained their own understanding through participation, formed their own views, and integrated this adjustment based on understanding with their own teaching practices.

2. Focus on the Practical Problems Encountered by Teachers

The promotion of "The Human Researches" in the United Kindom absorbed the lessons learned from its promotion in the United States, paying more attention to teachers' acceptability and focusing on improving teachers' professional level. It designed a promotion and training program consisting of curriculum concept framework and curriculum resources. In the morning, training personnel and trainees discussed together the teaching concepts and framework of "The Human Researches" curriculum. In the afternoon, they discussed in groups the teaching material resources of the curriculum, found out the relationship between teaching material resources and teaching principles and

---

1 Fullan, M. *Change Forces: Probing the Depths of Educational Reform*[M]. Translated by China National Institute of Education Sciences. Beijing: Educational Science Publishing House, 2004.

methods, and discussed how to apply them to practice.

3. Ensure the Continuous Teacher Training

Teacher training took place mainly in the form of training workshops, both national and local. The national training workshops were held once or twice a year in different places across the country, focusing on helping teachers develop a habit of research and thinking. Local training work was undertaken by a group of teachers from schools or colleges across the United Kingdom who sacrificed their rest time to think about how to improve teaching and assist new teachers who were interested in participating in this plan to learn.

4. Turn Curriculum Promotion into a Conversation

British teachers participating in "The Human Researches" formed a contact network of professional development in education, so that school teachers could have direct face-to-face contact with curriculum extension workers, providing effective communication channels among teachers, between teachers and promoters, enabling the program to be adjusted in a timely manner according to the actual situation and providing guarantees for broader curriculum promotion.

(3) Reflections on the Promotion Strategy of "The Human Researches"

Based on the experience of promoting the "Humanities Project", the promotion of "The Human Researches" in the United Kingdom strengthened the interaction among curriculum implementers and among curriculum promoters so that implementers could ask questions to curriculum promoters or peers at any time when encountering problems, and teachers could share teaching strategies with each other. However, this program was not well promoted, and the main difficulties were as follows:

1. External Training Is Difficult to Address Specific Classroom Problems

Although "The Human Researches" adopted many teacher training methods, many trained teachers still stated that they had not received real training in practical classroom teaching experience. They did not know how to apply the ideas from the seminars to actual classroom teaching and students, and problems encountered in classroom teaching could not be solved in a timely manner. It can be seen that training can hardly directly solve the problems encountered by teachers, but can only improve teachers' professional abilities and enable them to reflect and take actions by themselves to achieve changes.

2. Neglect the Communication and Exchanges among Teachers within Schools

The curriculum promotion strategy of "The Human Researches" adopted a phased and top-down approach, which was implemented through national and local in-service teacher training programs. This established a network between in-service training and professional development and was considered highly effective for teacher advancement and professional growth. However, the external contact network for curriculum promotion was an artificial and deliberately designed relationship, which was unreliable and not long-lasting. The communication and exchanges among teachers within the school were the important factors that had a long-term impact on teachers' curriculum and teaching behaviors.

3. Underestimate the Cultural Resistance of School Organizations

If a new curriculum reform program has no cultural resistance, it means that this reform is not "new", and "The Human Researches" is no exception. It involves essential changes in teaching methods, knowledge, teachers' roles and many other aspects, so conflicts and contradictions with the traditional culture of old schools will be inevitably caused in the classroom implementation. In the promotion of "The Human Researches", although communication channels between extension workers and teachers were established, it neglected the support from within the school, and unilaterally believed that curriculum promotion could be successfully completed as long as teachers changed classroom teaching. Meanwhile, it did not recognize the impact of administrative personnel's support and school organizational systems on curriculum promotion, and failed to coordinate curriculum promotion with the internal organizational systems of schools, resulting in trained teachers working in isolation during classroom implementation.

4. Lack of Sustained Financial Support

From 1972 to 1973, only 4 local education authorities, 19 schools and 50 teachers in the United Kingdom participated in the promotion of "The Human Researches" curriculum and by 1983, only about 100 primary and secondary schools in the United Kingdom had formally adopted this curriculum. Apart from the political changes at that time, the reason why this curriculum was not continuously promoted in the United Kingdom was also the lack of capital investment. The expenses for teachers' in-service training and textbooks were borne by the education administration, but the government's investment could not meet the needs of teachers, making it difficult to sustain the reform.

III. The Promotion Strategies for Chinese Curriculum Reform in Senior High School

In September 2004, Chinese curriculum reform in senior high school entered the experimental stage. Currently, 15 provinces and municipalities have implemented the reform, and many provinces have made beneficial attempts in promotion strategies.

(1) Adopt the Three-level Decentralized Curriculum Management Mode

On the one hand, more autonomy and curriculum implementation responsibilities were given to schools and local authorities to mobilize their enthusiasm for participating in the reform and creating experience. On the other hand, the provincial joint meeting system for high school new curriculum experiments was established, enabling implementers and the Ministry of Education to jointly face the difficulties and problems in the implementation of the new curriculum, forming a community of interests, strengthening local rights and responsibilities, and giving full play to the guiding role of the Ministry of Education.

(2) Conduct Comprehensive Teacher-centered Training

Before the new high school curriculum entered the experimental areas, a number of trainings had been first provided to the relevant persons in charge of the educational administrative departments, teaching and research personnel and school leaders in the experimental areas. The content covered the background and guiding ideology of the high school curriculum reform, and the new curriculum plan for ordinary high schools, with reference to specific aspects such as how to arrange courses and select courses. In order to reduce the disparity in training effects at each level, many provinces concentrated all first-year senior high school teachers involved in the new curriculum in the capital cities for training. Some other provinces took the approach of sending training to the countryside and organized training groups composed of university experts to conduct on-site training in the experimental provinces. In this way, curriculum extension workers had more opportunities to contact the teachers who implement the new curriculum at the front line, strengthening the dialogue between extension workers and implementers. On the one hand, it made it more convenient for front-line teachers to communicate with extension workers and designers about the problems in implementation, and on the other hand, it improved the pertinence of training on new curriculum. Clearly, it took a process from knowing, understanding to internalizing the reform, and implementers needed to constantly generate new understandings in practice.

(3) Focus on the Research Related to High School Curriculum Issues

The curriculum reform in senior high school is a complex project, and many problems will inevitably arise during the promotion process, such as how to promote research-based learning, how to implement the credit system, and the design and implementation of optional courses. There is also the issue of the college entrance examination, which influences the systems of school curriculum and teaching, even personnel management and teacher evaluation. In order to conduct forward-looking and guiding research on the college entrance examination issue, the Ministry of Education has organized relevant experts to set up a research group on college entrance examination plan before the promotion of the high school new curriculum. After the new curriculum entered the experimental areas, each experimental province also established a specialized institution for college entrance examination research, which on the basis of extensive consultation with local schools, formulated as stably as possible the college entrance examination plan of each province to ensure the consistency between the college entrance examination plan and the high school new curriculum plan. At the same time, local realities were also taken into account.

(4) Use Modern Information Technology to Promote and Popularize the New Curriculum

Relying on the rapid development of information technology, many information technology means have been used in the promotion of this high school new curriculum. The Internet, multimedia and other means have been used in teacher training and the publicity of new curriculum concepts, providing efficient ways to promote the new curriculum. For example, online training was carried out through the network so that teachers from different regions and schools could have access to the same information. The high school new curriculum website was established to publicize new curriculum concepts and strengthen the interaction among managers, designers, instructors and implementers.

IV. The Enlightenment of "The Human Researches" on the Promotion Strategies of China's High School Curriculum

As "The Human Researches" and China's new curriculum reform are large-scale curriculum changes, it is valuable to analyze the advantages and disadvantages of the curriculum promotion of "The Human Researches" for enriching and improving China's curriculum promotion strategies.

(1) Increase the Financial Investment in the Curriculum Reform in Senior High School

In addition to increasing the national capital investment, local governments should actively cooperate with national policies and raise funds through multiple channels. Especially in the promotion of the high school new curriculum in urban areas, they should increase funding in a planned manner, give more policy and financial support and provide sufficient financial and training quality guarantees for teacher training to ensure the promotion of the new curriculum. Obviously, investment alone is not enough. The management of the use of funds should also be strengthened to make the limited funds obtain the maximum promotion benefits. In this regard, many curriculum reform experimental areas have accumulated rich experience and local governments should timely organize personnel to summarize, refine and exchange the experience and form a set of experience that can be widely promoted.

(2) School System Is an Important Factor Affecting Curriculum Promotion

The school system is linked to the transformation of national curriculum policies and classroom teaching and is a key factor affecting curriculum promotion. The promotion of "The Human Researches" neglected the role of school organizations and systems, resulting in the obstacles at various levels. A sufficiently new curriculum will inevitably be resisted by the old school culture during promotion as stability and passive acceptance are the inertial traditions of many old school cultures. Fullan believes that in a situation where the structure is essentially unchangeable, it is unrealistic to expect success by taking one reform measure after another, or even some major initiatives, and it wil only be a discredit to the reform[1]. The promotion of the new curriculum undoubtedly requires the creation of an internal school organization suitable for curriculum promotion and makes it a learning-oriented organization. In order to change the organizations and systems of the school, the principals should firstly change their attitude, establish the sense of identity with new curriculum, and play the role of persuader and pioneer in the promotion, giving sufficient material and spiritual support to teachers, who, in particular need the leaders' affirmation and recognition in case of any frustration.

(3) Focus Constantly on the Implementers of the Curriculum - Teachers

Teachers are the final implementers of the curriculum. What they think and believe has a powerful impact on the process of curriculum reform and the transformation of curriculum policies into curriculum practice[2]. In addition to focusing on the establishment of multi-level and multi-form training networks in the promotion of China's high school curriculum, attention should also be paid to the role of teacher culture in the promotion. Teacher culture includes the attitudes, values, beliefs, habits, assumptions and ways of doing things shared by teachers in specific groups, and is an important factor in changing teachers' behaviors[3]. Classroom teaching is the key to determining whether substantial reforms occur and the establishment of a teacher culture of cooperative development is an important driving force for the in-depth promotion of the new curriculum. However, it takes a long process to develop a spontaneous and

---

1 Fullan, M. *Change Forces: Probing the Depths of Educational Reform*[M]. Translated by China National Institute of Education Sciences. Beijing: Educational Science Publishing House, 2004.

2 Xu Jicun. Curriculum Policy and Teaching Culture in the United Kingdom[J]. *Studies in Foreign Education*, 1999(5):1-5.

3 Hagreaves, A. & Fullan, M. U*nderstanding Teacher Development*[M]. New York: Teachers College Press, 1992.

cooperative teacher culture in the traditional teacher culture, which requires the active cooperation of school organizations. Teacher development requires schools to establish mechanisms that encourage teachers to cooperate in research and try innovations and the principal's guiding principles for school running and attitude towards reform also play a vital role.

(4) Seek the Support from Parents and Society Outside the School

High school education has a high social sensitivity and the college entrance examination is related to the interests of thousands of families. The promotion of the high school new curriculum can go further only with the understanding, recognition and support of society, parents and more people, which requires that in the process of promotion, the opinions of curriculum experts, school leaders and teachers should be constantly followed, as well as the opinions of parents and people from all sectors of society on curriculum reform. The establishment of a democratic mechanism with wide participation of schools, parents and people concerned about curriculum reform in society is also quite crucial for the smooth promotion of the curriculum.

[Originally published in *Journal of Hebei Normal University (Educational Science Edition)* 2008(10) (Lv Lijie & Du Caihong)]

4. Curriculum Deliberation in Basic Education Curriculum Development: A Practical Rationality Approach

In 1969, Schwab introduced the concept of curriculum deliberation. Since the 1970s, this concept has been a commonly used research and decision-making approach in the practice of curriculum development. The development of new curriculum in China's basic education curriculum reform was the most participatory in the nation's history. It was also a curriculum research process that fully attempted curriculum deliberation. In this regard, the author interviewed more than 20 participants in the development of curriculum standards, including curriculum managers of relevant projects in the Ministry of Education, senior curriculum theory researchers and subject experts. With the assistance of relevant departments, this study also collected some meeting transcripts in the development of curriculum standards. From these materials, the author extracted the reflective understanding of this practical process, hoping to contribute to China's current and future curriculum research.

I. The Approach to Curriculum Deliberation in New Curriculum Development

(1) Pursue Diversity: The Composition of Deliberation Teams

Participants in the new curriculum development hailed from various backgrounds, including universities, basic education teaching and research departments, and frontline primary and secondary school teachers. University participants were further categorized into subject experts and curriculum experts. Among them, curriculum experts generally came from normal universities and educational research institutes with pedagogical, psychological or curriculum theory background, and subject experts were generally subject professional researchers in normal universities and ordinary universities. The teaching and research staff and primary and secondary school teachers among the expert members were also the backbones in their respective positions, and some were nationally renowned special-grade senior teachers. Publishing house researchers were frequently part of curriculum standard groups due to their in-depth knowledge of China's historical and current curricula and teaching materials. Indeed, many curriculum developers had complex professional and occupational backgrounds, making it challenging to categorize them into specific expert types. For instance, in the compulsory education mathematics curriculum standard development group, there were 31 members from 14 provinces, with 29 specializing in "mathematics education", one in "basic mathematics", and one in "pedagogy". Among the "mathematics education" researchers, some had undergraduate degrees in mathematics and postgraduate degrees in pedagogy or teaching theory. Others had conducted research at universities and had extensive teaching and management experience in primary and secondary schools. Some developers, previously involved in scientific research at normal universities, are now managing curriculum reform. The multiple backgrounds of these developers made it possible to think about curriculum design from different perspectives.

In addition to the core researchers, those participating in the new curriculum deliberation also included scientists, sociologists, members of the National People's Congress and the Chinese People's Political Consultative Conference, as well as media organizations, social examination intermediaries, and relevant administrative departments of the Ministry of Education and various provinces.

The knowledge structure and social status of different researchers determined their different roles in curriculum design. Regarding these roles, a curriculum expert in China believed that generally speaking, curriculum experts, subject experts and teachers were the core members of the curriculum design group, while school administrators, educational administrators, media experts, students, parents and representatives of relevant institutions or industries were all the objects that could be consulted when the curriculum design group was in operation[1]. Judging from the composition of the new curriculum design team, it was quite similar to the conclusion of this expert.

(2) Seek Common Ground among Differences: Negotiation among Curriculum Deliberators

The deliberation group was a combination of people with different research directions, different statuses, different roles, and from different regions. Its rationality lay in the fact that the integration of different perspectives and levels could achieve complementarity, which was the significance and ideal result of deliberation. However, the process of forming complementary views had always been accompanied by the conflicts and communications of the deliberators. Clarifying problems was a difficult process. Therefore, disputes, negotiations, compromises, persistence and even "bargaining" made the process of creating culture itself form a unique deliberative culture.

1. Conflicts and Communications among Designers

The concept of the new curriculum was "for the rejuvenation of the Chinese nation and for the development of every student," focusing on students' "innovative spirit, practical ability, scientific and humanistic competencies", etc.. Behind such macro ideals, everyone's deepest and most profound understanding of the curriculum, their own understanding of the subject, habitual ways of thinking, academic schools, and even their emotions towards the subject to which they had contributed a lot would be expressed in arguments and negotiations. In addition, the conflicts of values and interests among designers from different regions and occupations ran through the entire process of curriculum design. These confrontations came from many aspects, such as: between teaching and research staff and university teachers; among researchers with different professional directions within a subject; between subject experts and curriculum experts; among subject experts, curriculum experts and

1 Hwang Jenq-Jye. *Curriculum Design*[M]. Taipei: Tung Hua Book Co., Ltd., 1991.

government officials.

Taking the communication between subject experts and curriculum experts as an example, both types of professionals had strong theoretical foundations, that is, they both mastered the instrumental discourse used in communication and had a certain degree of professional confidence with quite different theoretical structures, which determined that the integration of their perspectives was an even more difficult process. In the interviews, they expressed their views on each other's roles in curriculum design.

A subject expert said:

I think many problems in curriculum theory are very idealistic and many things in curriculum theory are not feasible in practice. We should consider both the contents put forward by curriculum experts and the ideas of those of us who work in the subject. We can't completely follow what curriculum experts say, after all, a subject has its own logic and regularity.

A curriculum expert said:

A Chinese language expert has ever said that what else can Chinese people do if they don't learn *Chinese Language* well? I think his idea is too extreme. According to the curriculum standard for compulsory education, it's right to learn *Chinese Language* well, but how many children will work in the field of Chinese in the future? Don't always think that since I'm a Chinese language expert, *Chinese Language* is the most important. A geography expert would say: people are in contact with the earth from birth and will return to the earth when they die. They spend their entire life interacting with the earth. Do you think geography is important or not? A foreign language expert said: I won't say how important foreign languages are. Anyway, the state leaders have said that foreign languages should be taught from childhood.

The previous interviewee, a subject expert in the curriculum standard group, believed that curriculum experts' understanding was "idealistic", while subject experts followed the "logic and regularity of the subject itself". Curriculum experts, on the other hand, believed that it was the logic of the subject that brought bias to their understanding. In terms of the arrangement, selection and presentation forms of curriculum content, the criteria on which these two groups based were different. When designing the curriculum plan, the curriculum expert group was logically and even chronologically ahead of the design of the curriculum standard, so that the subject experts in the "confrontation" felt constrained.

In fact, the core of the debate between curriculum experts and subject experts was how to view the role of curriculum experts, and the essence of this debate was their disagreement on curriculum ideals. Subject experts and curriculum experts had different theoretical backgrounds, so their curriculum ideals were also different. Since the birth of the curriculum professional field in the early 20th century, curriculum experts had been playing an important role in the field of curriculum design, especially in the practice of progressivism education, while after the 1960s, subject experts replaced the position of curriculum experts. Experts from various subjects replaced the traditional theorists in the curriculum field and became decision-makers and reformers, and neither private foundations nor official institutions believed that curriculum scholars could lead curriculum reform[1]. The curriculum professional field was on the verge of decline. However, the curriculum reform in the United States in the 1960s was not satisfactory, as the attempts of subject experts to scientize the curriculum design process and content led to a decline in students' academic performance. In the 1970s, Schwab, who was originally a subject expert, "learned from the bitter experience" and put forward the practical curriculum research paradigm with deliberation as the core, revitalizing the position of curriculum experts in the curriculum design field. After the 1970s, the emergence of phenomenology, critical theory and other researches in curriculum

---

1 Zhou Peiyi. *From Social Criticism to Postmodernity: A Study of Jihu's Curriculum Theory*[M]. Taipei: Normal University Academy Co., Ltd., 2000:56.

research field had brought the American curriculum research into a new stage of a hundred schools of thought.

China's curriculum system is different from that of the United States, and the history of curriculum research and development is also different. In the history of China's national curriculum design, it was the first time that a large number of curriculum experts participated, or it was the first time that subject experts and curriculum experts cooperated by adopting the deliberation method. So, how did curriculum experts view their own roles in curriculum design?

A curriculum expert believed:

When formulating standards, the curriculum experts play a role conceptually and technically. First of all, curriculum standards should be made based on the logic of the curriculum system itself. Subject experts are used to considering issues from the perspective of subject content, while curriculum experts are more willing to consider from the perspective of children, so dialogue is needed. Agreeing with either side will not work and both sides should consider issues from an intermediate position. Subject experts emphasize that all problems should be solved and stress "double basics". In such dialogue, curriculum experts must have their positions and play their roles. Secondly, curriculum development requires technical support and curriculum development, design, and curriculum planning are all a series of technical issues. Curriculum experts can provide support for subject experts, including what action verbs are used in curriculum standards, then we provide these verbs to subject experts, who sort them out according to this form.

Obviously, this curriculum expert had reflected on this issue. He divided the role of curriculum experts in curriculum desigh into two levels, the conceptual level and the technical level, which were exactly what the concept of curriculum development itself contained. He believed that curriculum experts should play a role in the entire process of curriculum design. This role was a framework of concepts and thinking, which was superior in logic and was inherently required by the nature of the curriculum. Because of the differences in professional perspectives, the differences in two curriculum design concepts had become very obvious. Therefore, the two forces should jointly act on the curriculum design process. In the dialogue, the professional boundaries were the obvious standards for different schools. Each discussant's original cognitive structure determined the information he selected and the scale for making choices between students and subjects. The cognitive structure provided what hermeneutics calls "legitimate prejudice" for all designers to understand curriculum elements, which means that it was legitimate because without prejudice, understanding was impossible. Prejudice was the prerequisite for people to understand the world and intellectuals were chosen to play the role of creating culture because they possessed this unique and legitimate "prejudice". This "prejudice" should not hinder the cultivation and development of common culture. The key was that while presenting their "prejudice", discussants should be willing to listen, empathize, and understand the rationality of another "prejudice".

A subject expert believed:

When formulating the curriculum standards for compulsory education, I initially felt rather uncomfortable with those who studied pedagogy and psychology and believed that what they put forward were sometimes irrelevant. Later, I came to think that they were quite reasonable. It's quite good to combine the two aspects and promote each other. Their concepts, such as the three-dimensional educational goals, had already been realized by us in the past, and now they put them forward and systematized them, which was a very good promotion.

This subject expert's change in understanding curriculum experts, from "irrelevant" to "quite reasonable" and "a very good promotion", was due to his understanding of the concepts advocated by curriculum experts and what they have done. He began to accept and even use the thinking logic of "those who studied pedagogy and psychology" to view curriculum issues. Therefore, his conclusion was that "it's quite good to combine the two aspects and promote each other".

2. The Generation of Decision-making

Within each curriculum standard design group, the seminar discussion ran through the entire process. How did the decision-making link come about after conflicts and communications? Different developers gave different answers.

An expert in the curriculum standard group said:

Everyone would try their best to express their opinions, but later, a core would gradually be formed within the group, then the core figure would eventually emerge as there had to be someone to make the final decision. This role was usually played by someone from a university. For example, when we were arguing about the curriculum structure, particularly on whether to set up a basic part, one teacher insisted the most strongly: Because we did the preliminary research, we knew the current situation in China best, and we proposed that there should be a compulsory and basic part. This view was rejected at the third and fourth meetings, and then he didn't say much. Afterwards, whenever he spoke, he would state this reason. By the fourth and fifth meetings, we still came to an agreement. Anyway, the person who had studied the issue the most deeply was more likely to have his opinion adopted.

Another expert in the curriculum standard group said:

There was no so-called decision-maker. It was just that everyone argued together, and take the opinion of the majority as the standard, a scientific decision-making process instead of being decided by the project leader. For example, no one can decide the content choice, which was finally confirmed after repeated argumentation. You put forward your views, and I put forward mine. In the process of arguing, our thinking gradually became clear, and finally, everyone reached a consensus, which I think was very reasonable. There wasn't anyone to make the final decision. Anyway, this was how our curriculum standard group worked, which was scientific and democratic.

In the first statement, there was an obvious decision-making center, which was an authority emerging during the discussion, but the authority was not the convener. As the formative authority and the final decision-maker, he had two characteristics: (1) His preliminary research was the "most" in-depth, so his views were likely to be the closest to rationality; (2) He persisted and patiently "stated the reasons", waiting for everyone's understanding to reach a unified level. Consensus didn't come out of thin air but was based on common beliefs, theories, purposes, procedures and other common positions. When it was impossible to make a choice based on positions, empirical data was the most convincing for basic research. This petitioner mentioned here had done a lot of "preliminary research" and was therefore very familiar with "current situation in China". As Dewey said: "The child and the curriculum are the two ends of the educational process", and "the present standpoint of the child and the facts and truths of studies"[1] define "instruction". In other words, the petitioner's judgment on the child's (student's) level in the preliminary research could determine that a "basic compulsory part" should be set up in this subject curriculum. Since this decision-making center was not the same as the convener (administrative person in charge), opponents could keep "opposing" without too many concerns, and finally they naturally reached a consensus on the premise of gradually understanding the existing research.

In the second statement, there was no obvious decision-making center. The interviewee kept mentioning "everyone" and "consensus" and different people's opinions were adopted for different problems. After eliminating the authority of the administrative person in charge, they naturally generated conclusions to problems in the process of arguing. The reason why was called a convener instead of the group leader was to weaken the consciousness of the designated decision-maker and follow the principles of democratic participation and scientific decision-making. In a team with a relatively loose and free administrative organization, the decision-making power was in the hands of

---

1 Dewey, J. *The Child and the Curriculum*[M]. Translated by Lin Baoshan & Kang Chunzhi. Taipei:Wu-Nan Book Inc., 1990:107.

those who dared to express their own opinions, even in a stubbornness manner. As sociologists said: "Autonomy is a very important feature in leadership authority. Only when a person trusts and cherishes his own special tendencies can he produce valuable things"[1]. Of course, this stubbornness and self-confidence were not blind.

An expert in the curriculum standard group said:

Before formulating the curriculum standards, we have written several sets of senior high school textbooks and done empirical research projects for three years, so we felt particularly entitled to speak. Subconsciously, we felt that we had done this before, that we had empirical research, and that we had written textbooks. I think all of these are helpful.

Another expert in the curriculum standard group said:

Once, when a certain gentleman was giving a lecture on curriculum design, he said that who should we listen to in curriculum reform? Whoever speaks the loudest gets heard. I think "speaks the loudest" refers to the recognition of one's professional level in this circle or group, that is, what he said was reasonable. There were often many problems that couldn't be resolved in the curriculum standard group. In such cases, the opinion of the person recognized by everyone was the dominant opinion.

Some curriculum designers had gone through the deliberation process of curriculum design, and in retrospect, they all reflected on how to make decisions reasonably. Their answers were the same whether it was the accumulation of research or professional level. It seems that if we put aside "human" factors such as interpersonal relationships, one or more informal organizational decision-making centers would emerge in a design team, which was not the administrative

---

1 Cooley, C. H. *Human Nature and Social Order*[M]. Translated by Bao Fanyi & Wang Yuan. Beijing: Huaxia Publishing House, 1999:200.

organizational structure maintaining the bureaucratic system but was generated by the persuasiveness of their views. If all members in the team could reach such a consensus that stating one's own proposition was not only a right but also a responsibility and obligation, and all members can respect knowledge, science and truth, then such a decision-making center was considered legitimate by the designers.

II. Understanding of Curriculum Deliberation

The development of this new curriculum can be regarded as a process of localization of the deliberation method in China. Curriculum deliberation is a very distinctive research method in the design of new curriculum. Through the examination of deliberation in the context of Chinese culture, we can see the characteristics shown by curriculum deliberation in the new curriculum design.

(1) Curriculum Design Based on Deliberation Is the Pursuit of Practical Rationality

Deliberation is not about solving theoretical problems but about considering the feasibility in practice. Cognitive rationality can pursue non-contradiction in thinking and can pursue absoluteness. Therefore, there will be a solution to a theoretical problem, and it is the only correct one. However, practical problems are different. For a curriculum plan, it may be a good solution in urban areas but not necessarily in rural areas; it may be feasible for large schools but not for small schools; it may work for gifted children but not for ordinary children. "There is no correct answer in deliberation, but there is the best approach."[1] The formulation of a plan is determined by the actual situation and such judgment and decision are rational judgments based on a deep understanding of practical problems. Therefore, the more specific and real the understanding of the actual situation is, the more reasonable the intuitive

---

1 Schwab, J. J. *The Practical: A Language for Curriculum*[M]. School Review, University of Chicago Press, 1969:1-23.

judgment tends to be. Solutions to practical problems are also different from that to theoretical problems. Pre-existing theories and logical judgments in thinking can be used to test the degree of theoretical problem solving, while practical problems can only be truly eliminated after the facts and after actions have been taken. In fact, when Schwab mentioned curriculum deliberation, he mainly referred to curriculum design at the school level because it could be closer to specific situations and had more practical significance. In contrast, China's new curriculum design adopted such research method at the national level, which compared with the school curriculum design deliberation, the information characteristics used are different, but the theoretical basis and attributes of deliberation are the same.

(2) Basic Research Is the Basis of Curriculum Deliberation

In the new curriculum design, each curriculum standard group has conducted current situation investigations, comparative studies, social need surveys, subject development studies, and student psychological development studies about their own subjects. These studies sort out existing theoretical research and help experts grasp the actual situation of relevant curricula, which are the basis of curriculum deliberation as these knowledge and information are the basis for judgment. Researchers in the deliberation need such a basic and consensual platform, which was defined as "platform" by the American curriculum scholar Walker. He believed that each curriculum designer dealt with the activities in curriculum development with certain beliefs and values. They would have a certain understanding of their work, have an idea of what the main problems are, determine what kind of prescription would be given and what commitments they are prepared to pursue and argue about[1]. Generally speaking, the platform often becomes clearer in the discussions of deliberation. Basic

---

1 Marsh, C. J. *Key Concepts for Understanding Curriculum*[M]. The Falmer Press, 1992:123.

research does not lead to complete agreement in curriculum deliberation, but it does improve relative consensus. The discovery of theoretical difficulties by researchers in the deliberation and their limited understanding of the practical problems of the curriculum have stimulated researchers' deeper and more persistent desire for curriculum inquiry. It can be said that there was a mutually constructive relationship between curriculum research and the deliberation in curriculum design.

(3) The Process of Deliberation Should Be Decentralized, Rejecting yet Relying on Authority

The "center" here refers to the administrative power center in the traditional bureaucratic system. Toffler once mentioned that due to the durability, hierarchy, and division of labor of the bureaucratic system, individuals pinned their prospect on the future of the organization, developed long-term loyalty to the organization, and eventually became tame and ineffectual. After the bureaucratic system, human society will form a "temporary system" (also translated as "special organization"), which refers to an organization established to solve a specific problem and quickly dissolved after the problem is solved. In this system, administrators and managers play a coordinating role among professional teams. They will be familiar with the terms of different expert groups, and convey information between groups by transforming one language into another in writing or orally[1]. In this system, "the traditional sense of loyalty disappears, and is replaced by a sense of loyalty to the profession" with more innovation and adventure, and professionals will be rewarded from their professional circles and work. Toffler believed that such people were already present in the embryonic forms of some of our organizations today. The "temporary system" depicted by futurologists indeed has great homogeneity

---

1 Toffler, A. *Future Shock*[M]. Translated by Meng Guangjun. Beijing: Xinhua Publishing House, 1996:123.

with the expert groups in curriculum design. In the “temporary system”, the thinking viewpoints and discourse positions of design experts have no administrative responsibility to obey and the deliberation relies precisely on the autonomy and ambiguity of each expert to generate meaning and achieve development. The rejection of authority in deliberation arises because the prerequisite for deliberation to occur is a relaxed public opinion space, a democratic and equal interpersonal atmosphere where every designer has the right and ability to express themselves. Therefore, there can’t be an absolute command center in the deliberation team. However, the deliberation process is often characterized by a stalemate of various opinions. Since the theory can’t judge the validity and rationality of the plan, which has not been tested by implementation, during the deliberation process, the opinions of the deliberator who is “recognized” as having a high theoretical competence and truly and comprehensively understanding the practical information of the curriculum will play a role of implication and influence on everyone.

(4) The Integration of Horizons Is a Difficult Process, Which Requires the Strategies of Tolerance, Patience and Even “Bargaining”

Various viewpoints in deliberation will not be easily integrated. Behind the seemingly identical curriculum values of each designer, there are profound differences in experience backgrounds, thinking paths and judgment principles, which will be manifested through the discussion, judgment and decision-making of specific issues. In communication, the value of the design subject lies in reflecting its own characteristics. The dispute itself is a kind of communication and, in fact, also a kind of mutual training. Finally, the particularity of the subject is blunted to achieve unity. There are two ways to resolve disputes. First, the prerequisite reflection that suddenly flashes in the argument - a transcendent understanding, which then elevates multiple subjects that are opposed and contradictory at the same level, makes them abandon their inherent prejudice, and leads everyone’s thinking to a new level. Second, “the success of the deliberation process requires all participants to bring certain standards or expectations in the process, which include listening attentively to the views and arguments of others, carefully accepting or rejecting rather than agreeing or rejecting without thinking, compromising in convincing the rupture of one's own position and the value of others' positions, and committing to deliberating the standards finally accepted. These are not something that dogmatists and non-cooperators can do"[1].

(5) Deliberation Requires Designers to Have Multicultural Competencies and Positive Cultural Psychological Reconstruction

The way and extent to which curriculum design connects reality and ideals determine the quality and level of curriculum products. Curriculum designers should have abundant curriculum culture reserves and use them as one of the backgrounds of thinking. Meanwhile, they should be familiar with the actual curriculum environment and predict the possible situations of reform. This characteristic implies that curriculum research is long-term, routine and latent, and that cultural reserves of curriculum researchers should be diversified. Because the actual curriculum activities are in a complete situation while the sources of any theory are limited, curriculum judgment and action will use complex research methods, and knowledge, theories and principles are all sources of information[2]. During the deliberation process, we can see the dilemma of mutual recognition caused by cultural differences among curriculum designers. The reasons for this lie in the paradox between the relativity of social situations and the transcendence of truth, and the difficulty of "commensurability" among different knowledge structures. In fact, this split in cultural identity, which sometimes even appears as the contradiction of an

---

1 Short, E. C. *Shift Paradigms:Implications for Curriculum Research and Practice/Paradigms Debate in Curriculum and Supervision: Modern and Postmodern Perspectives*[M]. Jeffery Gland, Linda S, Behar Hohenstein, 2000.

2 Ilene, H. *Deliberative Inquiry: The Arts of Planning*[M]. E.C.Short, Forms of Curriculum Inquiry, State University of New York Press, 1990:285-303.

individual's self-identity, comes from the "duality of the education received by intellectuals, or the deviation between the education received and local experience itself"[1]. Deliberators need to achieve psychological reconstruction in the long-term, routine curriculum research with the interaction between theory and practice.

(6) Deliberation Determines that the Curriculum Design Is an Organic Unity of Pre-formation and Generation

Pre-formation is manifested as the shaping and restriction of people's development activities by the existing curriculum culture. In addition, curriculum deliberation groups have limited knowledge of curriculum theory and practice, and are short of deliberation resources (mainly time and funds). Another challenge is the ability of deliberation, which refers to the power to execute the results of deliberation. When the deliberation group lacks the power of decision-making and execution, the viewpoints obtained through deliberation can only influence curriculum executors to a certain extent. Of course, on the other hand, if the deliberation ignores the intentions of the curriculum decision-makers, it would also be a waste of time.[2] All of these will become inalienable influencing factors in the deliberation process. Generation is manifested as the reconstruction of the new curriculum by human creativity. The decision-making process in deliberation is not a one-way linear determinative relationship, but a two-way and multi-interactive thread in which no one can or has the power to preset a given result. Weighing and creating among various possible options is the essence and significance of deliberation.

[Originally published in *Educational Research* 2005(2) (Lv Lijie & Ma Yunpeng)]

---

1 Tao Dongfeng. *Social Transformation and Contemporary Intellectuals*[M]. Shanghai: SDX Joint Publishing Company, 1999:39.

2 Walker, D. F. *Fundamentals of Curriculum Passion and Professionalism*[M]. Mahwah, New Jersey: Lawrence Erlbaum Associates, 2003:217-23

5. The Logic of Curriculum Organization in School-based Curriculum Development

Since the new curriculum reform began more than ten years ago, many schools have developed multiple school-based curricula. However, there exists a common problem in the development process in which schools tend to simply pile up curriculum contents with great arbitrariness and thus affects the value and effect of the entire curriculum. In fact, in the process of school-based curriculum development, it is crucial to reasonably arrange and combine the content elements of the curriculum, which is exactly what curriculum organization needs to accomplish.

I. Understand the School-based Curriculum Organization

(1) Definition of School-based Curriculum Organization

The meaning of curriculum organization must take its function as the entry point. Tyler, the father of modern curriculum theory, pointed out four basic problems in curriculum development in 1949, which briefly speaking, are stating objectives, selecting learning experiences, organizing learning experiences and evaluating the curriculum. Curriculum organization is regarded as a classic step in curriculum development. Tyler stated: "In order for educational experiences to produce a cumulative effect, they must be so organized as to reinforce each other... Curriculum organization is the process of organizing learning experiences into units, courses of study, and teaching plans."[1] A curriculum should have clear design goals and rich curriculum elements, which need to be "woven" together. Different ways of weaving will result in different presentation forms of the curricula with different educational functions. Just as the view of modern system theory suggests, the whole is composed of parts, but not the

1 Tyler, R.W. *Basic Principles of Curriculum and Instruction*[M]. Beijing: China Light Industry Press Ltd., 2008:73.

mechanical addition of all parts. When the elements remain unchanged, the structure of the elements determines the function of the system, and when the structure is reasonable, the function of the whole should be greater than the sum of all parts.[1] Curriculum organization is the structure of the system, and only the proper one can closely connect all parts of the curriculum, form a certain order, and improve the quality of the entire curriculum.

Curriculum organization is also a multi-level concept. Many curriculum researchers, such as Skilbeck[2] and Goodlad[3], have attempted to define curriculum organization from different levels or divide curriculum organization into different levels. Posner believes that the macro meaning of curriculum organization refers to the curriculum relationships among different stages of education (such as primary school and secondary school) and among different types of education (such as vocational education and general education). Its micro meaning refers to the relationships among specific concepts, facts, skills and other elements in the class. There are many different levels of curriculum organizations between the macro and the micro.[4] At the school level, the curriculum organization mainly involves three levels: first, the organization of the school's entire curriculum system; second, the organization of a specific curriculum; third, the organization of curriculum elements in a certain class. The school-based curriculum development needs to consider the issue of curriculum organization at all three levels. In this article, the author mainly discusses the organization of school-based curriculum at the second level, that is, the

---

1 Li Jinsong. *System Theory, Information Theory, Control Theory and Education Reform*[M]. Wuhan: Hubei Education Press, 1989:21

2 Skilbeck, M. *Curriculum Organization* in A. Lewy. *International Encyclopedia of Curriculum*[M].Oxford: Pergamon Press, 1991:342-346.

3 Lin Zhizhong, *et al. Curriculum Organization*[M]. Beijing: Educational Science Publishing House, 2006:2.

4 Posner, G. J. *Analyzing the Curriculum*[M]. Xi'an: Shaanxi Normal University General Publishing House, 2005:128.

organization of curriculum elements in the development of a certain curriculum, namely how to organize themes or concepts, knowledge, general rules, skills, and values in a certain curriculum.

(2) Principles and Methods of Curriculum Organization

Curriculum researchers seem to be more consistent in their views on the standards and methods of curriculum organization. Regarding the common principles of curriculum organization, Tyler called them the standards of effective organization and was the first to put forward the ideas of continuity, sequence and integration. After that, researchers have continuously enriched the principles and standards of curriculum organization. Professor Lin Zhizhong in China has summarized them as scope, sequence, continuity, integration, balance, cohesion, and learning context.[1] Generally speaking, curriculum organization should take into account the logic of the subejct itself, as well as the cognitive characteristics, interests and needs of learners, and the possibilities of curriculum resources in the environment.

The way of organizing curriculum can be generally divided into vertical organization and horizontal organization. Hermo, Posner, Lin Zhizhong and others believe that in vertical organization, according to the logical relationships among contents, there can be discrete, hierarchical, linear, spiral and other forms.[2] (See Figure 1 - 4)

---

1 Lin Zhizhong, *et al. Curriculum Organization*[M]. Beijing: Educational Science Publishing House, 2006:8-18.

2 Posner, G. J. *Analyzing the Curriculum*[M]. Xi'an: Shaanxi Normal University General Publishing House, 2005:133.

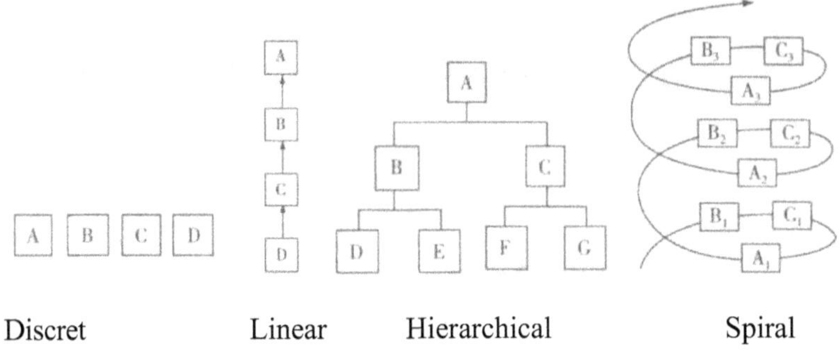

Figure 1-4 Forms of Curriculum Vertical Organization

Horizontal organization manifests itself in different degrees of integrated curriculum. In the integrated organization of curriculum, the forms of organization are more diverse. Drake and Burns, based on their research experience that people integrate curriculum from different bases and starting points, defined the approaches of integrated curriculum organization as multidisciplinary, interdisciplinary and transdisciplinary.[1] Obviously, there are various approaches for curriculum integration, and many researchers understand integration as a continuous concept. Jacobs[2], Wahl[3], Erickson[4], and Drake[5], etc., have all attempted to arrange a series of curriculum integration approaches in a certain logical order to form a continuous curriculum integration process with an increasingly deepening degree of integration. For example, Fogarty used

---

1 Drake, S. M. & Burns, R. C. *Meeting Standards Through Integrated Curriculum*[M]. Translated by Liao Shan, Huang Jinghui & Pan Wen. Beijing: China Light Industry Press Ltd., 2007:9.

2 Lin Zhizhong, *et al. Curriculum Organization*[M]. Beijing: Educational Science Publishing House, 2006:106-107.

3 Lin Zhizhong, *et al. Curriculum Organization*[M]. Beijing: Educational Science Publishing House, 2006:108.

4 Drake, S. *Creating Standards-based Integrated Curriculum: Aligning Curriculum, Content, Assessment, and Instruction*[M] Thousand Oaks, California: Corwin Press, 2007:27.

5 Ibid.

various mirrors as metaphors, with periscope, opera glasses, 3D glasses, eyeglasses, binoculars, telescope, magnifying glass, kaleidoscope, microscope, and prism representing ten curriculum organization ways that gradually tend to be integragted.[1] Specifically, they refer to the fragmented organization of separate disciplines, the juxtaposition of subjects within a discipline, focusing on multiple skills within a discipline, arranging consistent concepts in different disciplines, shared planning or teaching for different disciplines, widely organizing elements around a theme, connecting elements in series with "big ideas", forming new models through interdisciplinary integration, filtering disciplinary content according to learners' experiences and interests, and establishing internal connections among experiences and among disciplines based on learners' academic perspectives. (See Figure 1-5)

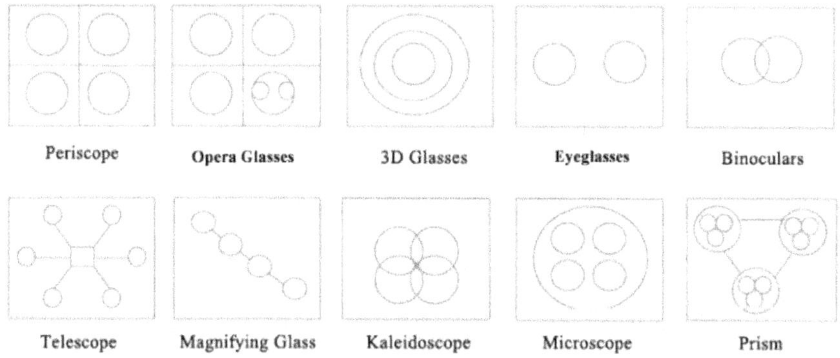

Figure 1-5 Fogarty's Ten Curriculum Organization Ways for Integrating the Curriculum

II. "Organization" Practices in the Development of Two School-based Curricula

U-S cooperation refers to the cooperation between universities and primary and secondary schools to jointly improve primary and secondary schools. University researchers, with their theoretical advantages and professional

1 Fogarty, R. Ten Ways to Integrate Curriculum[J]. *Educational Leadership*,1991(2).

backgrounds, help primary and secondary schools condense their educational philosophy, improve curriculum and teaching, and promote teachers' professional development. As a university staff member, the author has experienced two complete school-based curriculum developments in cooperation with N Primary School and F Primary School. Through jointly constructing and developing school-based curriculum with principals and teachers, it was found that university researchers and teachers need to play their unique roles and demonstrate their values in the curriculum organization stage. Both N Primary School and F Primary School develop their school-based curricula with the initial intention of realizing their own educational philosophy and distinctive culture. Although the two schools organize their curricula in different ways, they all demonstrated the significant importance of effectively arranging and integrating the curriculum content for the achievement of curriculum goals, the feasibility of implementation, and the availability of resources.

(1) Concentric Circle Pattern - The Organization of the School-based Curriculum *Chinese Symbols* in N Primary School

N Primary School is an ordinary primary school in Changchun. After the new curriculum reform, the school independently offered some school-based curricula of interest and specialty, such as optional courses in the game of Go, roller skating and instrumental music. In 2005, the school offered a Chinese studies course and hoped to make it a characteristic course of the school. In 2008, with the financial allocation from the local education bureau, the school built new school buildings. Based on the brand-new educational environment, the school further planned the direction of running the school and took "cultivating students' Chinese emotions" as its educational philosophy and characteristic. In order to highlight this characteristic in the school culture, many beautiful woodblock prints on the theme of "Chinese symbols" were hung on the walls of the corridors of the new teaching building, including elements such as the Four Treasures of the Study, the Abacus, the Compass and the Terracotta Warriors.

How could the Chinese symbols in the school's physical space be transformed into the qualities that students could identify with and possess? The principal hoped that students in each class would study the "Chinese symbols" hanging outside their classrooms. Therefore, in the discussion with teachers, we proposed to turn the scattered "Chinese symbols" observation and inquiry activities into a school-based research-oriented learning curriculum systematically offered by the school. In the first round of discussion, the school required each class to report a "Chinese symbol" selected by the teachers and students of the class as the research theme, forming a preliminary curriculum content structure. (See Table 1 - 1)

Table 1 - 1 The First Round of Curriculum Content Structure Designed by N Primary School Teachers

11.	Drum	2.1	Lanterns	3.1	Chinese Calligraphy	4.1	Four Treasures of the Study	5.1	Square-hole Coins	6.1	Bronze Ware
12.	Abacus	2.2	Fan	3.2	Cloisonné	4.2	Stone Lion	5.2	Jade	6.2	Terracotta Warriors
13.	Chinese Knot	2.3	Lion Dance	3.3	Erhu	4.3	Cloisonné	5.3	Silk	6.3	Ancient Lock
1.4	Paper-cutting	2.4	Peking Opera	3.4	Peking Opera	4.4	Jade Pendant	5.4	Jade Pendant	6.4	Tripod

We discussed this plan with the curriculum development team of N Primary School and believed that although this content took into account the wishes of teachers and students and was in line with the school's physical space, the content composed of 24 symbols lacked sequence and logic, and the repeated content would also make it difficult to have continuity in the curriculum implementation. Therefore, we carried out structured processing on the content in combination with the wishes of teachers and students. In the vertical direction, the contents were in a hierarchical relationship. Under the major theme of Chinese symbols, there were six research themes adapted to six grades, and under each research theme, there were sub-themes for each class to study. In terms of horizontal organization, the content was integrated from a transdisciplinary perspective, emphasizing the design and development of content according to children's life situations, and connecting relevant elements with larger theme concepts from the perspective of Fogarty's "magnifying glass". Eventually, it was designed into six major themes with 24 Chinese symbols elements. (See Table 1 - 2)

Table 1 - 2 The Curriculum Content Structure Designed in the Second Round

Traditional Cuisine		Traditional Folk Customs		Chinese Calligraphy		Quintessence of Chinese Culture - Peking Opera		Silk Road		Ancient Civilization	
1. 1	Dumplings	2.1	Lanterns	3.1	Four Treasures of the Study	4.1	Erhu	5.1	Tea	6.1	Bronze Ware
1.2	Mooncakes	2.2	Chinese Knots	3.2	Famous Calligraphers	4.2	Drum	5.2	Jade	6.2	Terracotta Warriors
1.3	Glutinous Rice Balls	2.3	Lion Dance	3.3	Calligraphy Schools	4.3	Facial Masks	5.3	Silk	6.3	Square-hole Coins
1.4	Zongzi	2.4	Paper-cutting	3.4	Masterpieces of Calligraphy	4.4	Role Types (in Peking Opera)	5.4	Porcelain	6.4	Tripod

The curriculum organization planning for the *Chinese Symbols* is mainly based on the following considerations:

1. The Pemise of Curriculum Organization Is the Consideration of Curriculum Goals and the Content

The goal orientation and content selection of this school-based curriculum are clear and easy to operate. The content obviously serves the school-running feature of "cultivating students with Chinese emotions", which is the direction to establish the overall goal of the curriculum. The selection of content themes mainly centers on the most representative Chinese elements, considering their relevance to real life, so that students can see the past and future of Chinese culture based on today's life. In fact, there are abundant optional contents.

2. Consider Children's Cognitive Level to Form a Sequential Cognitive Path

The curriculum cannot cover all aspects of Chinese traditional culture, but it should be representative. The content with this "representativeness" uses children's cognitive level as the connecting standard to form six themes for six grades: Traditional Cuisine, Traditional Folk Customs, Chinese Calligraphy, Quintessence of Chinese Culture - Peking Opera, Silk Road, and Ancient Civilization. These six themes correspond to children in six grades, and as their life horizons expand, the above themes become the representative "symbols" for their understanding of Chinese culture. From the food, folk games and activities encountered in family life and festival activities in the lower grades, to the Chinese calligraphy learned in school in the middle grades and the quintessential art often seen in public media, and until the ancient civilization learned from history in the upper grades of primary school, the curriculum unfolds layer by layer from the near to the far with the expansion of children's horizons, forming a stable curriculum gradient, with representative Chinese elements running through it all. (See Figure 1-6)

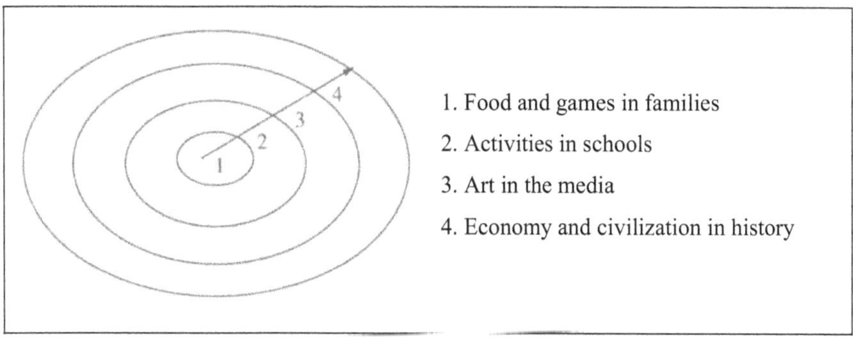

Figure 1-6 Sequence of Concentric Circle School-based Curriculum

3. Cognition, Experience and Emotion Serve as Both Ends and Means for Each Other, Forming a Structure for Children's Development

The curriculum gradient includes the diversity of implementation methods. For example, the first grade takes Chinese cuisine as the research theme, which is closely related to children's family dietary life and is an activity that children are "willing" to engage in and share. The implementation of the curriculum is mainly based on experience with some optional activities, such as inviting parents to make dumplings together, sharing mooncakes with classmates after the Mid-Autumn Festival, and telling stories in groups. In the second grade, with traditional Chinese folk customs such as lanterns, Chinese knots, lion dances and paper-cutting as the research theme, students can feel and initially appreciate these folk cultures through activities like drawing and cutting. In the third and fourth grades, students need to use the Internet and other means to search for texts, photos and other materials, sort out information, and communicate and present in the class. In the fifth and sixth grades, students should experience the complete process of research-based learning and "study" Chinese elements through the following steps: raising questions, determining topics, formulating research plans, collecting, sorting out and presenting materials. In this process, children have a cognition of Chinese culture and an experience of Chinese culture, and their emotions are sublimated in the process of cognition and experience. Cognition, experience and emotional arousal and sublimation are both the goals of the curriculum and the means to achieve the curriculum goals. The three aspects serve as both ends and means for each other and jointly play roles in the changes of children's competencies.

4. The Themes of Each Grade Correspond to the National Curriculum, Forming a "Correlated Curriculum"

In the curriculum plan for the national compulsory education, there are no class hours for comprehensive practical activities (including research-based learning) in the first and second grades of primary school. Then, the traditional cuisine in the first grade can be offered in combination with the *Morality and*

Life course, and in the second grade, the *Art* course can be processed in a school-based way so that the content can be integrated into the *Art* course. Starting from the third grade, the *Chinese Symbols* can directly rely on the comprehensive practical activity courses and correspond to the *Calligraphy* course offered by the school. Peking Opera appreciation and singing can also be added to the music class in the fourth grade, and the silk road and ancient civilization in the fifth and sixth grades also have corresponding contents in the *Morality and Society* and *Chinese Language*.

After two rounds of implementation of the *Chinese Symbols* school-based curriculum, we had a discussion with teachers. They believed that students liked this curriculum and teachers were also very "enthusiastic". However, each class had a different research theme and teachers of the same grade couldn't share resources, which increased the workload of teachers and was not conducive to the display and communication of results among the same grade. In addition, during the implementation, teachers found that students showed great enthusiasm for some research contents, while they were collectively indifferent to some other contents. Based on this, the school curriculum development team agreed to further plan and design the content structure of the *Chinese Symbols* school-based curriculum, forming a curriculum structure model with one research theme and two specific research contents for each grade. (See Table 1 - 3)

Table 1 - 3 The Curriculum Content Structure Designed in the Third Round

Grade	Theme	Content	Subject Arrangement	
			Major Subjects	Ancillary Subjects
Grade 1	Chinese Cuisine	Dumplings, Mooncakes	*Morality and Life*	*Chinese Language*
Grade 2	Traditional Folk Customs	Lanterns, Paper-cutting	*Art*	*Chinese Language*
Grade 3	Calligraphy Art	Poetry, Calligraphy	*Comprehensive Practical Activities*	*Calligraphy, Art*
Grade 4	Peking Opera Culture	Famous Peking Opera Artists, Facial Masks	*Comprehensive Practical Activities*	*Music, Art*
Grade 5	Silk Road	Tea, Jade Articles	*Comprehensive Practical Activities*	*Chinese Language, Morality and Society*
Grade 6	Ancient Civilization	Bronze Ware, Terracotta Warriors	*Comprehensive Practical Activities*	*Chinese Language, Morality and Society*

At present, the school-based curriculum *Chinese Symbols* in N Primary School has been implemented for multiple rounds, and teachers have explored the implementation methods of the curriculum for each grade, as well as several student research methods and teacher guidance methods for different research stages of the same theme. It can be seen that after the standardized and structured attempts in the curriculum design process, the teacher team has begun to think about curriculum issues systematically, and the professional level of the curriculum itself is improving.

(2) Spiral Ascending Pattern - The Organization of the School-based Curriculum *Chess Culture* in F Primary School

F Primary School is an ordinary primary school in Anshan. Since 2002, the school has carried out characteristic activities of "chess education". After more than ten years, the school's chess activities have had a great influence in the city, and its competitive achievements are also among the top. The school has consistently provided chess classes (technique classes) for students. In the first and second grades, popularized courses are offered, and all students attend chess classes. After the third grade, optional courses are offered for children who are good at chess and like playing chess. During the discussion, we jointly refined the educational philosophy of "Happy life, Wise life" for children with the school. Its meaning lies, on the one hand, in the characteristic of chess education. The chess education is popularized in the first and second grades to cultivate each child to learn the common techniques of three kinds of chess (Chinese chess, the game of Go and international chess) and to cultivate their interest in chess, making it a future life interest - "happy life". After the third grade, children who like playing chess and have special talents are cultivated to improve their skills, understand the chess spirit, and map out strategies - "wise life". On the other hand, all curricula provided by the school and all the work done are for the students' "happy life and wise life". Under the guidance of this concept, the principal and teachers reflect on the following question: are children moving towards happiness and wisdom in the life of chess? It seems that children are missing something in their chess life. For example, nowadays children care too much about rankings and are unwilling to admit defeat. They often quarrel because of retracting a false move, and even during competitions, parents watching the games also get involved and quarrel to fight for rankings for their children. It seems that with only chess techniques, children cannot achieve "happiness" and "wisdom". The principal decided that we would jointly develop the school-based curriculum *Chess Culture* with the teachers to let students understand the history of Chinese chess culture and the civilization it contains, and to cultivate their minds with chess culture.

What content should the school-based curriculum *Chess Culture* include? After several brainstorming sessions with the principal and teachers, it is agreed that three types of content must be contained. First, the extensive and profound Chinese characters and literature contained in chess, such as poems, proverbs, couplets and idioms related to chess. Second, the etiquette and moral cultivation in chess culture, such as no regrets after making a move and following the norms. Third, the psychological qualities of children, such as being strong, being able to resist setbacks, correctly treating success and failure, and being patient, which are also the psychological qualities that children generally need nowadays. In this way, the basic prototype of the content of the *Chess Culture* is formed. (See Table 1 - 4)

From the perspective of horizontal integration, this curriculum adopts the "telescope" integration method. Centering on the theme of chess culture, it connects relevant contents in subjects such as *Chinese Language*, *Morality*, and *Psychology*, and widely organizes various content elements. Then, in what order should these contents be presented vertically? Our suggestion is to present the order of contents in a spiral ascending manner, adding contents of characters, literature, etiquette and morality, and psychological qualities in the lower, middle and upper grades, and gradually expanding the depth and breadth of the contents in each grade. (See Figure 1-7)

Table 1-4 Prototype of the Content Structure of the *Chess Culture* Curriculum

First-level Concept	Second-level Concept	Executor
A. Characters and Literature in Chess	Poetry, Proverbs, Couplets, Idioms, Famous Sayings, Stories	*Chinese Language* Teacher
B. Etiquette and Moral Cultivation in Chess	No Regrets after Making A Move, Being Practical and Realistic, Following Norms, Keeping Silent While Watching Chess	*Morality* Teacher
C. Psychological Qualities in Chess	Being Strong, Resisting Setbacks, Adapting to Changes, Remaining Calm in Face of Honors and Disgraces, Being Patient, Not Being Indecisive	*Psychology* Teacher

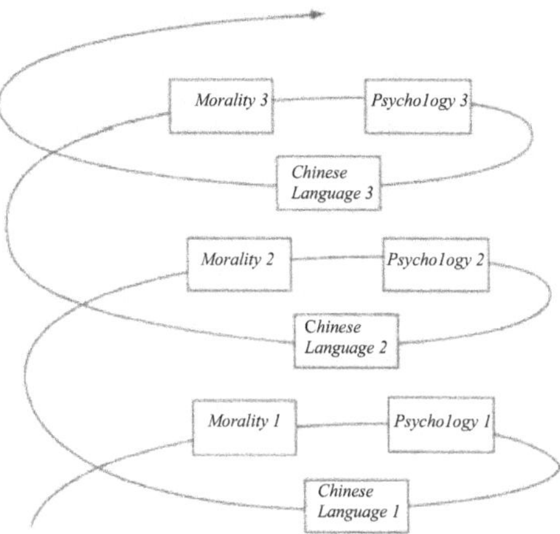

Figure 1–7

Under such ways of thinking, teachers in F Primary School begin to select and arrange the curriculum content. But new problems arise. The teachers have found a lot of materials, but how should they be arranged to achieve the spiral ascending effect? After dividing the work according to the curriculum content, how to integrate the content together? After discussing with the principal and teachers, we form a structural diagram that unifies the content structure and the class-hour structure, expanding the first-level concept of content into seven fields, such as historical stories, etiquette cultivation, characters and literature. Meanwhile, it is determined that *Chess Culture* is a compulsory course in the first and second grades, with six classes per semester, and an optional course from the third grade to the sixth grade, with eight classes per semester, combining the content fields and the class-hour allocation into a two-dimensional matrix diagram. Teachers in the curriculum development group divide the work according to their subject specialties and the grades they are in, with two to three teachers being responsible for one content field. They sort, rewrite and edit the curriculum content according to the content volume in the structural diagram and the corresponding grades, and finally integrate everyone's work together. (See Table 1-5)

Table 1-5 The Conceptual Structure and Temporal Structure of the

School-based Curriculum *Chess Culture*

Content Field	Grade 1	Grade 2	Grade 3	Grade 4	Grade 5	Grade 6
	Cultivation of Competencies (Compulsory)		Promotion of Wisdom (Optional)			
Historical Stories	+	+	+			
Etiquette Cultivation	+	+	++	+	+	+
Characters	+++	++				
Literature		+	++	+	+	+
Strategies			+	++	++	++
Anecdotes of Figures			+	++	++	++
Spiritual Growth	+	+	+	++	++	++
Total Class Hours	6	6	8	8	8	8

The design of the *Chess Culture* is relatively difficult because the content does not rely on a certain definite subject. It cannot directly borrow the logical system of the subject itself and needs to creatively select and organize the content starting from the curriculum goals. Many knowledge elements related to chess require the designer to distinguish the age groups of the learners they are suitable for, or the designer needs to rewrite them. While rewriting, factors such as implementation methods and curriculum resources also need to be considered. All of these pose great challenges to the teachers in the curriculum development group.

III. Considerations on Organizational Issues in School-based Curriculum Design

(1) Teachers Remain the Main Body of School-based Curriculum "Organization"

Teachers are the main body of school-based curriculum development. Even in the system where universities and primary and secondary schools cooperate to develop school-based curriculum, this subjectivity still has practical and value necessities. The school-based curriculum is developed for students in schools and is generated in schools, and only teachers can best grasp all the complex factors of the curriculum. In the design process of school-based curriculum, the "organization" is a technical link often overlooked by teachers, and the intervention of university theoretical researchers is effective. However, the role of the intervention is to provide a thinking framework, not to replace teachers in completing the development of school-based curriculum. Teachers should improve, sort out and perfect the curriculum content following the framework of the curriculum structure and gain curriculum development experience with theoretical content. In this process, the practical wisdom of both sides is needed. On the one hand, university personnel need to understand the demands of school curriculum and see the focus of their actions. On the other hand, school teachers need to understand the applicability of theories, and find feasible and normative action paths between theoretical frameworks and real resources.

(2) Curriculum Consciousness Determines the Degree of Teachers' Attention to Curriculum Organization

In the development of school-based curriculum, the main reason for ignoring the organization link is the potential bias of teachers' curriculum consciousness. When teachers act as curriculum designers, they often start from the curriculum content and choose what they think is valuable to students. Although this content is indeed effective for students, the effect may be partial and scattered. Therefore, teachers need to start from the overall function of the curriculum for children's development, understand what value the curriculum structure system can bring to students, what function a school-based curriculum undertakes in the structure, and how to achieve such a function. Only under such a thinking framework can the issues such as the logic of the content, the situation of children, implementation methods and possible resources be integrated and planned.

(3) Continuously Correct the Premise of Curriculum Organization - Curriculum Goals

Tyler's Principle clearly explains the general idea of developing a curriculum based on goals, which can also represent the logic of the school-based curriculum development process. The organization of school-based curriculum should be based on curriculum goals and possible curriculum elements. The goals of school-based curriculum need to target the school's philosophy and school-running characteristics, and responde to students' interests and needs as well as the needs of the times in social development. Among them, students' interests are indeed the logical premise of school-based curriculum development, but this premise should also be a bottom-line premise, or a basic premise, a necessary but not sufficient premise. Children's interests are extensive, diverse and highly variable. The same problem can arouse or eliminate interests in different situation or with different methods. Therefore, when determining the goals and content of school-based curriculum, children's needs should also be a prerequisite factor worthy of emphasis. Tyler gave the answer to how to consider children's needs: "the difference between the present condition of the learner and the acceptable norm"[1], that is, "need". In other words, children's "need" is the current deficiency of children which needs to be judged by curriculum designers. Of course, the understanding of children's interests and needs needs to be continuously improved after the implementation of the school-based curriculum. The implementer - the teacher will have a deeper understanding of whether the curriculum meets children's interests and needs, and naturally, the selection and organization of curriculum content should be continuously improved after the curriculum implementation and evaluation.

(4) The Organization of School-based Curriculum Needs to Be Weighed in a Multiple Organizational Community

As far as the organization of a certain school-based curriculum is concerned, how to arrange the knowledge, information and activities in the content elements

---

1 Tyler, R. W. *Basic Principles of Curriculum and Instruction*[M]. Beijing: China Light Industry Press Ltd., 2008:6

into a continuous and sequential system requires considering not only the logical order of the content elements themselves but also several related structures. (See Figure 1-8)

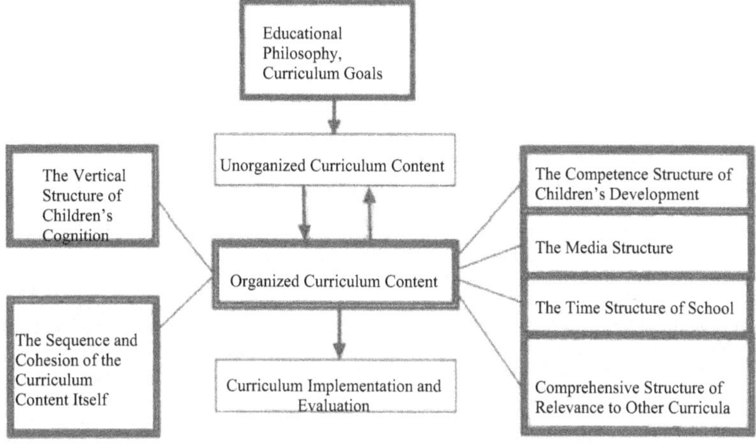

Figure 1-8 The Multiple Organizational Structure of the School-based Curriculum Content System

First, the vertical structure of children's cognitive abilities and cognitive characteristics. The depth and breadth of the curriculum content should be consistent with the possibilities of children's cognition. Second, the competence structure of children's development. The goal of any curriculum is not merely to increase children's knowledge or just improve a certain skill of children. Therefore, the arrangement of curriculum elements should take into account the improvement and development of students' competence structures in aspects such as knowledge, skills, emotions and abilities. Third, the media structure. The media structure refers to the teaching methods through which this curriculum will be implemented and the resources that will be utilized. Different teaching methods and curriculum resources directly affect the competence structure of children's development. Therefore, the media structure needs to be diversified and form its own structure, which influences the selection and arrangement of curriculum content. Fourth, the time structure of the curriculum. When creating a school-based curriculum, it is necessary to consider the school's time resources and the appropriate curriculum time for each grade. Therefore, the arrangement of curriculum elements should be incorporated into the time structure of the curriculum. Finally, there is the comprehensive structure of relevance to other curricula in the school. In the curriculum system of basic education in China, the national curriculum is still the main body of the school curriculum. The nature of the school-based curriculum is to assist the national curriculum in achieving the goal of educating people and realizing the educational philosophy. If the content of the school-based curriculum can cooperate with the national curriculum to form a correlation among curricula, it will inevitably produce a comprehensive effect, save time, and give students an overall understanding.

[Originally published in *Educational Research* 2014(9) (Lv Lijie & Yuan Qiuhong)

Topic Two: Curriculum Transformation of Competency-Oriented Objective

6. On the Approaches to the Curriculum Transformation for the Goals of Talent Cultivation

How today's education addresses the talent needs of future social development and the challenges of the new era is the focus of educational reforms promoted by developed countries and international organizations around the world. The systematic, organic, continuous, and complete penetration and integration of talent cultivation goals into the curriculum is the strategic guideline for the realization of talent cultivation. The implementation of talent cultivation goals in the curriculum is the issue of curriculum transformation, which refers to the morphological changes, transmission clues, and implementation degrees of the ideals of curriculum reform among different curriculum hierarchies. The process of implementing national talent cultivation goals at different levels such as curriculum standards, teaching materials, and classrooms is the process of curriculum transformation.[1] Curriculum standards and teaching materials are important carriers of the curriculum, and their development is an important link in the curriculum transformation of cultivation goals which need to be implemented in the curriculum, reflected through those carriers and realized in school education and teaching activities. They serve as the intermediary bridge between cultivation goals and education and teaching activities. Whether they can embody the orientation of cultivation goals and fulfill the function of educating people is related to the direction of education and teaching practice as well as the specifications and quality of future talents. Curriculum standards and teaching materials should adhere to the fundamental task of fostering virtue in education and actively explore the transformation of talent cultivation goals in the new era within the curriculum.

---

1 Lv Lijie & Li Gang. Study on Hierarchy of Key Competencies in School Curriculum Transformation[J]. *Curriculum, Teaching Material and Method*, 2016(11):50-56.

I. The New Era Proposition of Talent Cultivation Goals

Today's education must face the challenges of human social development. General Secretary Xi Jinping emphasized at the National Education Conference that "we should focus on improving students' comprehensive qualities and cultivating innovative, compound, and applied talents who can adapt to the development of the new era", clearly indicating the basic qualities of socialist builders and successors with all-round development in morality, intelligence, physique, aesthetics and labor. He proposed that to fully implement the Party's education policy, we must work hard on strengthening ideals and beliefs, deeply boosting patriotism, enhancing moral cultivation, increasing knowledge and insights, cultivating the spirit of dedication, strengthening comprehensive qualities, establishing the educational concept of "health first", comprehensively improving school aesthetic education, and promoting the spirit of labor among students. By sorting out the talent cultivation goals in China and other countries or organizations, we summarize them into four aspects: values education, basic competencies, key ability and 21st-century concepts.

(1) Values Education

The world pattern filled with multiculturalism is no longer one of regional independent development but of cultural joint symbiosis. However, the global village that has become one has led to value identity crises in ethnic culture, ideal and belief in some nation-states. Concepts such as global citizens, universal values, and supranational identities have weakened citizens' cultural identities and national cohesion. This has made many countries in the world, such as Japan, South Korea, France, and Denmark, attach great importance to citizens' values education in talent cultivation. In China, it is emphasized to fully implement the Party's education policy, implement the fundamental task of fostering virtue in education and develop quality education in the 19th CPC National Congress report. Meanwhile, the national curriculum also emphasizes the education of socialist core values, further highlights the education of fine traditional culture of the Chinese nation and revolutionary traditions and strengthens education on the rule of law, national security, national unity and ecological civilization.

(2) Basic Competencies

The purpose of education is not only to enable people today to accept and overcome the challenges from the changing world and prepare for different social roles they will face in the future but also to make individuals obtain happiness and pleasure and become active and responsible social citizens. Although the competence frameworks under different role requirements and social traditions show diversified characteristics, the basic competencies for human survival and life in the contemporary social context must be considered firstly. For example, with the continuous inheritance of social civilization, the mutual integration of diverse cultures, and the increasing richness of the human spiritual world, there is more frequent thinking, interaction, and understanding between people and texts, between people and the world, and between people and themselves. Basic text reading ability and arithmetic ability remain the basic prerequisites for people to integrate into society. Moreover, the rapid development of communication technology has pushed human society into the information age, and real life has been swallowed up by the digital torrent created by the "Internet +" technology. Everyone has become a "digital citizen". Digitalization has become the basic way of contemporary life, and the ability to use digital tools has become a basic ability in life. In addition, although the highly developed modern society has kept people away from the embarrassment of being unable to meet food and clothing needs, over-reliance on advanced technology has led to the degeneration of human limbs, and the high incidence of various diseases has prompted humans to shift their attention back to national sports and public health. Health competence has become a basic competence related to survival and life.

(3) Key Ability

In the era of information explosion, the total amount of knowledge is growing exponentially. People can no longer go through the development process of every field, so the focus has shifted from only cultivating students' professional abilities to improving individuals' general abilities, especially the cultivation of key abilities among general abilities. In 2017, the General Office of the Communist Party of China Central Committee and the General Office of the State Council issued the *Opinions on Deepening the Reform of the Educational System and Mechanism*, which clearly proposed to strengthen the cultivation of students' key abilities, namely cognitive abilities, vocational abilities, cooperative abilities, and innovative abilities in the process of cultivating students' basic knowledge and basic skills. The 21st-century skills in the *Framework for 21st Century Learning* in the United States are also high-order abilities higher than basic competencies, including three categories: learning and innovation skills, information, media, and technology skills, and life and career skills.[1] In 2018, the Organization for Economic Cooperation and Development (OECD) released "The Future of Education and Skills Education 2030", emphasizing cognitive and metacognitive skills such as critical thinking, creative thinking, learning to learn, and self-regulation; social and emotional skills such as empathy, self-efficacy, and collaborative ability; practical and physical skills such as using new information and communication technology devices; and emphasizing the abilities to change society and shape the future, such as creating new value, coordinating contradictions and difficulties, and taking responsibility.[2] These key abilities are necessary to adapt to social changes in the information age, as well as to innovate and create on the basis of basic competencies.

(4) 21st-Century Concepts

Artificial intelligence, big data, knowledge economy, and information

---

1 Zhang Hua. On the Connotations of A Key Competence[J]. *Global Education*, 2016(4):10-24.

2 Meng Hongwei. OECD Learning Framework 2030[J]. *Journal of Open Learning*, 2018(6):9-12.

society have become new core issues in people's life. It is difficult to highlight their importance in the traditional subject curriculum system, and they have become new contents and concepts in the talent cultivation goals for the 21st century. For example, from the late 20th century to the 21st century, people's living standards have significantly improved, household incomes have continued to grow, and the mode of production has also changed greatly. The rapid expansion of the knowledge economy has completely changed people's concept of wealth. Meanwhile, people have also suffered from major crises in human history, such as the global financial bubble in 2008. In the face of the huge wealth accumulated in human history, the retention of wealth can no longer be used as a bargaining chip to meet the challenges of the 21st century. Instead, it should be the creation of wealth. Citizens in the 21st century must have a clear understanding of the economy itself and realize that the rapid development of the economy does not rely on primitive accumulation but on continuous flow and creation. The *Framework for 21st Century Learning* in the United States proposed to cultivate students' financial competence. The *OECD Learning Framework 2030* included entrepreneurship in it. Finland even proposed in the *National Core Curriculum for Basic Education* to cultivate students' vocational abilities and entrepreneurial competence.[1]

II. The Metaphorical Features of the Talent Cultivation Goal System

Deeply examining the metaphorical features of the times contained in talent cultivation goals is an important yardstick for better grasping the direction of curriculum transformation.

(1) Iceberg Metaphor - The Holistic Feature of Talent Cultivation

1 Finnish National Board of Education. *National Core Curriculum for Basic Education 2014*[M]. Porvoon Kirjakeskus, Helsinki, 2016:32-44.

Goals

The iceberg metaphor vividly points out that human abilities and qualities consist of the visible parts floating on the water surface, such as knowledge and skills, and the invisible parts hidden under the water surface, such as attitudes and cognition. The cultivation goals also have characteristics similar to an iceberg with visible contents such as knowledge and skills on the surface and invisible contents such as attitudes and cognition inside. Neither can be neglected, and they jointly constitute the entire content of talent cultivation goals. To cope with the ever-changing world, the talent cultivation goals in the new era aim at cultivating people with all-round development, taking into account the cultivation of multiple abilities and qualities in morality, intelligence, physique, aesthetics and labor, and attaching importance to forming a complete cultivation goal positioning system covering three aspects: depth of knowledge, width of ability, and breadth of cognition. The holistic feature of talent cultivation goals in the new era emphasizes that what students have learned should not be limited to the completion of visible cultivation goals such as mastering knowledge and observing phenomena, but also to the attainment of invisible cultivation goals such as values and methodologies for understanding and transforming the world.

(2) Driving Metaphor - The Situational Feature of Talent Cultivation Goals

The driving metaphor of talent cultivation goals refers to the characteristics of the process of achieving talent cultivation goals, which requires creating situations in the educational process so that students can improve their abilities through experience, inquiry and application. Driving a car requires obtaining a driver's license for the corresponding model before one can drive on the road. After passing the theoretical knowledge test and the on-site driving test, candidates need to take the road driving test, that is, to have their driving skills assessed in a variety of real road situations. When actually driving a car, in addition to these knowledge and skills, one also needs to have the ability to judge directions and speeds in complex environments, as well as the "essential character of polite driving and the value concept of respecting life".[1]

Many of the talent cultivation goals mentioned above are high-order concepts, abilities and competencies based on knowledge and skills. Students need to comprehensively use knowledge and skills in created situations through experiences, enlightenment and practice, and independently construct concepts, abilities and qualities. Achieving talent cultivation goals should not be just about indoctrination and accumulation but about understanding, enlightenment and dialogue, so that students can acquire abilities that they can take away instead of heavy schoolbags that they can't bear, enabling them to adapt to changes in situations and make timely adjustments and responses when facing the real world of real life.

(3) Ripple Metaphor - The Evocative Feature of Talent Cultivation Goals

Ripples in the nature refer to the phenomenon that water waves continuously spread outward after objects like stones fall into the water. The talent cultivation goals in the new era are just like the stones thrown into the water, stirring up ripples that continuously spread outward and are several times or even dozens of times larger in area than the stones themselves. These ripples, summoned by the cultivation goals and continuously developed and organized by students, are life skills broader than the talent cultivation goals themselves in adapting to both individual development and social development.[2] The talent cultivation goal itself is not a master key but an initial tool that can create the keys to match the lock cores.

---

1 Cui Yunhuo. A Study on the Curriculum Meaning of Key Competencies [J]. *Global Education*, 2017(10):24-33.

2 Cheng Shangrong. The Chinese Expression of Key Competence[N]. China Education Daily, 2016-09-19.

Talent cultivation goals are the key abilities and essential qualities that students should possess, and their key and essential nature lies in the evocative structure generated by students based on these goals. Different students can summon different knowledge, abilities and emotional attitudes according to different combinations, and then build their own open competence structures, enabling students to successfully solve various problems they encounter and gradually construct a developing, complete and happy life edifice.

III. Ways of Curriculum Transformation of Talent Cultivation Goals

(1) Transformation of Talent Cultivation Goals in Curriculum Standards

The curriculum standard is the policy text that is formulated based on the propositions of the times for talent cultivation, reflecting the will of the state, highlighting the subject concepts, and condensing the subject systems. It is the subject expression of the national education guiding principles. The subject curriculum system is different from the subject system, and the construction of the subject curriculum system should not only take into account the logic of the subject itself, but also the needs of social development, the laws of children's growth, etc. The function of the subject curriculum is not only to transmit subject knowledge but, more importantly, to cultivate people. Therefore, it is necessary to make overall plans for what qualities, concepts, abilities, skills to be cultivated through the subject curriculum so as to form a joint force among subjects and different learning stages. This is where the value of curriculum standards lies. Firstly, the curriculum standard is the subject decomposition of cultivation goals. Textbook compilation and teachers' classroom teaching can further implement the overall requirements of cultivation goals based on the concepts and contents of the curriculum standard, enabling teachers and students to accurately internalize the state will, social values, and key abilities in the transmission of subject knowledge, and practice fostering virtue in education in the way of the subject itself. Secondly, the curriculum standard makes overall plans for the development ideas of subject curriculum over a period of 9 or even 12 years. Multiple versions of textbooks are selected and designed according to the subject curriculum concepts and characteristics in the curriculum standard to ensure that different versions have different styles but the same goal orientation. The same version of textbooks for different learning stages are based on the subject competence in the curriculum standard to ensure that the textbooks as a whole are orderly, logically connected, and progressing in a gradual manner.

1. Structured Decomposition and Synthesis

Talent cultivation goals need to be scientifically and reasonably infiltrated into the curriculum standard. Continuity, sequence and integration are the clues and passwords for the transformation of cultivation goals in the curriculum standard. The curriculum compilation principles put forward by Tyler based on the curriculum reform experience of the "Eight-Year Study" in the United States[1] have provided important inspirations for curriculum and textbook development for more than half a century. The cultivation goals in the curriculum standard are not the aggregation of scattered points but an orderly and organic organization with certain structural relationship among them. On the one hand, the gradual progress of learning and the phased nature of growth require that cultivation goals continuously and successively guide the selection of curriculum contents in different learning periods. In other words, the achievement of each goal and the cultivation of each ability need to be continuously and progressively reflected in the curriculum standards of each learning stage progressively in order to have an impact on students. On the other hand, this clue does not mean that goals and abilities are only presented in a single linear manner in the curriculum standard. The comprehensiveness and complexity of human development also require transcending the boundaries of

1 Tyler, R. W. *Basic Principles of Curriculum and Instruction*[M]. Beijing: China Light Industry Press Ltd., 2008:1.

subject systems, forming a network structure that spreads and extends among different subjects. Different subjects cooperate with each other according to their characteristics and form a joint force to have an integrated impact on students. In the process of developing the curriculum standard, talent cultivation goals can be decomposed into learning stage goals and subject goals of the corresponding subjects at primary school, junior high school, and senior high school by combining the nature and functions of different subjects. Or, different learning stages and subjects can "claim" cultivation goals according to the content characteristics and learning focuses to form a goal structure that is intertwined vertically and horizontally and interconnected with each other.

2. Content Loading

The curriculum standard is the basis for teachers to design teaching, the basis for academic evaluation, and the basis for textbook compilation. The transformation of talent cultivation goals in curriculum standards should not only be reflected in the goal system but also in the content system. The content in the curriculum standard is not an aggregation of knowledge points but a carrier with the orientation of educating people. In such guiding documents as curriculum standards, there should be designs and prompts on which aspects of abilities, concepts and qualities of students can be cultivated by different contents. For teachers who design teaching, textbook compilers, and evaluation proposition personnel, the inescapable curriculum element is curriculum content. If there is no programmatic document that directly regulates and prompts the educational goals corresponding to the content, these users of curriculum standards need to consciously define the goal functions of the content in their respective work processes. Deviations in the understanding of different people will lead to the attenuation of the effectiveness of curriculum implementation. Or, if the users of the curriculum do not consciously and systematically reflect on the purpose of education, then the talent cultivation goals will be useless, and the teaching and examination processes will degenerate into a process of teaching knowledge, memorizing knowledge and examining knowledge. Only when curriculum standards systematically consider and establish contents that carry talent cultivation goals can the goals be implemented in the teaching and evaluation processes.

(2)Transformation of Talent Cultivation Goals in Textbooks

Textbooks are the main basis for teachers to design teaching and organize classroom teaching, so the design of textbooks should provide appropriate support for teachers' "teaching". Firstly, the concepts, propositions and principles selected in the textbooks are the medium for teacher-student interaction in the classroom. The exercises, experiments and situations provided in the textbooks provide materials for teachers to design exercise activities, experimental activities, discussion activities and inquiry activities in the classroom. Secondly, in order to help teachers better organize classroom activities, textbooks should give guiding prompts for the teaching activity process, that is, textbook designers should appropriately decompose and present the thinking process, activity process and inquiry process to help teachers obtain corresponding teaching strategies. Finally, as a medium for "education", textbooks should have the potential function of comprehensive education, help teachers understand and explore the ideological values behind subject knowledge, and provide materials for cultivating interdisciplinary abilities.

The compilation of textbooks should reflect the stage nature of the learning process, provide scaffolds for the occurrence of learning, and provide assistance for in-depth learning. Firstly, the basic logic of textbook compilation should be internally consistent with the laws of students' cognitive development, and the contents should be arranged in a progressive or spiral ascending manner according to the phased characteristics of children's cognitive development. Children's cognitive characteristics, reading habits and aesthetic needs determine that textbooks for different learning stages have different presentation methods and style characteristics. Secondly, textbook compilation should consider the context in which learning occurs. The learning process takes place in context, a process of extending and expanding experience and internalizing new knowledge. The context provided by textbooks can be connected with learners' past knowledge, mobilize learners' pre-conceptions, and allow learners to "confront" the confusion of new knowledge with past experience in the context. Finally, the textbook should be a guide for students' inquiry activities. Centering on new knowledge, textbook designers can design a large number of in-depth and wide-ranging inquiry activities. What is presented in textbooks are the materials for inquiry activities and the requirements for key steps, and blanks are left for the results of each action, allowing learners to generate in-depth, wide-ranging and guiding inquiry learning in the interaction process with textbook texts. It is necessary to systematically transform the requirements of textbooks to carry out talent cultivation goals.

1. Intermediate Transformation of Talent Cultivation Goals in Textbooks

Textbooks are the basis for teachers to design teaching activities in the classroom and the map for students to carry out inquiry activities. Textbooks should carry and reflect cultivation goals, but they do not directly state these goals and intentions. Talent cultivation goals are abstract and need to be reflected through the cooperation of various content elements to guide classroom activities and students' learning activities and ultimately achieve the goals. For example, the cultivation of ideas and the formation of values are the results of a combination of conceptual cognition, emotional resonance and post-action comprehension. The role of textbooks lies in presenting materials that can carry cognition, resonance and comprehension. This material is the intermediary, and the story can be such an intermediary. This story should be familiar to students and commonly exists in life, while at the same time, the plot of the story can trigger a clear thought or reflections on moral creed, with a dilemma in the judgment of the conclusion. The compilation of textbooks does not lie in how to directly express these target moral items but in selecting and writing such stories with carrying capacity. With these materials, students, with the help of teachers, analyze familiar life events, compare the demands of different value subjects, and thus clarify their own values and learn the process of value establishment. Another example is that the formation of cooperative ability cannot be achieved simply by putting forward the requirement of cooperation. The premise of cooperation is purposeful group activities and clear division of labor, and inquiry activities are the intermediary for forming cooperative ability. When designing inquiry activities based on the unit content, the compiler should preset a complete inquiry process, and the problems dealt with in the activities are the cognitive key points of the unit content. Through the prompts and blanks in textbooks, the group divides the work to collect materials, compares materials and record actions, making the text lead students' activities to cooperate in activities, obtain conclusions in cooperation, and construct new knowledge in discussion and reflection. In this process, students learn inquiry methods, develop thinking habits, and form cooperative ability.

2. Multi-modal Transformation of Talent Cultivation Goals in Textbooks

Different subjects can have the same cultivation goals, but due to different subject characteristics, each subject has different abilities to express certain abilities and different abilities to present certain ideas or concepts. Talent cultivation goals can be presented as the background of learning content, which can be scattered infiltration, coherent linear system presentation, or a three-dimensional form where knowledge and behavioral experiences are intertwined, etc., forming different impacts on students' cognition, emotion and behavioral intention. Briefly speaking, the same talent cultivation goals can have multiple manifestations in textbooks. For example, for the cultivation goal of promoting fine traditional culture, there can be multiple transformation ways in textbooks. It can replace the context in math example problems, such as traditional Chinese math problems like "chickens and rabbits in the same cage" and "measuring a well with a rope", and present cultural elements as the background of learning content. It can also keep the theme content unchanged and mention terms such as the Four Great Inventions in ancient China and historical celebrities in the texts of *Chinese Language*, *Geography* and other textbooks to form a scattered presentation of cultural elements. In addition, it can also take Chinese literary achievements in different periods such as the poetry of Tang Dynasty, the iambic verses of Song Dynasty, the drama of Yuan Dynasty and the novels of Ming and Qing dynasties as one of the main contents and run through the textbooks to form a linear presentation of cultural elements. Moreover, in the exercises of geography textbooks, students can also be asked to collect photos, pictures and related stories of famous scenic spots and historical sites in various parts of China that they have visited, and form a three-dimensional form that is intertwined with the geography subject through displaying, communicating, feeling and experiencing the thickness and richness of Chinese culture.

3. Focused Transformation of Talent Cultivation Goals in Textbooks

In recent years, the "big idea" (also translated as "big concept") proposed in the field of science education represents a focused approach to the transformation of talent cultivation goals in textbooks, which aims to systematically cover and integrally process the information, knowledge, skills and other contents that give rise to the scientific concept under the umbrella of the scientific concept. The "big idea" (big concept) serves as a bridge connecting the cultivation goals and textbooks and is the anchor point for focusing the grand goal abilities in textbooks. Firstly, it is a specific manifestation of competence, which is a high-level cognition involving attitudes, values, and ways of thinking based on facts and knowledge.[1] Secondly, the big concept contains a clear content system of knowledge, skills, etc., which can integrate the learning process by selecting, editing and organically organizing with the help of the content scope and logical sequence of relevant subjects. Introducing the concept of big idea in textbook design helps students grasp the key threads of the subject

1 Wiggins, G., Mctighe, J. & Alexandria, V. *Understanding by Design*[M]. Association for Supervision and Curriculum Development, 2005:66-78.

through understanding and applying the big idea. Meanwhile, it simplifies the cumbersome knowledge points in the content system, reduces the content volume, and corrects persistent problems in the curriculum such as being overly complicated, biased and outdated. Promoting the focused construction of cultivation goals with the idea of big idea clarifies the overall thinking of textbook system design and forms a connection system of scientific concepts with the help of the textbook content network composed of big idea groups. Taking the life cycle in science education as an example, during the learning process, students may be very familiar with the specific contents of the four developmental stages of a specific organism like a butterfly. However, when parents ask what they are learning, they may only answer that they are learning about the developmental stages of the butterfly, without realizing the scientific big idea that all living things have a life cycle consisting of birth, growth, prosperity and death. The redundant fragments of knowledge obscure the key points in the entire scientific learning process, while using the big idea to focus on the cultivation goals in textbooks can avoid the complexity of relevant contents and reconstruct the process for students to achieve the cultivation goals.

4. Multi-level Transformation of Talent Cultivation Goals in Textbooks

The real world that students live in is complex and diverse. Correspondingly, talent cultivation goals are also comprehensive and rich, including orientations in multiple aspects such as knowledge, skills and values. Therefore, textbooks should provide possibilities for learners to have multi-level interactions with the texts, and the same unit content can be designed with multi-level goals. Firstly, textbooks should clearly express subject contents. The starting point of any talent cultivation goal is based on basic concepts, knowledge and skills, which need to be acquired through practice and practical activities. These are all instrumental aspects that textbooks can present. Secondly, the same subject content can be designed to cultivate subject thinking and interdisciplinary abilities through reading materials, inquiry activities and discussion activities. In addition, experiences and reflections after reading and activities can lead to thinking about individual values, social values and historical values. All of these should become the "potential curriculum" with designs and intentions in textbooks. For example, in the statistics section of the German primary school mathematics textbook, the meaning of fractions is first reviewed through the context of pizza, and basic operation exercises are carried out, followed by activity designs. Students work in groups to conduct investigations in the whole class, discover mathematical problems in class life, collect information, make questionnaires, record information and sort out materials. After obtaining the materials, the results of the investigation activities are used to learn the core mathematical knowledge of this unit: how to make tables, count frequencies, and make various statistical charts. Next is the application of mathematical knowledge with very extensive application contexts such as using the acquired statistical knowledge in fields related to science, technology and life like geography, economics and astronomy. Finally, there will be hierarchical level tests. From the textbook design, it is easy to find that mathematical statistical knowledge is integrated into a multi-level goal category, and problem-solving, cooperative ability, financial competence, etc. run through the formation and training of mathematical knowledge and skills. Meanwhile, the real, complex and difficult materials in the application exercises of mathematics enable students to deeply understand the value of mathematical knowledge to science, technology and life while practicing new knowledge, understand the meaning of new knowledge, and even the meaning of mathematics. It is not difficult to see that the design goals of textbook designers are clear, rich and diverse.

Ensuring the quality of textbooks and guaranteeing their orientation, scientific nature, and suitability are the core issues in textbook construction. During the process of textbook compilation, new requirements and new structures of talent cultivation goals in the new era should be absorbed, and ways for the systematic and scientific implementation and transformation of talent cultivation goals in textbooks should be explored. Managers of textbook construction should make overall plans to ensure that textbooks for different learning stages and different subjects can systematically, hierarchically, and integrally reflect the cultivation goals. For textbook compilers, they should not only have a clear ideological direction and a high-level understanding of the subject itself but also study the laws of textbook compilation, especially for adolescents, the growth laws unique to their age groups should be particularly respected. This is the most fundamental and professional guarantee for improving the quality of textbooks and achieving talent cultivation goals.

[Originally published in *Educational Research* 2018(12) (Lv Lijie & Li Gang)]

7. Cultivating Subject Core Competencies: the Value Demand of Curriculum Implementation

In 2014, the *Opinions of the Ministry of Education on Comprehensively Deepening Curriculum Reform and Implementing the Fundamental Task of Fostering Virtue in Education* pointed out: "Implement core competencies in subject teaching to promote students' all-round development with individuality." Since then, core competencies have become one of the hot topics in educational reforms, especially in curriculum reforms, with subject core competencies emerging as the primary value pursuit of curriculum implementation. Therefore, this paper intends to address the following questions in the actual curriculum implementation field: What is the teaching modality for cultivating subject core competencies? What is the theoretical foundation implied in such teaching?

I. Subject Core Competencies: The Link between Cultivation Goals and Curriculum Implementation

(1) Subject Core Competencies: Decomposition of Cultivation Goals

Core competencies are the current goals and directions in basic education. The *Core Competencies for Chinese Students' Development* officially released by the Ministry of Education in September 2016 has become the general reference for talent cultivation goals in all educational stages in China. As cultivation goals that focus on the all-round development of people, core competencies emphasize fundamentality, universality, identity and interdisciplinarity, constituting a relatively abstract overarching concept. To bridge the gap between top-down cultivation goals and bottom-up curriculum implementation, research on subject core competencies has emerged, and each discipline has individually outlined the constituent elements of its core competencies. For example, the subject core competencies of mathematics can be divided into mathematical abstraction, logical reasoning, mathematical modeling, intuitive imagination, mathematical operation and data analysis; those of physics are divided into physical concepts, scientific thinking, experimental inquiry, scientific attitude and responsibility, etc. Subject core competencies are the disciplinary-specific articulation of quality standards for talent cultivation. They originate from the extraction and condensation of disciplinary essence, aiming to enable students to acquire important thinking qualities, concepts and abilities that they should possess when facing themselves, others and the world through learning specific subject knowledge and skills, comprehending ideas and values, acquiring methods and being influenced by attitudes and emotions. Some scholars believe that the relationship between core competencies and subject core competencies is that of the whole and the part, the common and the individual, and the abstract and the concrete.[1] Different from core competencies, subject core competencies emphasize disciplinarity and uniqueness, which are specific expressions and requirements of core competencies at the subject level and in practical aspects and also serve as a transitional bridge for core competencies to enter the curriculum implementation process.

(2) Subject Core Competencies: The Direction of Curriculum Implementation

As the decomposition of students' development core competencies, subject core competencies connect the requirements of cultivation goals upwards and guide the direction of curriculum implementation downwards. If students' development core competencies need to be embodied and realized in the process of school education, then subject core competencies need to be embodied in the process of curriculum implementation (specifically classroom teaching).

Then, where is the core point of curriculum implementation directed at

---

1 Zhong Qiquan. Curriculum Development Based on Core Competencies: Challenges and Issues[J]. *Global Education*, 2016(12):3-25.

subject core competencies? It is written in the *Framework for 21st Century Learning* in the United States: "Education in the 21st century should be based on core knowledge, but the subject knowledge here does not refer to storing a pile of facts but refers to subject concepts and ways of thinking, with the aim of enabling students to think like subject experts."[1] Obviously, the education in the 21st century here mainly refers to subject education and teaching, and its goal orientation is consistent with the subject core competencies we advocate. The shared value pursuit is that subject teaching should go beyond the mere transmission of knowledge and skills, delving to the origin, development, value and meaning of knowledge as well as the internal essence and laws of the subject, guide students to understand the world and analyze problems from a disciplinary perspective, and form disciplinary awareness and thinking habits. Curriculum implementation directed at subject core competencies originates in but transcends it, representing students' profound grasp of disciplinary essence and laws through curriculum learning. Characterized by durability and transferability, these competencies empower students to apply the acquired subject knowledge and skills to daily life and help them think and solve problems from the subject perspective.

Returning to the reality, what does the curriculum implementation directed at subject core competencies look like? How to get students to think like subject experts in this process? What is the implied theoretical foundation? This study takes three teachers' different approaches to teaching the same lesson as a case and attempts to analyze and discuss these topics.

---

1 Zhang Hua. On the Connotations of A Key Competence[J]. *Global Education*, 2016(4):10-14.

II. Distinguish the True from the False: What Kind of Teaching Can Realize the "Implementation" of Subject Core Competencies?

What does the teaching based on subject core competencies look like? This study takes three junior high school mathematics teachers' different teaching practices in the same lesson as examples to analyze what kind of teaching can cultivate students' subject core competencies and what cannot. The teaching content in the case is the learning of the system of linear equations in two unknowns in the second year of junior high school, and three teachers conduct different practices to guide students to learn. The first part of the three practices is to use the "chickens and rabbits in the same cage" problem in the textbook to guide students to the learning of the system of linear equations in two unknowns, but the starting points, focuses and the target orientations are completely different. The three approaches to the same example problem represent three typical understandings of the teaching meaning. From the perspective of the teaching transformation of subject core competencies, these three classes also represent what should the teaching directed at subject core competencies be and be not. For the convenience of narration, the three teachers are temporarily numbered as A, B and C.

(1) Teaching Directed at Problem-solving Skills

The teaching starting point chosen by Teacher A is the conditions and questions in the example. The teaching process follows the logical steps of solution, and students acquire fixed calculation methods and operational skills. In Teacher A's mind, the primary goal of teaching is how to find the "solution". No matter what the question is, what learners need to do is to quickly find the known quantities, remember the formulas, list the equation, master the algorithms skillfully, and obtain the answers. In this way, the learning process is completed. Under the domination of this teaching concept, the learning content is "streamlined" into theorem knowledge and algorithm skills. What students experience is learning one solution through examples and then learning more solutions through more exercises. Obviously, the process of teaching and learning lacks interest and real thinking. The teaching goal only stays at the level of acquiring problem-solving skills, and what students obtain are just methods to cope with exams.

(2) Teaching Directed at Knowledge Application

The teaching analysis of Teacher B needs to be considered from three aspects. Firstly, Teacher B's teaching design reflects the care for students' interests. In the lead-in part, Teacher B introduces an interesting TV program, and the class immediately becomes active. However, by further analyzing the content of this video and the way it is used, it is not difficult to find that Teacher B just uses it to introduce the topic, and the logic of all the subsequent learning content has no substantial connection with the video content, or rather, the video does not bring learners to think but only plays a role in enlivening the atmosphere.

Secondly, Teacher B absorbs new ideas of reform in the application of teaching methods. After presenting the question, students are asked to find two solutions and then compare and think about the characteristics of the two methods through discussion and presentation, leaving students with a certain amount of tension in their thinking. In this way, students have a more comprehensive experience and perception of the role and function of the new content - the system of linear equations in two unknowns. The idea of designing teaching methods from the perspective of students' learning is worthy of affirmation.

Finally, although this teacher guides students to think independently, if we deeply explore what students are actually thinking about in this class, it is easily to find that students' thinking just stays at the application of the equation system method, lacking a real understanding of the equation's origins, practical applications and their connections with the real life.

(3) Teaching Directed at Subject Core Competencies

Teacher C "takes great pains" in the part of guiding students to understand the mathematical meaning in the question, that is, to find the equivalent relationship. First, Teacher C inspires students to represent the relationship between the elements in the question by using the word description method and the pattern method. Then, students are asked to solve the problem by using the arithmetic method, the method of linear equation in one unknown, and the method of the system of linear equations in two unknowns which is the key content and make analogies, comparing the algorithm value of the system of linear equations in two unknowns. Finally, Teacher C extends the solution to a mathematical model. From finding the equivalent relationship to connecting all possible mathematical methods and then to modeling the methods, Teacher C's teaching implies such a thinking logic:

Firstly, the teaching starting point for Teacher C to deal with the problem is the mathematical element and mathematical relationship contained in the story itself, that is, to discover mathematical problems in the story and think about how to solve them. The thinking activity designed by Teacher C is to express the equivalent relationship in the real situation by using natural language or semi-symbolic language (graphics), so that students can understand that the essence of an equation is an equality relationship established between unknown number and given number in order to find unknowns. Students establish a connection between the intuitive abstraction process and the learning of equations, understanding that the difference between the linear equation in one unknown and the system of linear equations in two unknowns is not essential but just more complicated in terms of algorithms.

Secondly, when students review the several solutions they use and master, Teacher C explains the comparison of these methods as the significance of mathematics in solving problems in life, and that this significance can generate a more universal form, that is, a class of problems can all be solved by equation method. This universal form is symbolic expression. Students complete the second abstraction of equation modeling through understanding the significance.

Finally, Teacher C helps students establish subject ideas. On one side are problems in life, and on the other side are a series of method systems that can solve the problems and the general model of the methods. There is a span and also a connection between the starting point and the ending point of this teaching, through which students experience the mathematical abstraction idea, the classification idea and the model idea in an orderly manner, and understand the significance of mathematical development to the real life. If this learning experience that touches the essence of the subject continues to accumulate, it will be further internalized into students' subject concepts, guiding students to view the surrounding world and analyze problems from a subject perspective.

So, what is the teaching directed at the cultivation of subject core competencies? From the previous analysis, we can know that subject core competencies are the understanding of the essence, characteristics, laws and values of the subject formed after the accumulation of subject knowledge and experience, as well as the general views to the world. Teaching directed at the cultivation of subject core competencies does not mean narrowing the teaching goals, reducing teaching to the solution of example problems, simplifying students' learning to mechanical imitation and memory, catering for students' interests formally, and "wrapping the unpalatable things with sugar coating and letting students swallow them whole".[1] The teaching focuses on experiencing knowledge discovery and understanding knowledge's deeper meaning. It is a process of connecting old and new knowledge by retrieving previous experience, a process of obtaining learning experience through independent thinking or inquiry, and a process of generalizing and improving the acquired general views on subject values, natural laws, and social problems after the accumulation and

---

1 Dewey, J. *Democracy and Education*[M]. Translated by Wang Chengxu. Beijing: People's Education Press, 2001:64.

advancement of subject experience.

III. Deep Focus: What Theoretical Foundation Contain the Teaching of Cultivating Subject Core Competencies?

(1) The Starting Point of Teaching: the Internal Relationship with Experience

At the starting point of teaching, it is necessary to arouse children's interests. "If individual's initiative, enthusiasm, participation and doubts cannot be integrated into learning, their learning interests and motives will disappear in the boring and monotonous classroom learning, and their sense of doubt and critical spirit will be completely wiped out by the ideas they believe, follow and adhere to."[1] More importantly, it is the connection between interests and new knowledge. Every child has a world picture in his heart, and all learning and development are the expansion, extension, and transformation of this world picture. The starting point of teaching is children's life experience or cognitive experience, which seems to be a sentence we often repeat. But what is the significance of this starting point for learning? Contemporary learning researchers believe that "when learning concepts and methods, a new piece of information is rarely inserted into the ranks of the knowledge already mastered. The existing knowledge will reject all ideas that cannot resonate with it... When the received information seriously shakes his perception of the world, he would rather give it up. The learner may record this information but will never use it."[2] Therefore, for the teaching starting point in relation to students' experience, it not only arouses students' interests and attention but also reveals the structural alignment between prior knowledge and new concepts, ensuring that "empty

---

1 Ernest, P. *Philosophy of Mathematics Education*[M]. Translated by Qi Jianhua & Zhang Songzhi. Shanghai: Shanghai Educational Publishing House, 1998:203-217.

2 Giordan, A. *Nature of Learning*[M]. Translated by Hang Ling. Shanghai: East China Normal University Press, 2

associations" are replaced with purposeful cognitive links. In order to learn new knowledge, it is necessary to find the students' existing knowledge ranks or concept systems. Effective teaching not only requires teachers to establish the "association" but also needs to make students feel this association, which should also be created between old and new methods for solving problems, and between new concepts and current phenomena. Only by establishing this "association" can "personal ideas be directly confronted with objects, experiences, or the preconceived concepts of other learners"[1]. The process of confrontation is the process of deconstructing the original concepts, that is, the process of increasing new knowledge.

In the above case, Teacher C asks students to identify the equivalent relationship in the example problem by using language and then abstracts it into graphics to draw the equivalent relationship. This process "retrieves" the relevant common sense systems and concept systems which are necessary associations for learning new knowledge in students' cognitive structures. Therefore, at the starting point of students' learning, the teacher should not only set an appropriate situation to arouse students' experience but also retrieve the knowledge system in the experience so that profound learning can be possible.

(2) The Support of Teaching: Deep Interaction with Texts

In teaching design, teachers' different ways of using textbooks reveal their different views on textbooks, and different understandings of curriculum and textbook by teachers will lead to different teaching plans. Some teachers use textbooks in a way that completely rely on textbooks, replicating all the textbook content as teaching content and simply converting the text content into audible content. Under such circumstance, students only understand the textbook based on their own cognitive levels. Some teachers rely on textbooks to add or subtract

---

1 Dewey, J. *The School and Society and The Child and the Curriculum*[M]. Taipei: Wu-Nan Book Inc., 1989:119.

content or adjust the order to vividly represent the textbooks, activating the solid texts and turning them into vivid experiences for students. Some teachers go beyond the superficial expressions of textbook texts and carry out "deep interaction" with the texts, thinking about the profound meanings carried by the texts from the perspective of subject experts. Such teachers use the materials in the texts to connect students' experiences, guide students to understand and explore the ideas behind the materials, and then inspire these vivid experiences and insights into contemplative wisdom, which is manifested as the integration of previous and subsequent principles, so that students can achieve a thorough understanding from observing phenomena to suddenly realizing general rules.

The case in this study reflects the different ways in which teachers use textbooks under the guidance of different textbook views. Simply reading the example problem, students only learn the solution samples of the current examples. "Generalizing" the example problem to a problem class, students can learn the solutions for similar problems. Connecting the old and new knowledge and establishing the thinking of equivalent relationships based on the example problem, students can learn the core of the whole equation thought. This perspective has already touched the essence of the subject, and students can make broader transfers of problems based on this, with far-reaching significance of learning.

(3) The Way of Teaching: Active Exploration of the World

Dewey compared the content of textbooks to a map, "A map is a summary, an orderly arrangement of previous experiences, and can serve as a guide for future experiences."[1] Although a map is convenient for "memory" and "observation", it is detached from the various situations when it was originally discovered, while real learning is an exploration with reference to the map.

---

1 Dewey, J. *The School and Society and The Child and the Curriculum*[M]. Taipei: Wu-Nan Book Inc., 1989:119.

Therefore, in teaching, teachers should consciously guide students to carry out active exploration of the unknown world by relying on the "map".

In the case, Teacher A teaches the example problem in a verbatim manner and students just identify the logical relationships in the example, memorize the knowledge points in it, and continuously repeat this fixed and limited logical relationship in subsequent exercises to deepen the memory of the knowledge points. In such a learning process, it is difficult for students to transfer knowledge and use the learned knowledge to explain and solve problems. For this reason, Teacher A asks students to do a large number of exercises to cope with the problem of inability to transfer knowledge, which enables students to spontaneously construct a knowledge system in the exercises to cope with different examination questions.

Teacher B clearly illustrates the characteristics of a problem class represented by the example problem, the reasons for choosing methods, and the skills for solving problems in the teaching process, which is equivalent to presenting a complete "map" to students. Students understand the whole picture of the "map" and learn to use the "map", but their thinking is still limited to the abstracted results on the "map". In fact, students only carry out superficially "thorough" learning.

Teacher C guides students to experience all the solutions one by one around the question, and lets students experience and reflect on the continuity and transition of methods in the context of a coherent thinking process, perceiving the thinking space and tension in the face of the problem. In addition, Teacher C positions the focus of teaching on finding the equivalent relationship, which is the core of the equation thought, so that students can go beyond the summary elements of the "map" and concentrate on experiencing the adventure of drawing the "map". The process in which students draw their own "map" about equation question by themselves is a process of subject core competencies cultivation. How competencies are generated requires not only the ideas themselves but also the establishment of understanding these ideas.

(4) The Destination of Teaching: Encounter with the Essence and Meaning of Knowledge

Subject core competencies are the goals of subject teaching. Transcending simple knowledge indoctrination and skill training, and establishing subject concepts and subject thinking are the teaching goals emphasized by the current curriculum reform. For students, the elevation of subject knowledge to subject core competencies means placing knowledge in historical, current and future lives, and recognizing, understanding, grasping, experiencing and applying it with a holistic and developmental mindset, that is, encountering with the essence and meaning of knowledge. At the same time, it is also necessary to be able to explain the world with systematic knowledge and thus establish an attitude towards nature, society and others. Therefore, subject core competencies are related to knowledge itself, the logic of knowledge and the meaning of knowledge.

Firstly, teaching design should establish a connection between students' existing cognition and new knowledge. It is necessary to think about what new knowledge learners will accept based on their existing cognition, because new knowledge is the broader picture of the world, which is the nature, society and others related to oneself, and is what students need to know and want to know. Learners feel the significance of new knowledge to themselves and want to explore new knowledge. Therefore, Whitehead said "Learners want to accept a new knowledge not to prove its correctness but to prove its value."

Secondly, the destination of teaching lies in guiding students to fully understand the origin and development, essence, laws, values and meaning of knowledge, helping students establish the connection between knowledge and historical, current and future lives, and letting students feel how to flexibly use knowledge to solve practical problems in life. "Ideas that cannot be utilized are positively harmful... Interrelated truths are utilized en bloc, and the various propositions are employed in any order, and with any reiteration... When children prove and utilize a certain knowledge, they should have no doubt when it is proving and when it is utilizing."[1]

Teacher B's class in the case enables students to learn the solutions to equations, but the significance of learning the solutions is still limited to being able to answer the questions designed by others. Teacher C connects the graphic method, arithmetic method, the linear equation in one unknown and the linear equations in two unknowns, so that students can experience the differences between the linear equations in two unknowns and other methods, especially the arithmetic method. Students can also feel what changes in thinking would be brought about by each development and transformation of methods, thus understanding the value and application of the equation thought and even the mathematical thought. In this way, new knowledge is placed in a coherent context of thinking. Standing at the height of an observer, students see the connection and significance between previous learning methods and current new knowledge methods like experts, and can even reserve a cognitive structural space for future learning. Students not only experience the significance of new knowledge in solving current situational problems but also establish a more profound way and concept of viewing the world.

(5) The Challenge of Teaching: "Moderate Game" with the Relationships between Elements

Whitehead compared how to choose teaching methods to the "rhythm" of teaching. Rhythm includes the sequence, time and frequency of various ways, methods and activity arrangements in teaching, as well as the artistry of the use of ways, methods and activities. That is, when they are generated, whether they match the content, whether they are consistent with the teacher's style, and whether they are in line with the students' needs.

---

1 Whitehead, A. N. *The Aims of Education*[M]. Translated by Zhuang Lianping & Wang Lizhong. Shanghai: Wenhui Publishing House Co., Ltd., 2012:6-7.

1. Knowledge and Thinking Ability

Which is more important between knowledge and thinking ability is not a new controversial issue in the field of education. The relevance and mutual constitution of the two determine that both should be the central purposes in education and teaching. In Whitehead's view, on the one hand, the student's mind is not a "box" that can be ruthlessly filled with various unfamiliar concepts. On the other hand, orderly acquisition of knowledge is the natural "food" for students' developing minds. It is important for students to acquire knowledge, which is the natural "food" for enriching their minds, but students are not simply "boxes" in which various "foods" are stored. Whitehead described the main purpose of intellectual education as imparting knowledge and developing wisdom. "Wisdom is the way to master knowledge", which involves the processing, selection and application of knowledge. That is to say, although it is important for students to obtain "food", it is more important for them to acquire "wisdom". Furthermore, Whitehead compared the acquisition of wisdom and knowledge to freedom and training, "The only avenue toward wisdom is freedom in the presence of knowledge. But the only avenue toward knowledge is by discipline in the acquirement of ordered facts."[1] He believed that these were two elements of education, and the rhythm of education was the adjustment of freedom and training. "Freedom and training, these two principles are not opposed and should be adjusted in children's lives to adapt to the natural changes in their personality development."[2]

Therefore, freedom and training, that is, the development of thinking ability and the consolidation of knowledge in teaching are both necessary. "In a perfect educational system with an ideal structure, the goal should be to make training

---

1 Whitehead, A. N. *The Aims of Education*[M]. Translated by Zhuang Lianping & Wang Lizhong. Shanghai: Wenhui Publishing House Co., Ltd., 2012:43.

2 Dewey, J. *The Child and the Curriculum*[M]. Translated by Lin Baoshan & Kang Chunzhi. Taipei: Wu-Nan Book Inc., 1990:112.

the spontaneous result of free choice, and freedom should be enriched with opportunities because of training." Freedom and training are included in the same teaching activity. Without exploring the essence of problems, it is impossible to consolidate knowledge, and without facing the essential attributes of knowledge, there is no way to train thinking. Just like the three-dimensional goals we mentioned, it is not a matter of first training knowledge and skills in a class, then emphasizing the process and method, and highlighting the emotional attitudes to form values in the last five minutes before class is over. Instead, the same teaching activity already contains goal orientations in different dimensions.

2. The Essence of the Subject and the Learner-centeredness

The current classroom reform emphasizes the transformation from "teaching" to "learning", a concept that is reasonable and progressive. In a broad sense, the teaching process is actually also a part of the orderly learning process of students under the planning and guidance of teachers, which requires teachers to arrange the learning content in the classroom and choose appropriate learning methods according to the psychological logic of students' learning. However, in response to the call for reform, the current teaching reforms in many schools emphasize students' independent learning and cooperative learning, blindly weakening teachers' instructions. Some schools even require teachers to instruct as little as possible and let students discuss more. Teachers' instructions must occur after students' discussions and must be a summary of students' independent learning. These practices do have a certain effect on changing the deep-rooted cramming teaching habits, but is this the ideal classroom learning mode?

Conceptually speaking, teachers' teaching is to help students construct their own knowledge structures. The perfect interpretation of teachers does not mean that students will have good learning effects. But can breaking the integrity of teachers' interpretation surely guarantee the high quality and efficiency of students' learning? Such a proposition is certainly unreasonable. A large amount of time can be arranged in the classroom for students' independent learning and cooperative discussion, but the premise is to understand what students are learning and discussing - is it the essential issue of knowledge? Whether the new knowledge constructed by students points to subject concepts? Whether the unique thinking mode of the subject is used?

Both the essence of the subject and learner-centeredness should be considered when teachers design teaching. The relationship between the two is as Dewey said, "The child and the curriculum are simply two limits which define a single process. Just as two points define a straight line, so the present standpoint of the child and the facts and truths of studies define instruction." The transformation of the classroom is from "teaching-centered" to "learning-centered", not from subject-centered to student-centered. The core of teaching is student learning, and the purpose is the growth of students' core competencies. However, learning and growth are not empty, nor can they be superficial. The essence of the subject and learner-centeredness are not a matter of who determines who, or who comes first and who comes second, but a matter of unification in teaching.

[Originally published in *Curriculum, Teaching Material and Method* 2017(9) (Lv Lijie, Han Jiwei & Zhang Xiaojuan)]

8. Study on Hierarchy of Key Competencies in School Curriculum Transformation

It has become an international trend to promote curriculum reform based on students' key competencies, and international organizations such as the European Union and many countries and regions in the world have paid great attention to it. In 2014, China promulgated the *Opinions of the Ministry of Education on Comprehensively Deepening Curriculum Reform and Implementing the Fundamental Task of Fostering Virtue in Education*, defining key competencies as "the essential qualities and key abilities that students need to adapt to lifelong development and social development". The establishment of the key competencies system for students' development has a guiding value for grasping the direction of school running and for the development of national curriculum and school curriculum. Key competencies need to be transformed into school curriculum, teachers' teaching understanding and individualized student development plans through national curriculum and the school philosophies.

I. Key Competencies and School Educational Philosophy

(1) Characteristics of Key Competencies

1. Criticality

Key competencies are critical competencies, which are the most critical and central competencies among the numerous competencies required for an individual's lifelong development. Key competencies are not comprehensive competencies but indispensable competencies in response to the needs of life situations. Their criticality ensures that they are both universal and fundamental. Key competencies are the common competencies that everyone must possess and the foundational competencies for an individual's future development. Its criticality is not determined by individuals but by the whole, a concentrated reflection of the requirements for individual competencies in a specific time and space. Although the concept of key competencies is newly proposed, it is a concept that can span thousands of years, and the manifestations of its criticality will change in different eras. For example, physical health was a key competence in the agricultural era and an important competence for human survival and reproduction at that time, but in the information age, it can only be seen as a basic competence, not a key competence.

2. Comprehensiveness

The comprehensiveness of key competencies is manifested in two aspects: static comprehensiveness and dynamic comprehensiveness. The static comprehensiveness means that key competencies are the comprehensive manifestation of the requirements on students' knowledge, skills, emotions, attitudes values and so on. Key competencies do not point to independent knowledge, nor independent ability and independent thinking, but the combination of all these aspects. Key competencies are no longer the fragmentation of the three-dimensional goals, but the correction of the previous educational bias of emphasizing knowledge, neglecting ability and ignoring emotional attitude and values, paying more attention to the integrated and continuous cultivation. The dynamic comprehensiveness means that key competencies show a certain degree of comprehensiveness in individual actions and situations. No single key competence can solve problems independently. In order to achieve a certain goal, key competencies intersect and combine with each other and form problem-solving strategies and solutions according to a certain logical order.

3. Relevance

Key competencies combine individual development with social development, and connect individual value with social value. On the individual side, the acquisition of key competencies enables individuals to better realize their own value and better adapt to the development and changes of future society. On the social side, key competencies are the products of social development and at the same time the cornerstones of social development. The healthy development of society is inseparable from the improvement of individual qualities. Key competencies reflect the requirements of individual development for itself and the requirements of social development for individuals, and its dual connotations endow key competencies with important status and important roles. This relevance of key competencies has positive significance for both individuals and society.

4. Generativeness

Within a certain period of time, key competencies are stable, while over a period of time, key competencies are generative. The generativeness of key competencies includes two aspects: the cumulative generativeness and the transitional generativeness. The cumulative generativeness means that for a certain key competence, its formation is phased, not achieved overnight, requiring continuous development and improvement and reflecting different development tiers at different development levels of students. The transitional generativeness refer to the key competencies required by the development needs of the times, which did not exist before and are incorporated into the student development system after being recognized.

(2) Student Competencies in the School Educational Philosophy System

Each school should have its own educational philosophy, which is the value pursuit of education by the educational subject of the school - the principal and all teachers. The philosophy is unique, a personalized understanding of the common educational policy or a personalized value expectation of the educational significance by specific educational subjects, which will be manifested in the form of the characteristic culture of specific groups. Where people gather stably for a long time, there must be a social structure and generate social interactions. In people's social interactions, standards, practices and value orientations for people and things are naturally formed. Different schools will have different characteristic cultures and different educational philosophy, which potentially and powerfully dominate the educational behaviors of school educators and even form clear and unique pursuits of educational significance.

In recent years, many schools in China have consciously reflected on and clearly put forward their own educational philosophy. This study searched the websites of 20 national demonstrative senior high schools and analyzed the school development plans they provided. It can be found that when schools formulate their own development directions, there are usually two levels of expressions: the macroscopic educational goal and the specific expected student state. At the first level, the macroscopic educational goal is put forward in the form of educational philosophy, which is a general description of the ideal person. The most common expressions are “all-round development”, “individualized development”, “harmonious development”, “diversified development” and so on. The educational philosophy puts forward the direction of student cultivation and contains the school’s value pursuit of the uniqueness of student development, serving as a fundamental guiding principle for the school’s educational work and the orientation and basis for the school’s curriculum planning and school-based curriculum development. At the second level, the macroscopic educational direction is decomposed and described as the student character and ability that the school attempts to shape through education, which is the educational result that the school hopes to obtain through its own educational process. From the school plans of these 20 demonstrative high schools, each school has expressed this appeal clearly or implicitly. Some schools directly call this appeal the student competencies to be cultivated, some imply it in the overall curriculum goals of the school and some imply it in the educational goals. Some schools focus on the content of competencies, such as “learning to care, learning to create, leadership qualifications, sound personality, national emotions, international norms, innovation ability” and so on, and some focus on the quality of competencies, such as “gifted”, “potential”, “full development of individuality” and so on.

(3) The Student Competencies Pursued by the School Are

Individualized Key Competencies

The school's educational philosophy carries the national educational policy and cultivation goals, and also reflect the school's own development needs and characteristics, a distinctive expression of the national guidelines for running schools. The student competencies appeal put forward by each school should be the decomposition of the school's educational philosophy, and at the same time the individualized and distinctive expression of the student's key competencies. That is to say, before the country put forward the key competencies, many schools have begun to consciously explore the issues of students' common competencies and key competencies. The proposal of national key competencies is not a change of the educational goal, but a further clarification. The student competencies put forward by the school are the individualized and distinctive competence parts put forward on the basis of promising to cultivate students' common competencies and key competencies in accordance with the national educational goal and in accordance with the differences in educational stages, school characteristics and student needs.

II. The Role of Student Competencies in the Transformation of School Curriculum

The school's educational philosophy needs to be transformed into the school's curriculum system, curriculum content and teaching behavior. American scholar Goodlad, in response to the hierarchical characteristics of the curriculum, divides the curriculum into five domains: ideological curriculum, formal curriculum, perceived curriculum, operational curriculum and experiential curriculum.[1] In addition, curriculum scholars such as Glatthorn, Brophy J.E and Posner also have their own classifications of the hierarchy of the curriculum. If the educational philosophy is regarded as the ideological

---

1 Goodlad, J. I. *Curriculum Inquiry: The Study of Curriculum Practice*[M]. New York: McGraw-Hill, 1979:58-64.

curriculum, then there is a problem of curriculum transformation between each hierarchy of the curriculum. Student key competencies are both the purpose and the intermediary of curriculum transformation.

(1) About Curriculum Transformation

What is curriculum transformation? Hwang Jenq-Jye, a scholar in Taiwan, China believes that it refers to "the process of gradually planning valuable abstract ideas into specific and feasible curriculum based on the principles of teacher teaching and student learning for teachers to teach effectively and students to learn effectively".[1] At present, there are two important discussion focuses in curriculum transformation. One is the curriculum transformation of multiculturalism or multicultural education theory, and the other is the curriculum transformation that curriculum decides the hierarchy. Among them, the curriculum transformation of multiculturalism refers to the introduction of previously unemphasized and unexplored issues, such as nationality, race, gender, religion and so on, into the original school curriculum system in three ways: infusion, integration and specialization.[2] The infusion curriculum transformation refers to placing new curriculum ideas and contents in the original curriculum and infiltrating them into curriculum objectives, curriculum contents, curriculum texts and curriculum evaluations to influence student learning. The integration transformation refers to connecting new ideas with the current curriculum and merging them together, but with insufficient penetration. The specialization transformation refers to opening up special topics for a certain idea, allowing students to explore in depth and learn in a targeted manner. Generally speaking, the curriculum transformation of multiculturalism refers to the curriculum changes at the same level, that is, infiltrating or adding the

---

1 Tsai Ching-Tien & Chen Yen-Hsin. Curriculum Transformation of the Key Competencies for Nationals[J]. *Curriculum & Instruction Quarterly*, 2013(3):65.

2 Hwang Jenq-Jye. The Exploration of an Integrated Investigation Conceptual Framework for Curriculum Transformation[J]. *Curriculum & Instruction Quarterly,* 2013(3):11.

curriculum elements of multiculturalism into the original curriculum system. Curriculum transformation between hierarchy is to change the existing form of the curriculum and maintain the internal consistency of curriculum elements among various curriculum forms. The process of transforming abstract ideas into specific plans is a process of transforming the written curriculum into teachers' understanding and the teaching behavior, and of transforming the designed curriculum into the curriculum for students' experiences. In practice, curriculum elements will decay, distort, be misinterpreted, or expand and enrich between several hierarchies of the curriculum.

(2) The Role of Student Competencies in the Transformation between Curriculum Hierarchies

The variation of curriculum between hierarchies is due to the break between abstract ideas and specific plans, between the macro and the micro, and between the text and the operation. The participation of key competencies can play an intermediary messenger role. Key competencies are the concrete, explicit and systematized embodiment of educational goals, and the curriculum transformation process can be transcribed and translated between two hierarchies of the curriculum with the help of key competencies, a metaphor inspired by the intergenerational inheritance of genes in biology.

If we compare the educational philosophy to the gene DNA of the curriculum, the key competencies are the intermediary that transmits DNA-messenger RNA. The function of messenger RNA is to accurately transmit the genetic information in DNA, and this transmission process includes two steps. The first is transcription. Messenger RNA transcribes the information in DNA into a single strand with sequence to become a template. The second is translation. This template with genetic information sequence carries gene information to guide protein synthesis, or acts as a template when new proteins are synthesized. Transcription and translation are the key ways for intermediary messenger RNA to transmit genes. We can take the gene transmission mode of messenger RNA as a metaphor to describe the role of key competencies in the process of curriculum transformation. Just like RNA that transmits gene information, key competencies can also guide and frame the connection and transformation between curriculum hierarchies through transcription and translation.

At the school level, the school's appeal for student competencies is the messenger RNA of the school's educational philosophy, which is used to convey the school's direction, idea and orientation in running school. The appeal for student competencies expresses the educational purpose contained in the philosophy in the form of explicit results, and lists and describes these expected results clearly, that is, transcribes them to make philosophy explicit and serialized. This explicit sequence carries the school's understanding and pursuit of education to guide and frame the educational process including curriculum teaching, that is, translation. The competence system gathers the curriculum elements in its own structure, selects the valuable parts to match the competence system and achieves consistency with the competencies. This translation process can guide and frame the formulation of the school's curriculum planning and curriculum system, as well as guide and frame teachers' understanding and comprehension of the connotations and meanings of the current curriculum and formulate individualized guidance plans for student development. The process of curriculum hierarchy transformation mediated by key competencies is shown in Figure 2-1.

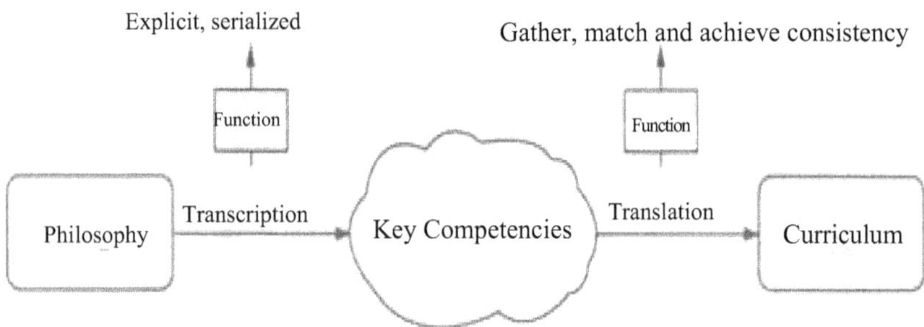

Figure 2-1 The Process of Curriculum Hierarchy Transformation Mediated by Key Competencies

III. Three Hierarchies of Curriculum Transformation at the School Level

(1) Transformation from Intention to Plan: School Curriculum Structure Based on Student Competencies

The first transformation is from the school-running concept to the school curriculum plan, and from educational concepts and educational intentions to a systematic and organized school curriculum system. What is obtained after the transformation is the curriculum structure planned by the school, also known as the school curriculum map. Starting from students' development competencies and centering on the structure of students' competencies to plan the school's curriculum structure is a logical way of thinking, a way to decompose the concept into specific implementation paths and to make educational means reflect the school-running intentions. Although schools will consider the requirements of the college entrance examination, the requirements for students to apply for foreign universities and make use of traditional school ceremonies and activity courses when establishing the curriculum system, these requirements should be integrated into the main idea of the school curriculum structure. The curriculum should be constructed based on the fundamental mission of school education and the value appeal of school education. It has been more than ten years since the senior high school curriculum reform, and many high schools have made efforts, offered many school-based curricula, and also formed complete school curriculum plans. However, there still exist some problems when some schools plan the school curriculum.

1. Plan the Curriculum According to the Actual Function of the Curriculum

The curriculum systems in many schools are piled up according to the actual functions or curriculum sources. For example, the curriculum system of a certain school is divided into basic curriculum, extension curriculum, moral education curriculum, speciality development curriculum, and advanced placement curriculum. Among them, the basic curriculum is the national compulsory curriculum, and the extension curriculum is the elective and intensive extension parts around the college entrance examination. The moral education curriculum is traditional ceremony education as well as newly opened career planning education and labor education, and the speciality development curriculum is aimed at art and sports specialties as well as competitions and club activities. The advanced placement curriculum refers to credit-bearing courses taken in advance to apply for foreign universities. From the perspective of the categories of curriculum offered, the contents are relatively rich and will have significance for the all-round and characteristic development of students. However, this kind of curriculum classification lacks a consistent idea with the school educational philosophy, and it is impossible to see how the philosophy is implemented and how the appeal for students' competencies is realized through ways of education.

2. Plan the Curriculum According to the Management Hierarchy of the Curriculum

The curriculum of some schools is divided according to the hierarchy of national curriculum, local curriculum and school curriculum, or is classified as national curriculum, local and school curriculum. This classification can show the work done by the school for curriculum development, but it still cannot show in a structured way the idea of offering curriculum, the expected functions, the reason why so many school-based curricula are offered, what knowledge and abilities of students are to be cultivated, and what curricula are offered to which types of students.

3. Plan the Curriculum According to the Division of Work

Some schools plan their curriculum system according to the school's internal work management system. For example, the curriculum is divided into national curriculum, moral education curriculum, club curriculum, and teacher curriculum, among which the teacher curriculum refers to the training courses for the professional development of teachers. This curriculum system divides the curriculum types according to the work of several departments in school management, such as teaching management, moral education management, club management, and teacher management. Although it is convenient to correspond to the work of managers, the value orientation of the curriculum itself is not clear. The problems of this curriculum plan are as follows: on the one hand, teacher curriculum is not suitable to be included in the school curriculum plan. The school curriculum plan is the implementation path of the educational philosophy and cultivation goals. The educational subjects of the school are teachers and principals, and the educational objects are students. The curriculum system is planned for the development of the educational objects - students, so the teacher curriculum should be arranged separately in the school plan. On the other hand, there will also be the problem of duplicated contents among the other three types of curriculum.

The school curriculum plan should not only combine the existing curriculum foundation but also consider the requirements of the educational philosophy and educational goals, integrating the curriculum that has been offered and has a good foundation into the system of school-running ideas. "It is particularly important to use a more systematic and sustainable transformation method, which can change learning experiences and curriculum goals."[1] Therefore, this curriculum system should be structured, with the appeal for students' competencies as the basis for planning the curriculum system and the student competence system as the template to collect and organize the school curriculum structure. This study believes that the school curriculum structure can be organized and constructed from at least two dimensions. One is the learning areas aiming at achieving key competencies. On the basis of the eight

---

1 Hwang Jenq-Jye. The Exploration of an Integrated Investigation Conceptual Framework for Curriculum Transformation[J]. *Curriculum & Instruction Quarterly*, 2013(3):11.

domains of the national senior high school curriculum, a universal curriculum content domain with characteristics is formed based on the student competence system demanded by the school. This includes common competencies such as humanistic competencies, scientific competencies and artistic competencies, together with school-characteristic curriculum such as survival abilities and leadership abilities. In addition, the school curriculum structure also needs to consider the other dimension, that is, the curriculum type. For example, according to the degree of classification and integration of knowledge and ability, it can be divided into extension curriculum, expansion curriculum, integrated curriculum, inquiry and experience curriculum and autonomous curriculum. Competencies, especially basic competencies and key competencies, are characters and abilities after integrating knowledge, skills and attitudes. Different types of curriculum have different functions in cultivating competencies. A comprehensive knowledge system that integrates experiences on knowledge, skills and attitudes can more directly contribute to the generation of competencies. These two dimensions can be presented in the form of a two-dimensional chart. This curriculum system clarifies the type of student competencies targeted by the curriculum in the vertical dimension, while in the horizontal dimension, national curriculum and school-based curriculum are not strictly distinguished, and the basic curriculum will also have the content of school-based treatment of the national curriculum. However, from left to right, the content of school's independent development gradually increases, and at the same time, the ways of curriculum implementation gradually become more open and comprehensive. Of course, some comprehensiveness must be cross-content integration. Incorporating all curricula of the school into such a structure facilitates the educational subjects of the school to reflect on whether the curriculum nutrition provided to students is balanced and whether it reflects their school-running intention, so as to correct deviations and add what is missing. At the same time, it provides a clear curriculum map for everyone who wants to know the school, indicating what the school curriculum is based on and what competencies students can be cultivated along the path.

(2) Transformation from Text to Experience: Teaching Understanding Oriented towards Student Competencies

Student learning is a process of transforming the textual curriculum into experiential curriculum, which requires the guidance, instruction and assistance from teachers. The design of teaching by teachers is to think about how to transform the materialized textual curriculum into students' experiences based on students' existing experiences. This design process includes teachers' comprehension of the textual curriculum and teachers' implementation of the comprehended curriculum.

In recent years, great changes have taken place in classroom teaching in China, and some new reform models have emerged, but problems still exist. For example, some teachers are accustomed to streamlining the curriculum content into several knowledge points, the derivation of several theorems, and the application of several rules based on their existing teaching experience or only according to the requirements of the examination syllabus, without considering the subject ideas, subject methods behind the knowledge points and the extensive social significance related to the content. Even though some changes and updates have been made in teaching forms and teaching methods, teachers' comprehension of the value of the curriculum content itself has not changed. As a result, in some seemingly reformed classrooms, the changes in students' experiences are still greatly limited. Another example is that the use of learning guides for students has increased the purposefulness and independence of students' learning, with which students can preview the content, practice independently in the classroom, discuss in groups, and present their results. However, when we analyze the content of the learning guides, we find that some so-called guides are just exercise sent to students in advance, such as the theorems to be mastered in the preview stage, exercises to be completed in the classroom group discussion, and the conclusions to be drawn in the presentation. With the implementation of school standardization construction, multimedia equipment in school has become more and more advanced, and information technology has been more widely applied. However, the purpose of using some information technology is still to help students remember and reproduce the knowledge, theorems and laws that have already presented in the textual curriculum. Without appropriate teaching methods and teaching means, the teaching content cannot achieve the teaching purpose, and students' understanding of problems is not profound. Even if teachers use methods that conform to the learning characteristics of students, they still cannot achieve the teaching goals if their understanding of the curriculum text is narrowed. Therefore, in the process of comprehension, design and implementation, teachers need to think about the fact that they are based on the curriculum text, but the purpose is not directed at the curriculum text but at students' competencies. The curriculum text is just a tool to achieve students' competencies, and how to use this tool needs to be developed by teachers.

Taking the goal of teaching - students' competencies as the thinking template for teaching design requires exploring the educational potential in the curriculum text. As a person's character and ability, competencies are comprehensive and are formed in the interaction between students and the environment. The curriculum aimed at students' competencies should be experiential and comprehensive, requiring teachers to mobilize students' comprehensive abilities as much as possible and transform the curriculum from the text form to students' experience form in students' experiences. To form students' competencies, it is necessary not only to analyze the knowledge and its gradient that students need to learn in the textual curriculum but also to analyze the possibility of multi-dimensional and multi-level experience growth that the curriculum content may bring to students and match it with the expected student competence template. Schwab named the possibilities contained in the curriculum as "curriculum potential", that is, "the curriculum contained in the subject content that is helpful to the possible growth and development of students"[1]. Exploring and comprehending curriculum potential is the premise for teaching design. Only by exploring curriculum elements can valuable curriculum elements be collected and directed at the cultivation of students' competencies. Teachers' teaching design often starts with textbook analysis.

In teaching design, teachers need to explore and organize curriculum potential. American scholar Ben-Peretz[2] believes that compared with curriculum designers who interpret subject content from a single perspective, multiple groups interpreting subject content from multiple perspectives can reveal more useful information. As the "users and developers", teachers should bear part of the responsibility for curriculum development. Teachers have certain autonomy in curriculum implementation, so Ben-Peretz advocates that in the process of curriculum implementation, teachers should not only be the faithful executors of the curriculum, but their role is to adapt the curriculum to the actual teaching situation. She does not agree that teachers participate in the curriculum development of the practical model advocated by Schwab, believing that teachers should not conduct independent curriculum development in isolation from curriculum goals. The reason is that such participation ignores teachers' research level, time and energy. Teachers' voice in the curriculum is not reflected in the curriculum design process but in the curriculum implementation and teaching design process. By analyzing and interpreting different uses of curriculum content, teachers discover curriculum potential and infiltrate their own opinions and propositions into the prescribed curriculum. Regarding how to explore curriculum potential, scholar Deng Zongyi proposed four aspects to interpret curriculum potential based on the characteristics of the curriculum text content, namely inquiry framing, socio-cultural framing, psycho-

---

1 Schwab, J. J. The Practical 3: Translation into Curriculum[J]. *School Review,* 1973(81):501-522.

2 Ben-Peretz, M. The Concept of Curriculum Potential[J]. *Curriculum Theory Network*, 1975(2):151-159.

epistemological framing, and pedagogic translation[1]. Under the inquiry framing, teachers should clarify what are the themes and key issues pertaining to the module, what are the key concepts that underlie each of the themes and how are these concepts related to the concepts in other modules, and what could be the key and the related issues for exploration. Under the socio-cultural framing, the questions that teachers should think about are what significance do the related concepts, key issues and related issues have for students, the society and the world, how might these issues arise from various socio-cultural contexts, what different perspectives can be brought to bear on addressing these issues, what kinds of critical thinking can be encouraged, and what attitudes and values are worthy of cultivation. The psycho-epistemological framing prompts teachers to think about what prerequisite knowledge and skills are needed for learning the issues and concepts, how might the key issues and concepts connect with what students learn in other school subjects or from other learning experiences in the curriculum, what do students have already known and experienced in relation to these issues and concepts, and how might their existing knowledge and experience be drawn upon for learning the issues and concepts. The pedagogic translation focuses on what could be teaching and learning activities that could broaden students' perspectives and provide them with opportunities for problem-solving, independent learning, interdisciplinary learning and critical thinking development, what resources could be employed for achieving the instructional purposes, what tools are most useful for assessing student learning, and how could the results of assessment be used to inform instruction. These four aspects are the thinking framework for teachers to analyze and explore curriculum potential.

Using these thinking frameworks to analyze curriculum potential can provide teachers with tools to analyze and think about curriculum elements at multiple levels and dimensions. Teachers of different subjects and even with

---

1 Deng Zongyi. Revisiting Curriculum Potential[J]. *Curriculum Inquiry*, 2011(3):538-559.

different teaching styles may have their own paths to analyze the curriculum. However, when teachers analyze the curriculum, they need to have a common purposive orientation, that is, to cultivate the student competencies through their teaching. The student competence system may not necessarily correspond one-to-one to the teaching content and methods at the teaching design level, but as a purposive orientation, it can help teachers break away from the habit of narrowing the curriculum content and simplifying the teaching methods.

(3) Transformation from Universal to Individual: Student Development Planning Based on Student Competencies

Key competencies are the most critical part of student competencies. The appeal for student competencies put forward by the school is the competencies that the school hopes every student should possess. However, these universal competencies do not mean that every student acquires the same level of competencies. For the same competence, different students will also have different ways of achievement. The value of the school curriculum also lies in transforming the universal competencies into an individual competence system that adapts to the characteristics and needs of students, that is, transforming the universal competencies into an individualized competence system. The following issues can be focused on:

1. Implement the Selectivity of the Curriculum

In the new curriculum reform, elective modules have been added to the senior high school curriculum on the basis of the division of liberal arts and sciences to meet different needs of different students for the curriculum. After the adjustment of the college entrance examination system, there is no longer a division between liberal arts and sciences, and in principle, senior high school students can freely combine the subjects they study, taking a further step in catering to the tendencies of student competencies. However, compared with senior high school curriculum in other countries and regions, there are fewer applied curricula in China. In the new curriculum of the Hong Kong Special Administrative Region of China, in addition to traditional subjects such as chemistry and history, applied learning curricula have been added to meet the needs of different students, including the following six learning areas: creative learning; media and communication; business, management and law; service; applied science; engineering and production. Senior high schools in the Chinese mainland can provide students with such curriculum in the form of school-based curriculum. For senior high school students, giving each individual a different curriculum menu is the main way to meet the tendencies of student competencies. At the same time, even for the same competence, different students can achieve it through different curricula.

2. Differentiated Instruction

Differentiated Instruction does not only refer to dividing students into classes or groups according to their learning levels and abilities and applying different teaching contents. It can also be a strategy of providing different representational forms and teaching activity forms for the same content in teaching according to students' cognitive tendencies, interest characteristics and experience characteristics. The order of learning tasks can be adjusted, as well as the learning pace and time, and the members of student groups can be changed according to different subjects or contents. Students can be required and guided to express the results of learning and research in diversified ways. More praises can be given to some students, and different rewards can be given to different students.

3. Provide a Student Support System

With the popularization of senior high school education, its functions and characteristics will change, and more emphasis will be placed on the fairness of the educational process. The famous three principles of social fairness proposed by sociologist Rawls[1] state that on the basis of taking equality as the first

---

1 Rawls, J. *A Theory of Justice*[M]. Translated by He Huaihong, He Baogang & Liao Shenbai. Beijing: China Social Sciences Press, 2009:50-57.

principle, respect for differences and compensation for shortages should also be emphasized. The development of senior high school education should focus on not only the differences in the types of student competencies, but also the differences in the levels of student competencies. Individualized support should be given to students with academic difficulties and development obstacles. In the existing school system in China, there is a lack of the individual classroom and the system of special guidance teachers. The establishment of such a system requires schools to make corresponding adjustments in the teacher structure and teaching management on the basis of an abundance of teacher numbers and professional resources.

From intention to plan, from text to experience, and from universal to individual, these three types of curriculum transformations are the transformations of three curriculum hierarchies. Each hierarchy of transformation can use student key competencies as an intermediary template to plan and frame numerous curriculum elements, making the process of creating new curriculum forms more directional. This template makes the gap between curriculum hierarchies no longer a simple attenuated state.

[Originally published in *Curriculum, Teaching Material and Method* 2016(1) (Lv Lijie & Li Gang)]

Topic Three: Curriculum Implementation and Monitoring

9. Situated Teaching and Group Discussion —Observation and Reflection on Teaching Strategies under the Background of the New Curriculum

Under the guidance of the new curriculum, many teachers have reexamined on the significance of education and actively implemented it in their classroom teaching. As key agents and allies of the reform, experimental teachers' innovative attempts have provided excellent cases for our research on curriculum implementation. This paper will analyze, reflect on and discuss two common "self-evident" teaching phenomena in the new classroom teaching under the background of curriculum reform.

I. Situated Teaching

What is situated learning? Situated learning theory emerged in the West after the 1980s, against the background of cognitive psychology and the revolutionary view of knowledge. This theory holds that knowledge is context-bound—embedded in activities, backgrounds and cultural products. Knowledge is continuously applied and developed in activities and in its rich situations. The acquisition of knowledge is co-constructed by individuals and the environment, not a static fact. The different functions of situated learning and traditional learning methods are as follows: 1. Promoting transfer. Situated cognition can identify the difficulties and dilemmas in thinking and their generating contexts, revealing the intrinsic meaning of real-life situations in learning. In contrast, the knowledge background in traditional learning is simplified or idealized and generally cannot be realized in real life. Students' understanding of knowledge out-of-context is only limited to the literal level, and they only know how to use it to solve problems in class or on test papers. 2. Authentic understanding. The artificial and simplified "situations" in traditional learning are designed for fixed cognitive paths, which are preset by curriculum developers and teachers and are often considered to be natural, effective, orderly and scientific. However, research by psychologists shows that people tend to adopt practical strategies in daily environments. For example, when individuals purchase groceries, they basically construct their strategies through the environment and purchasing activities of the grocery store, rather than making the problem fit the strategy. They connect mental arithmetic, approximate values and the characteristics of the physical environment to make decisions.[1] 3. Construction of subjectivity. Students placed in a situation easily generate the desire to explore, the enthusiasm and sense of responsibility to solve problems. These motivational resources for learning prompt students to actively search for, prove, evaluate and even develop information elements, and independently construct a cognitive path, which is individualized and unique.

【Classroom Observation Record Excerpt 1】A First-grade *Mathematics* Class in Primary School

Teaching Content: Two-Digit Addition without Carrying and Subtraction without Borrowing

Teacher: Boys and girls, how much do you know about our school? Do you know how many classes we have? [Show slides (panoramic photos of the school)]

(Students are surprised and start talking.)

Teacher: Look how beautiful our school is! (Write on the blackboard: 6 classes in Grade One; 8 classes in Grade Two; 8 classes in Grade Three; Grade Four...) Who can tell me how many classes there are in total in the school?

(A student blurts out from his seat: Count the windows. The teacher doesn't reply, signaling the students to raise their hands to answer.)

---

1 Gao Wen. The Role of Context and Content in Situated Cognition: On the Theoretical Basis of Situated Cognition and the Design of Learning Environment (Part 1) [J]. *Studies in Foreign Educational Materials*, 1997(4).

…………

(Write the equation and calculate.)

Teacher: Do you know how many teachers we have in total? (Show the photos.)

(The students are surprised.)

Teacher: Here's the school faculty photo taken on last Teachers' Day. Please estimate first.

Students: (All talking at once) 150, 200, 300 ...

Teacher: How do we calculate the total number of teachers?

A boy: Just count the teachers in each class and add them all together.

Teacher: I'm afraid this method won't work. (Write on the blackboard: 18 female *Mathematics* teachers, 20 male *Mathematics* teachers; 38 female *Chinese Language* teachers, 10 male *Chinese Language* teachers) (Show a table: the number of teachers of other subjects)

…………

(Work with the students to write down the complex addition equations and calculate.)

【Classroom Observation Record Excerpt 2】A Second-grade *Mathematics* Class in Primary School

Teaching Content: To know Coins.

(The slide shows a picture of the situation: A boy is holding a banknote and talking to a supermarket cashier, and a girl waiting in line behind him, holding change of various denominations)

Teacher: Xiaoming wants to buy a pencil, but the cashier doesn't have enough change. What should we do?

Students: Go to the bank to exchange!

Teacher: (Signals the students to look at the picture) Please pay attention. Lingling behind Xiaoming is holding a lot of change.

…………

In the cases, both teachers adopt the strategy of situated teaching and try to break away from the traditional mathematics teaching pattern of "explaining formulas - memorizing formulas - practicing formulas". They both connect mathematical principles with students' lives and make the mathematics class relaxed and lively. By examining the curriculum implementation processes such as lesson preparation, teaching, and after-class reflection, we can see that they all achieve the redesign of the textual curriculum, and it can be inferred that these two teachers have established the concept of "teacher curriculum" and tried to go beyond the role of the "voiced replica of textbooks" in the past, attempting to construct a vivid classroom. In addition, the context is selected appropriately, connecting with the mathematical content on the one hand, and being selected from the real and familiar lives of the students on the other. Since the students feel close to the context, their participation and attention persistence exceed those of the traditional classroom. These changes are what we hope to see in the curriculum reform. However, when we examine and reflect on "situated teaching" as a meaningful concept rather than just a name, we believe that teachers' interpretation of the context in the case needs to be discussed and prompted.

In situated teaching, students are placed in it as conscious subjects. They design solutions for problems, search for meaningful information, and analyze, screen and organize the information until the problems are solved. This process should be open, in which individual meaning construction continuously provides feedback and exchange with the information in the context, and the tools, information elements, methods and thinking paths for problem-solving are also individualized. Therefore, there should be several key points in situated teaching: learners search for and screen information elements, extract their existing knowledge information, and construct problem-solving strategies by themselves. In Case 1, the teacher makes a lot of preparations to create the situation and setting up "knowing our school" as the situated question is indeed a good idea. Knowing the school is within the "zone of proximal development" of students' abilities, thus naturally igniting their enthusiasm for thinking and action, leading to swift immersion in the learning situation. However, after raising the question, the teacher directly gives the sufficient and necessary conditions for solving the problem (such as the teacher numbers of various subjects in Case 1 and the little girl with change that naturally appears in Case 2). As a result, the established information is reintroduced into the students' thinking tracks, and the students' thinking loses its dependence on the designed situation. Can we infer from this that in teaching practice, many teachers' understandings of situated teaching seem to be to incorporate fixed problem-solving ideas into stories, and to embody "newness" by highlighting the edited plot. The problem-solving process is unchangeable, which is the "duty" of mathematics classes. Although these two teachers make careful preparations for the situation, such as making slides, large photos and wall charts and other audiovisual products, the teaching process we see seems to be that the teacher guides the students to solve a complex applied problem. Of course, we cannot deny the importance of these carefully crafted "situated" elements in attracting the attention of students in primary school lower grade, but what we expect in the situation should not be limited to this. Taking Case 1 as an example, we imagine that after assigning the situation question, if the teacher asks the students to investigate the school in groups in appropriate time by asking the principal for data, counting the classes on each floor, or even counting the number of teachers in each office, then in the classroom, there will not only be multiple problem-solving solutions, but also students can understand the meaning of mathematics, at least the meaning of addition... We believe that this experience will make the understanding deeper and more conducive to knowledge transfer.

In the 1980s in China, there also emerged a situated teaching model that had an impact across the country, and that was mainly created for *Chinese Language* teaching. By simulating the situation in the texts and creating an atmosphere, students could experience the feelings of the authors of the articles. While this model had a unique role in humanities teaching, it is obvious that the teaching of *Mathematics* and other natural sciences cannot position the situation at creating an atmosphere and experiencing emotions. At present, many works on teaching theory in China also put forward "creating question situation" as a teaching strategy. However, the question situation only refers to the teacher giving a relevant and attractive example generally only in the lead-in part, not the same concept as the one mentioned above. Such "questions" aim not at solutions, but at "creating atmosphere", incapable of supporting the thinking in the process of new knowledge cognition. In this regard, under the background of the new curriculum and in the reform of curriculum implementation methods and learning methods, how to truly make students experience the value of mathematics, perhaps the Western situated learning theory since the 1980s is worth our appreciation and reference.

II. Group Discussion

Conceptually speaking, discussion is a good way of learning and exploring. If we trace back to the origin, the ancient teaching form was discussion such as the question-and-answer style of Confucius in China and the maieutic method of Socrates in ancient Greece. In addition, institutions like Yuelu Academy and Plato's Academy in Athens were not only famous for their unique discussion atmosphere in the world but also left precious cultural and ideological treasures for mankind. Indeed, discussion can go beyond the limits of the text to clarify an understanding, organize one's own thought, and gather everyone's wisdom as the starting point and pillar for one to keep thinking. The shift from tutorial systems to classroom teaching enhances education's social efficacy, which is due to the fact that the teaching form changes the slow rhythm of discussion, and teachers teach in a systematic and preset program. This transformation is not only rooted in the social requirements for an increase in the number of talents and the amount of individual knowledge possession, but also because people tacitly approve the maturity and commonality of human culture. However, for individuals, cultural inheritance cannot be directly inherited like physiological functions. The learning of existing knowledge is as arduous as the exploration in the early stage of human civilization and is a development process in which the subject's understanding constantly negates itself. Therefore, two hundred years after the prevalence of the class teaching system, scholars in Europe and America in the late 19th and early 20th century made reforms in schools. Reforms like the Dalton Plan pioneered small-group learning within classrooms to facilitate a discussion-based way of learning. Obviously, today's education system and curriculum content no longer allow the teaching form to completely replicate the ancient model, but this spontaneously generated teaching form of mankind can be organically integrated into today's teaching as an idea.

【Classroom Observation Records】 A Third-grade *Mathematics* Class in Primary School

Teaching Content: A Practice Activity Class on Area and Perimeter

Teacher: (After doing several consolidation exercises with students) Next, we will have a group discussion. Please take out the paper pieces and form groups of four with your neighbors. Let's discuss "How many rectangles can be formed at most with 16 squares".

(30% of the students show hesitation at first, but soon start to take out several prepared square paper pieces. 40% of the students do not discuss with others and operate by themselves. 10% of the students show indifference and are off-task. 20% of the students have discussions, but do not specify their reasons and still stick to their own views.)

The teacher quickly inspects the first two groups in the front row, then returns to the podium to organize the teaching aids for the next session. Two minutes later, the teacher signals to end the discussion and asks the students to raise their hands to answer the questions (representing themselves instead of the group).

The example given above is common in real teaching, and especially in open classes, it has become a necessary part of teaching design. Traditional teaching is criticized for mainly focusing on teachers' lecturing, where students' thinking is completely controlled by teachers, and their interests, imaginations and creativity are eroded in this teaching system. Curriculum implementation is not a process of experience and feeling, but a process of transmitting knowledge. What teachers care about is whether students pay attention to this knowledge and whether they have the ability to accept knowledge. For teachers themselves, it is important whether they have systematically presented the knowledge content and whether they have the power to make dozens of restless students quietly focus on the knowledge. Teaching in the new curriculum lies in returning the subjective status of students in teaching, and therefore, increasing the number of students' classroom speeches and arranging classroom discussions have become the preferred strategies for many teachers. From such teaching designs, we can feel that teachers are indeed trying to change their lecturing habits and obtain multiple teaching values through increasing classroom interactions among students. However, when we take the theoretical essence of classroom discussion as the starting point to observe the existing teaching, we also feel that there are some understandings worthy of clarification in these common teaching phenomena. The most obvious sign of a classroom with the teacher as the absolute main body is the teacher's monologue, so it is easy to deduce that giving students time is an important sign of changing the teaching mode. However, the subjective status and the quantity of speech are not an absolutely equal pair of concepts, because classroom discussion exits under the premise of giving students opportunities for independent thinking and mutual communication, not just a simple occupation of time. As we have observed in the case, most of the discussion groups do not have the collision of ideas and fierce debates, with some students even being a little tired and lazy. For the entire teaching process, the discussion does not affect the direction of the teacher's thinking, or it only plays an auxiliary role in completing the teacher's predetermined thinking.

Group discussion is an adaptation to and respect for the cognitive qualities of learners under the existing teaching system. It takes recognizing the subjectivity of students as the premise, and students enter the discussion with the status and identity of the subject. In the discussion, their individual subjectivities are dissolved, ultimately leading to individualized and subjective understandings. On the surface, the teacher in the case does not interfere with the discussion of any group. However, the students indeed disregard the discussion because they lost their subjective status. First, we need to identify how students enter the discussion. In the observation, the discussion session is designed by the teacher who has already "anticipated" the places where students' understandings differ before the teaching starts, and where all students in classes he or she teaches must have doubts and differences. As a result, some students in the classroom start to "discuss" before they even understand what is going on. Second, it is necessary to clarify whether the discussed question is worthy of controversy (the example question is from the book, and the conclusion is ready-made. If you have a different answer, you are wrong). Since discussion is a kind of communication, it should arise spontaneously. In a classroom that fully respects students' thinking, the teacher makes instant judgments based on students' behaviors and attitudes, allowing the discussion to emerge naturally. It may appear many times in a class, or not at all. It may be about the course content, or a strange question raised by a student. It may lead to a collective clarification of understandings, or end up diverging far from the topic with no solution... Group discussion does not serve to enrich and diversify the teaching form. It is a form in itself and should serve our teaching objectives.

III. Reflections on the Implementation of the New Curriculum

This curriculum reform is an all-round reform, from the curriculum management model to the curriculum development process, from the curriculum goals to the curriculum content, from the diversified curriculum structure to the curriculum implementation form. This reform is powerfully shaking people's (first and mainly teachers') deeply rooted traditional educational concepts. Through the comparison between the old and new curriculum, we can see from teachers' behaviors that they have recognized the significance of the new curriculum and are trying to change their established professional habits. However, just as the implementation of any reform is a difficult journey, the implementation of curriculum reform also requires constant examination and reflection.

1. Curriculum reform is first and foremost a profound transformation of educational concepts. Without experiencing a shock in thinking, the new curriculum can only be understood metaphysically and vulgarly. In practice, there are some latent ideas: (1) The teaching of the new curriculum must change the form, vary the patterns and enrich the teaching design. To this end, teachers have made a lot of efforts, such as showing the scenarios in the questions with slides and increasing the frequency of questioning. Such reform can only end up evolving into two "lesson types", performance lessons - for open classes, and traditional lessons - for daily teaching. The content of teaching design still emphasizes the systematic nature of knowledge and the authority of teachers, and the change in form is only to put a gorgeous coat on the criticized traditional teaching. The change in form is necessary, but form and content are always an inseparable pair of categories, and form serves content. (2) Attempting to demonstrate all new concepts simultaneously forces teachers into fragmented instruction. One moment they are training problem-solving, the next moment they are cultivating emotional attitudes, and then they are promoting communication... We believe that the curriculum goal is a synchronic expression of a diachronic concept, that is, the curriculum goal is the trend that students should ultimately achieve throughout their learning process, and all these trends are classified and expressed simultaneously. Compressing all concepts into one lesson resembles damming a river to capture its currents, which reflects rigid thinking.

2. The teacher teaches the flourishing and radiance of lives and the realization of the student subjectivity, which seems contradictory, but in fact, the former is the premise of the latter. In the classroom, teachers and students are a

pair of concepts that correspond to each other and are mutually causal, and it is difficult to distinguish which one is more “superior”. We have pointed out the drawbacks of the absolute center of teachers in traditional teaching countless times, but in the past hundred years, all the vital educational reforms in the world have been unable to cancel or diminish the role of teachers in the classroom. Classroom dynamics require careful equilibrium between teacher and student roles. Achieving this balance demands greater skill than traditional teacher-dominated instruction. It requires profound academic accumulation, a true sense of educational responsibility, lasting enthusiasm and educational wisdom that can assess the situation.

3.The sudden change in concepts and the gradual change in behavior are the characteristics of the reform. After the implementation of the new curriculum, the phenomenon of teachers’ conceptual recognition and behavioral lag is a common paradox. This illustrates the idea: things perceived may not be understood, and only those understood can be deeply perceived. Existing teaching behaviors are slowly formed and gradually changed like living habits. The teaching itself is the professional life of teachers and cannot be deliberately disguised. Teaching behavior is the natural manifestation of all his or her educational qualities. The true educational role of a teacher cannot be transformed overnight, but he or she needs to feel, reflect and understand in daily experiences and then express it in the unique and individualzed educational method. “Change is a process, not an event”[1]. Therefore, for the misunderstandings in the implementation of the new curriculum, we should carefully study and overcome then, instead of stopping the whole process.

[Originally published in *Research in Educational Development* 2002(10) (Lv Lijie & Ma Yunpeng)]

---

1 Fullan, M. *The Meaning of Educational Change*[M]. New York: Teachers College Press, 1982:41.

10. A Study on the Design of the "My Neighborhood Relationship" Thematic Unit from the Perspective of Theory of Variation

This study adopts the theory of variation to design instructional materials for the "My Neighborhood Relationships" unit in the *Morality and Society* curriculum, using students' developmental levels and lived experiences as entry points to scaffold their understanding of social complexity. The purpose is to enable students to examine interpersonal conflicts from different angles, think about how to handle such situations from multiple angles, and learn to live calmly, healthily and happily.

Morality and Society is a comprehensive course in the new curriculum system, offered in grades 3 - 6 of compulsory education. Based on children's social life, this course gradually expands into different life domains, with family, school, hometown (community), motherland and the world as clues to help children understand the main factors such as social environment, social activities and social relations in these fields. The course aims to promote students to form good moral characters, learn to live, and learn to live in society. The textbook design of *Morality and Society* follows a thematic unit structure, with one core topic for each thematic unit.

In many versions of textbooks, the topic like "My Neighborhood Relationship" is regarded as the first issue for children to understand society after leaving their families and schools. Various things that happen between neighbors usually leave different emotional experiences in children's hearts, which directly affect their views on interpersonal relationships and contribute to the formation of their moral values. A positive neighborhood relationship is conducive to children establishing a healthy outlook on life, and the diverse and trivial issues that arise in neighborhood relationships, if properly guided, are also conducive to cultivating children's ability to solve practical problems in life. At present, we see that many teaching designs position the concept of this thematic unit as "A neighbor nearby is better than a relative far away". However, in reality, the interpersonal relationships in neighborhood context are much more complex. Besides help and care, there are also tolerance, understanding, respect for public interests and protection of legal rights. Simple value indoctrination cannot guide children to recognize the multifaceted nature of life. The *Morality and Society* course should focus on solving the following problems: how to understand the complexity of social life through the stories of neighborhood relationships in the activities of the thematic unit, enabling students to learn to examine the interpersonal conflicts from different angles, think about how to handle such situations from multiple angles, and learn to live calmly, healthily and happily; how to guide students to learn to observe and understand society and learn to solve the numerous problems in life. The purpose of curriculum design is to design thematic units to avoid simple and superficial value indoctrination, improve students' cognitive qualities and achieve curriculum goals. The research group plans to use the theory of variation as the framework basis for the design of the thematic unit.

I. Inspiration from the Theory

Theory of variation was proposed by a research group led by Ference Marton, a scholar at the University of Gothenburg in Sweden. Their phenomenography framework, examines how individuals conceptualize and interpret phenomena or property in the world. They believe that learning is "an intrinsic relationship between an individual and the world"[1]. The purpose of school teaching is to prepare students for facing an increasingly complex future society. Thus, the most important form of learning is to enable students to view a learning object in different ways. Marton further points out that learning means

---

1 Lu Minling, Pang Yongxin & Zhi Peimin. *Catering for Individual Differences: through Learning Studies*[M]. Translated by Li Shuying & Guo Yongxian. Beijing: Educational Science Publishing House, 2006:10.

developing a way for students to view things (objects), and the establishment of this way is based on the discernment of the critical aspects of the learning object and the simultaneous focus on these aspects. It is precisely through variation that we can experience and distinguish the critical aspects of the learning object. When different variations appear at the same time, they enable learners to recognize the essence and characteristics of the learning object. The theory of variation believes that only when students, as learners, have direct contact with the learning content can they obtain an intuitive and profound understanding of things. The role of teachers is to act as guides for students' learning, guiding them to identify the critical characteristics and essence of things.

This pedagogical approach—identifying invariants across variations—has deep roots in Chinese education tradition. For example, variant teaching in the field of mathematics learning is consistent with the theory of variation in terms of function and purpose. The Hong Kong Institute of Education has applied and experimented with Marton's theory in subjects such as *Chinese Language*, *English* and *General Studies*. They use the theory of variation as a tool to guide teaching design, aiming to catering for individual differences among students, understand the critical attributes of students' learning difficulties, identify the differences in students' understanding, and then use appropriate variation schemas to design learning experiences to help students focus on the critical attributes and achieve a correct understanding of the learning content. Based on the theory of variation, the research of the Hong Kong Institute of Education has developed three different levels of variation[1].

The first level of variation: "Variation in students' understanding of the learning content". It emphasizes that teachers must start from students' different understandings, identify students' learning difficulties, and use them as the basis

---

1 Lu Minling, Pang Yongxin & Zhi Peimin. *Catering for Individual Differences: through Learning Studies*[M]. Translated by Li Shuying & Guo Yongxian. Beijing: Educational Science Publishing House, 2006:27.

for teaching design.

The second level of variation: "Variation in teachers' approaches to handling the learning content". Different teachers may approach the same learning content in diverse ways, and sharing these varied approaches can also bring about variation in teaching design.

The third level of variation: "Using appropriate variation as a tool to guide learning design". About the learning content, which attributes of things should be focused on, which attributes should be varied simultaneously, and which attributes should remain unchanged must be considered to achieve students' in-depth understanding of the problem.

Neighborhood relationship, as a microcosm of social interpersonal relationships, is a complex issue for children. Focusing on the critical points of the issue, understanding and evaluating from multiple angles and levels, and handling the critical points of critical events are ways to help them improve their understanding ability and increase the effectiveness of teaching. Therefore, the key to teaching design is to explore different perspectives based on students' existing understanding of the problem, help students improve the quality of their cognition of things, and then cultivate their ability to handle problems and construct a healthy moral concept.

II. Thematic Unit Design and Implementation under the Guidance of the Theory of Variation

Through pre-class surveys, we find that many students have experienced neighborhood conflicts like "water leaks upstairs and the downstairs suffers". The research group decides to use the "water leakage incident" as an entry story to analyze neighborhood relations and adopts the role-play activity to introduce the issue in students' activities and experiences. The teacher in charge design the teaching plan, and then through classroom observation, the research group finds the following problems in the teaching design and students' performance:

Firstly, the role-play activities run through the whole class, and there is almost no summaries and comments on the issue by the students.

Secondly, students' understanding of the incident is rather simple, and the information expressed in the role-play is repetitive.

Thirdly, the teacher's guidance is limited to summarizing the unitary moral rules at the end of the class, and values are indoctrinated "without thinking".

Based on this, the research group decides to redesign the course on the basis of the first class by using the theory of variation while the starting point remains the problem-solving approaches. The reasons are that, firstly, students are quite familiar with it and have life experiences, and secondly, the problem-solving approaches can reflect students' value orientations towards neighborhood relations. By contrasting resolution strategies, students discover how agentic choices shape communal well-being. The redesigned unit incorporates these variation-theory enhancements: some variations are made to the "plots", and through the comparison of different problem-solving approaches, students can experience how to construct a healthy and happy lifestyle.

(1) Selection of Learning Contents and Creation of Variation Space

The role-play performed by students require certain plot regulations, which serve as topics to guide students' thinking. The research group designs three themes, that is, three possible solutions: "Does the Winner Really Win?", "A Fair Solution", and "I'm Sorry", allowing students to experience the reasons and results of different approaches to the same incident in the same time and space. (See Table 3-1)

Table 3-1

Incidents	The State of Life after the Incident	Students' Reflection and Discussion
After the apartment is flooded by the Wen family upstairs, Mrs. Li goes to the door and quarrels fiercely, demanding substantial compensation. Mr. Wen, the elder brother of the Wen family, apologizes and offers to help clean up the apartment. But Mrs. Li refuses to give in and, along with several relatives, continues to pressure the Wen family. Ultimately, the Wen family has no choice but to meet the Li family's demands, but they feel very uncomfortable.	The Wen and Li families regularly run into each other in their neighborhood, creating an awkward atmosphere. The children from both families are also asked not to speak to each other. Both families live in a state of mutual hostility, and neither of them is in a good mood.	"Does the Winner Really Win?" How to create your own healthy and happy life?
The Li family's child upstairs, eager to watch TV, hastily wraps a leaking faucet with a cloth after washing fruit. When the Wang family's son downstairs notices water dripping into his kitchen, he goes upstairs. After being reminded, the Li child finds that the faucet is still running, and he immediately turns it off, but falsely claims that it has never been on. When the Wang family's investigation confirms the Li family's responsibility but is met with denial, they escalate the issue to the property management and authorities. Faced with evidence, the Li family finally admits fault and makes appropriate compensation.	"A Fair Solution" keeps life going.	Learn to safeguard your legitimate rights.

Incidents	The State of Life after the Incident	Students' Reflection and Discussion
The Li brothers find their apartment flooded, so they go upstairs to Wang's apartment to figure out the cause. After checking, the Wang family realizes that their negligence brings trouble to the Li family and immediately apologizes. They go down to the Li family to check the situation, help clean up the mess, and offer compensation. Since the Li family does not think they have suffered major losses, the two families reach a reconciliation.	The Wang family feels deeply sorry. From then on, the two families become good neighbors, always helping each other and getting along very well.	Neighbors should understand each other, tolerate each other, and live in harmony.

(2) Focus on Critical Features of the Learning Content in Discussion

Through discussion, students sum up their own principles for dealing with neighborhood relations from each role-play, and these principles should be conducive to building a healthy and happy life. However, in different incidents, these principles vary and require teachers to give proper guidance according to the specific situation. This process is carried out through the following four steps:

Step one: The teacher introduces the issue of attitudes towards dealing with conflicts from the practice in the previous class and further raises thought-provoking questions to trigger cognitive and moral conflicts in students' minds. Based on the fact that students' attitudes towards solving problems are rather overbearing in the first practical class, the teacher asks students to talk about examples of resolving neighborhood relations in a calm manner in life. Then several questions are raised to prompt students to think: in fact, people usually handle problems calmly in life. Why is that? We have also seen radical ways of solving problems, but what are the consequences of doing so? If the two sides in a conflict cannot reach a reconciliation on a certain issue, do you have other solutions?

Step Two: During the role-play, the focus is on guiding students to experience the problem-solving approaches and their impacts on people's lives. The first group's "Does the Winner Really Win?" focuses on the approaches of solving the problem (the Li family threatens and forces the Wen family), takes the problem-solving results as the basis (the Li family receives compensation and the Wen family shows superficial compliance), and takes the state of the neighbors' life after the incident as a reference (the awkward neighborhood life and the hostile state of life), showing students a way of handling the water leakage incident and the resulting life state. The second and third groups are also guided in the same way.

Step Three: Students are guided to make a three-dimensional comparison of the three role-plays, talk about their own feelings, discuss with classmates and summarize the principles for solving problems that they learn from each role-play. The key members of each group (for example, Mrs. Li in the first group) are invited to share their feelings after solving the problems. Finally, the teacher helps students to summarize and express it in appropriate words. From the first group, it can be concluded that when others infringe on one's own interests, one should express dissatisfaction in an appropriate way and safeguard one's rights, but should not take radical actions (such as quarreling, hitting people and threatening), which will only intensify the conflict, make both families angry and distressed, and affect their healthy and happy life. From the second group, it can be concluded that neighbors should abide by public morality, not bring troubles to neighbors and check the faucets at home regularly. One should take the initiative to admit the mistake if accidentally causing damages to others' homes, voluntary pay for loss if compensation is required, solve the problem calmly or deal with it through the intervention of judicial authorities if encountering unreasonable people. From the third group, it can be concluded that neighbors should be tolerant, understanding and mutually modest. If making mistakes, one should take the initiative to compensate and apologize to others, jointly building a harmonious, healthy and happy neighborhood life.

Step four: Let students further deeply experience the impact of healthy and unhealthy lives on people and help students acquire knowledge on how to deal with their own neighborhood relationships. However, it can also be seen from this class that the teacher's guidance for students is insufficient, resulting in students' not having a deep enough experience in the variation of incidents. Therefore, in the subsequent practical classes, we focus on guiding students to observe and experience the problem-solving approaches and their impacts on people's lives. Horizontally, we guide students to experience an approach (radical actions, through legal procedures, understanding each other) and its consequences, as well as the impact on people's lives (hostile, normal, harmonious). Vertically, we let students understand why there would be three different results for the same water leakage incident. The focus is on introducing the life state after the incident, so that students can realize that life is not static and that every action they take would have an impact on themselves and others, which would last for a period of time or even a lifetime.

(3) Variations at Different Cognitive Levels

1. Knowledge explanation. The teacher explains some knowledge in life to students in the form of lecturing and presenting, such as what harm would be caused to people's physical and mental health if they live in hostility for a long time, and the common legal knowledge that must be followed in neighborhood relationships and so on.

2. Emotional expression. Let students feel the power of understanding in the process of being touched. With the help of the story "A Different Melody" in the C-version textbook, the teacher read it with emotion to evoke emotional resonance and elevate students' feelings.

(4) The End of the Class: Neighborhood Dilemma Stories

Stepping out of the neighborhood incidents centered on water leakage, several groups of neighborhood dilemma stories are shown on slides to arouse students' cognitive and moral conflicts. Students are asked to make judgments according to their own rules to recognize the same attributes of different incidents and cultivate their ability to solve practical problems.

III. Analysis and Conclusions

(1) "Instruction" and "Perception" - Different Teaching Effects

Students without much life experience can hardly obtain real benefits and enlightenment from social life stories, and high-profile instructions only make them feel that it has little connection with the reality. How to guide students to perceive what significance life stories will have for themselves and others and choose the right life for themselves? The "post-life state" introduced in the revised course design is a critical element. Taking this as a dividing line and comparing the life before and after the incident, students can deeply understand the impacts of their problem-solving approaches on their life quality. Naturally, they will have such a feeling: we yearn for a peaceful and quiet life and don't want such a life to be disrupted. There are three handling ways for the three plots, bringing us three different lives. Therefore, although conflicts in life are inevitable, we can choose how to deal with them. The life state after dealing with the incident is largely related to our problem-solving approaches (see Figure 3-1). Under such guidance, students realize that their life attitudes are their own choices.

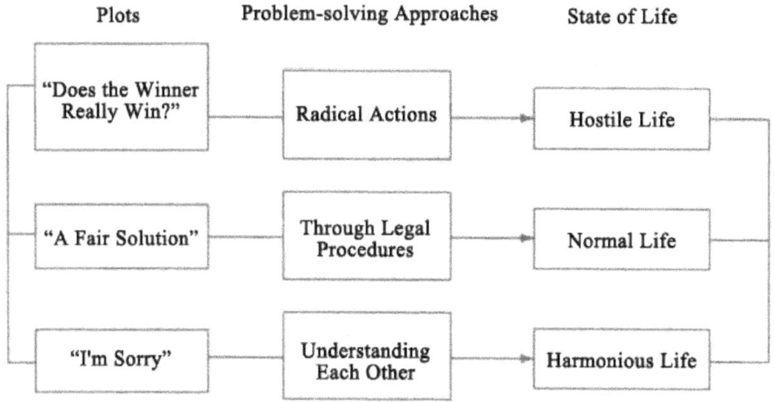

Figure 3 - 1 Problem-solving Approaches and Results

(2) Theory of Variation Is one of the Theoretical Bases for Teaching Design

The theory of variation provides a thinking framework for understanding complex issues. *Morality and Society* is different from other courses in that it starts from life phenomena, which not only pursues the essence of things in the objective world but also attaches greater importance to constructing an individual's value system in the subjective world of people. The design of thematic units, especially those for understanding complex social issues, presents students with varied life phenomena in a certain space, shows students diverse lifestyles, stimulates the collision of multiple values, guides students to identify in their own discussions and reflections, cultivates critical thinking and constructs multiple perspectives. Therefore, for certain learning contents, such as the design of thematic units for understanding complex social phenomena, the theory of variation can serve as a theoretical basis.

[Originally published in *Research in Shanghai Research on Education* 2008(3) (Lv Lijie & Zhao Tongyou)]

11. Children's Learning in Cooperation: A Study on Homogeneous Grouping in Primary School Cooperative Learning

Cooperative learning, emerging in the United States in the 1970s, is an innovative teaching strategy that reorganizes classroom dynamics. Its aim is to find a "reasonable way to greatly improve the academic performance of all students on a large scale" and to "establish positive and constructive interpersonal relationships among students of different races within schools and classes, and eliminate racial barriers, discrimination and indifference". After that, Slavin R E, the Johnson brothers (Johnson D W & Johnson R T), Sharan and others have done fruitful research on issues such as the essence, elements, group composition and strategies of cooperative learning. Since China's 2001 curriculum reform advocated "independent, cooperative, and inquiry-based learning", cooperative learning has gained attention in domestic educational practice. In recent years, many schools have put forward teaching model reforms such as independent learning and individualized learning, and cooperative learning is an important part or form among them. While definitions vary, this paper defines it as a component of classroom teaching organization. The cooperative learning is a teaching organization form mainly oriented towards student-student interaction, and is supported by a series of teaching theories, teaching strategies and teaching method system. In the attempts in recent years, people have recognized the significance of cooperative learning and also found some problems in it, such as the effect of cooperation, students' willingness to cooperate, ethical issues in cooperative learning, and the status and role of students with medium and low academic levels in cooperation. As a teaching organization form, cooperative learning is reasonable and progressive in improving the drawbacks of traditional teaching, but it needs the support and monitoring of a systematic and localized theoretical and strategic method system to guide the transformation of this form.

I. Core Issues of Cooperative Learning in Classroom Teaching

Generally speaking, more researchers believe that cooperative learning is effective. However, this does not mean that cooperative learning can become a general form of classroom teaching, because “cooperative learning is not always the best teaching organization form under any teaching conditions”, and “students’ individuality, subject characteristics, and characteristics of learning tasks are all different”. Cooperative learning is just one of the many teaching organization forms. The author believes that when using cooperative learning in classroom teaching, at least three questions should be asked: What kind of course content is suitable for cooperative learning? What teaching goals and student development goals has cooperative learning achieved? How to organize cooperative learning? These three types of questions each form a dimension, and they also support, influence and constitute each other.

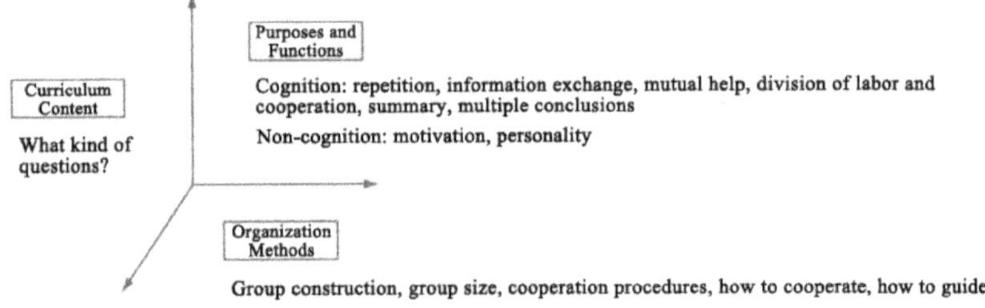

Figure 3-2 Three-Dimensional Questions in Cooperative Learning

Firstly, what course issues are suitable for cooperative learning? This is a prerequisite question, and how the same question is raised can better stimulate the interest in cooperative learning. For such questions, some scholars have summarized Rachel A. Lotan’s view that the tasks of cooperative learning should possess the following characteristics: “open-ended learning tasks, diversified learning contents, the completion of tasks requires positive interdependence among group members and clear division of individual responsibilities, and clear assessment standards for group achievements”, etc.

Secondly, what is the purpose and function of initiating cooperative learning? In response to this question, what teaching goals are expected to be achieved through cooperative learning and what roles does it play in student development? For example, in terms of cognition, is it to deepen memory by having members within the group repeat content, share and exchange information, help each other, with the "better" ones helping the "weaker" ones, or is it to divide tasks and cooperate with each other, and finally obtain results and multiple conclusions? In terms of non-cognition, is it hoped that students will acquire learning motivation in cooperation or an opportunity for personality growth? Western psychology has made a detailed classification of the cognitive processing levels in the cooperation process, which can be used as a reference index for examining the achievement degree of the cooperative learning effect. For example, Robyn M *et al.* proposed six levels of cognitive language strategies in the interaction during the cooperative learning process in 1998. They are: information repetition (repeating almost word for word what others have said), unstructured opinions (thinking aloud, but the opinions are not closely related to the theme of the discussion), specific opinions (stating facts related to the theme), evidence-based explanations (providing reasons), information summary (deriving conclusions or principles from the discussed information), and evaluation (comparing the values of multiple sources of evidence to obtain an answer).

Finally, how to organize cooperative learning? For example, how to form a group, by homogeneous grouping or heterogeneous grouping? What are the principles for forming a heterogeneous group? What should be the size of the group? What are the methods, procedures and strategies of cooperative learning? How to promote the cooperation? How does the teacher guide the process of cooperative learning? Many scholars such as the Johnson brothers and Slavin have done a lot of research in this area. Among them, research on group construction has always had different views because researches are conducted under different subjects and different learning task conditions, and students' individualized characteristics are also not completely consistent. For example, the Johnson brothers have always emphasized that heterogeneous grouping is better than homogeneous grouping, in which students can think more deeply and receive more explanations. John Baer, on the other hand, believes that students perform better in homogeneous groups than in heterogeneous groups because conversations are more likely to occur among students with similar knowledge and understanding levels. In the comparative study of students in high-ability, medium-ability and low-ability groups, it is generally believed that high-ability students perform excellently in both homogeneous and heterogeneous groups. Louetal. believes that medium-ability students perform significantly better in homogeneous groups than in heterogeneous groups, and low-ability students perform significantly better in heterogeneous groups than in homogeneous groups because low-ability students have a sense of collective incompetence in homogeneous groups. Bennett *et al.* believe that the performance of medium and low-ability students in homogeneous groupings is worrying, and low-ability students are easily ignored in heterogeneous grouping. Some researchers also believe that those who learn slowly can benefit the most and maintain their self-esteem in homogeneous groups because in them, students can see the level that they can reach through their own efforts instead of seeing perfect performances from the beginning.

II. Exploration on the Composition of Homogeneous Groups in the Primary School Course *Morality and Life*

The course *Morality and Life* is an activity-based comprehensive course for lower grades in primary schools, characterized by flexibility, openness and comprehensiveness. It advocates students' personal participation and experience and pays attention to the integrity and in-depth nature of the activity process. It includes collaborative tasks with low cognitive complexity, high openness, and real-life relevance, necessitating peer cooperation. These characteristics provide a prerequisite for attempts at teaching reform in cooperative learning. In the first semester of the second grade of a primary school, we conduct an attempt at cooperative learning with one class as a case. The successful implementation of cooperative learning involves many related issues, and this paper only discusses the issue of group composition structure. In Western empirical research, there is no consensus on which is more reasonable between homogeneous group and heterogeneous group. Based on the task characteristics of this course, we attempt to take cooperative learning as the main classroom organization form and homogeneous grouping as the grouping method in one semester to examine the advantages and disadvantages of homogeneous group and how to reduce the disadvantages through teacher guidance.

(1) Value Expectations of Cooperative Learning in the Thematic Unit

The thematic unit activities involved in this semester include: "How Big Is Our Body", "Playing with Autumn", "Reading Exchange Meeting", etc. Taking the theme activity of "How Big Is Our Body" as an example, this unit is a secondary theme activity in the thematic unit of "Taking Care of Our Body" in the national standard textbook of *Morality and Life* for the first semester of second grade of primary school published by Beijing Normal University. In setting the learning tasks, firstly, we should ensure that they are sufficiently challenging but not beyond reach, and can be completed through the joint efforts of group members so as to arouse the interest and desire for the activity. Secondly, groups were granted flexibility to avoid over-restriction and foster creativity. Finally, the learning tasks should be as continuous as possible, and relevant learning activities should be arranged in succession according to the different observation contents to ensure the continuous and in-depth research. The main content we set is to feel the actual size of the body through drawing. The teaching process is that students work in groups to jointly complete the task of drawing the body. That is, each group prepares a large piece of paper, with one lying on the paper as a model and others drawing the outline on the paper. Then all the students in the group design and draw clothes together. This formal cooperative learning structure spanned four class hours across the theme. This process allows students to feel how big their own bodies are in the experience of drawing and painting, and deepen their perception of the growth and change of their bodies. Compared with direct teaching, its significance is obvious in both cognitive and non-cognitive aspects. In the cognitive aspect, each student can have individualized experience conclusions about himself and his growth through action experience. In the non-cognitive aspect, students acquire learning motivation in operation and experience, improve their ability of interpersonal communication and interaction, and gain confidence in growth.

(2) Establish Groups

1. Group Size of 3-4 Students

Group size is a critical factor influencing cooperative dynamics and efficacy. How many people should be in a group? W. Johnson *et al.* believe that "In a two-person group, students must handle the interaction between the two. In a three-person group, 6 kinds of interaction relationships need to be handled, while in a four-person group, 12 kinds of interaction relationships need to be handled. It can be seen that as the group size increases, the interpersonal communication and group skills required to manage the interaction among group members will become more and more complex"... "The most important principle is that the smaller the group size, the better". For this reason, since students enter the second grade of primary school, we have also tried to discover the performance and value significance of student cooperation in different group sizes in the *Morality and Life* course observation. Smaller groups reduced conflicts but limited interaction and prolonged task completion. On the contrary, if the number increases, the workload of each student will be reduced with increasing mutual assistance, but more differences will also arise in forming a consensus and dividing tasks and cooperating. Group members will have to spend a lot of time on communication and coordination, and the overall effect of completing the learning task will not change obviously. Moreover, the phenomenon of "some people having nothing to do and some people not doing anything" is likely to occur. For students in the lower grades who have just started cooperative learning, they are not yet fully capable of solving the many problems brought about by too many group members, which undoubtedly increases the difficulty of group learning. Through comprehensive analysis, the author believes that for second-grade students, a group of 3-4 members is the most reasonable and effective in completing a task activity.

2. Group Construction with Homogeneous Willingness

At present, the generally recognized grouping principle is "heterogeneity within the group and homogeneity between groups" because "heterogeneous groups will have more advantages. Groups composed of students with different backgrounds, abilities and hobbies can enable students to view problems from multiple perspectives and obtain multiple solutions, and generate differences in cognition, which will stimulate students to learn actively and promote the continuous deepening of understanding". However, this grouping method has also encountered many drawbacks and problems in practice. For example, in some classes, the progress and development of medium and high-level students in heterogeneous groups are not obvious, and only low-level students benefit the most. In other classes, high-level students are unwilling to help and recognize low-level students and still work on their own, resulting in some students completing tasks alone while others being neglected and having nothing to do. Some people also raise the issue of educational ethics in heterogeneous grouping. Naturally, heterogeneous grouping requires excellent students to help students with difficulties, which will inevitably take up the time for excellent students to think further. Heterogeneous grouping has its limitations, but does homogeneous grouping necessarily compensate for the drawbacks and limitations of heterogeneous grouping? In practice, homogeneous grouping is mostly applied in the senior high school, and its main purpose is to stratify academic levels so that teachers can organize practice and guidance in a targeted manner. However, such homogeneous grouping will obviously bring problems, that is, it will make students have a sense of inferiority or a sense of comparison, which is not suitable for primary school students in lower grades. So we experiment with a method of voluntary grouping by students. Adhering to the principle of "homogeneity in willingness and heterogeneity in other aspects", we put forward the requirement of "forming a group with your favorite friends, preferably 3-4 members". It is found that the members in the formed learning groups are mostly good friends, with relatively consistent genders, similar personalities and hobbies, and even relatively similar academic levels. In such groups, children are full of expectations for the following work because they are with their favorite friends.

(3) Observation and Analysis of Learning Performance of Different Types of Students in Homogeneous Grouping

We select three typical groups - Group A, Group B, and Group C - for follow-up observation. Group A has four female students, all of whom are excellent in academic performance, are confident, possess strong self-management abilities, and can actively interact with others. We represent them as A1, A2, A3, and A4. Group B consists of three male students with medium academic performance, who exhibit a compliant demeanor in heterogeneous groups and don't take the initiative to express their opinions. We represent them as B1, B2, and B3. Group C has four students who do not voluntarily form a group. That is to say, during the voluntary group formation process, no group is willing to accept these four students, so the teacher ultimately combines them into one group, and we represent them as C1, C2, C3, and C4. The information collection methods include recording the whole process with a video camera and a recorder for each group. After class, the performance of the 11 students in the three groups is recorded one by one. At the end of each thematic unit, comprehensive sorting is carried out and we find that the students in all three groups have gained a lot in the learning activities of the homogeneous groups, although the dimensions of development are different. There are many reasons why homogeneous grouping is not widely recognized. Researchers believe that in homogeneous groups, significant progress is only limited to high-ability groups, and it is difficult for other students to meet the basic academic requirements. However, we find in our research that this is not the case.

1. Analysis of the Classroom Record of Group A

The four students in Group A show a positive willingness from the first cooperation, with an orderly learning process and excellent results. The record is taken from the first class of the thematic unit "Taking Care of Our Body", namely "How Big Is Our Body":

…………

A3: I want to draw the legs.

A4: I want to work on this part.

A1: I'll draw the body.

A2: Let's not do it this way. We should discuss it together. Look, this is our plan

diagram. First, who will draw the head?

A1: A3, you draw the head.

A3: Alright.

…………

A4: Let's put our markers together and use them jointly.

A3: Use mine. There are more colors.

A1: Let's use them together.

A4: Then how about we use our own first, and borrow the colors we don't have from each other?

A2: I Agree.

A3: That's it. We've finished discussing. Everyone, take your seat.

…………

A4: Let's speed up. We can also add a crown. I'll do it.

A1: When coloring, we can choose the colors we like as long as they match well.

A2: A1, you still need to make a decision. I'm just the model.

A4: The pants don't look good. Let's color them red. Be gentle when coloring, not

too hard.

A3: I'm not good at drawing.

A1: It's OK. We'll design it together.

A2: I'll help you later. My markers have special colors. Everyone can use them.

A1: Be sure to color in order so that it won't be messy.

A4: We can also make flexible adjustments according to what we discussed just

now.

A3: A2, thank you.

…………

The final result of Group A is of the highest quality, which is the same as expected. There are three outstanding aspects in the process of producing this excellent result. First, the group demonstrates excellent mutual recognition and coordination. Communicative languages such as "I agree", "I'll help you", "It's OK", and "thank you" run through the whole process. Second, everyone actively puts forward constructive suggestions and act strategically, such as "we should discuss it", what to do "first", and "speed up and make a decision". These driving words come from each member, and there are no disengaged individuals or a single decision-making center in the team. Third, they have a deep and specific understanding of the task content. They have a "plan diagram" and grasp the keys to drawing a good picture, such as "match well", "color in order", and "make flexible adjustments". The performance at these three levels sufficiently prove that the students in Group A are excellent in both cognitive ability and social development.

2. Analysis of the Classroom Record of Group B

The three boys in Group B have medium academic performance, are introverted and are not willing to show off. They are not strong in expressing themselves and lack courage. In the heterogeneous grouping, they are typical silent and obedient ones. Judging from the recorded process, the work of this group progresses smoothly. They are able to advance the work step by step according to the teacher's requirements, first discussing the division of labor, then drawing the outline, and finally decorating the clothes.

B2: Let's talk about who will outline the body in pencil first. Raise your hand if you agree with B1... Raise your hand if you agree with me.

B1: I'll do the outlining.

B2: I'll do the coloring. Is that OK?

B3: Let's color the edges together.

B2: We still need to discuss which color to use for each part.

…………

B2: You say first, which part do you want to be responsible for?

B3: The head part. Then you can color this part. After I finish coloring the head,

I'll help you color the body.

B2: Which part do you want to be responsible for?

…………

B1: I'll mark the part I'm responsible for with red.

B2: It's a bit difficult to draw the head. I'll circle it with green. Who wants to draw

the left side of the body? Raise your hand. Who wants to draw the right side? Raise your hand.

B1: Then I'll draw these parts.

…………

B2: I only have oil pastels, no markers.

B1: You can use the oil pastels to help me color.

B2: I have an idea. We can have a vote. B1 is the model. If everyone thinks his clothes are good-looking, we'll draw his clothes. If not, we'll use someone else's clothes.

B3: I think his clothes are good-looking.

B2: Raise your hand if you think B3's clothes are good-looking... Raise your hand if you think B1's are better... You can't raise your hand for yourself. Raise your hand if you think my clothes are good-looking.

…………

Since the three members are familiar with each other and have developed smooth communication habits in daily games, the most obvious feature during the task completion process is harmonious and democratic negotiation with "together", "discuss", and "agree" being the key words in their conversations. The performance of student B2 is particularly interesting. B2's usual performance is consistent with the overall characteristics of the students in Group B, but in this familiar team, he is obviously very relaxed and takes the initiative to play the role of a "democratic leader". He uses the word "raise your hand" nine times in his speech, indicating his attempt to lead and promote the progress of the cooperative work and happily organizing everyone to negotiate. B2's leadership role is naturally presented in such a group environment.

3. Analysis of the Classroom Record of Group C

The four students in Group C are often criticized by the teacher for not following disciplines and sometimes disrupting other students. In heterogeneous grouping, they are unpopular students and usually don't need to work for the group as long as they don't affect others. After Group C is formed, the first cooperation does not go smoothly. The followings are the classroom record spanning one semester and its analysis.

The Classroom Record of the First Class -

(While other groups are dividing the labor, the members of Group C don't respond

and keep playing, completely failing to focus their attention on this matter. In the end, the group still hasn't decided who would be the model, and the group members don't feel anxious about not having completed this task.)

Teacher: Record the group's division of labor on the card and have a discussion about how to do this quickly and well. Use a pencil.

C1: Just choose C4.

C3: Why should you decide?

C1: I just want to do it this way.

C2: Forget it. Let C1 go crazy by himself. He's too bossy.

C1: I'd rather ask someone else to draw than you (C2).

C4: I don't want to be the model.

C2: If you don't, I'll be.

C1: We all disagree with you being the model.

…………

Teacher: It's not that difficult. First, don't get angry. Let's discuss it again, OK?

C1: Job No. 3 is mine.

C2: I'm for Job No. 2.

C4: Who's for Job No. 4?

C4: What's my number?

C2: I don't know. Let's draw the clothes together, no discussion.

…………

C3: What do you mean by no discussion?

C2: I won't be in this group next time. I'm so unlucky.

C3: Why is C1 so bossy?

C4: Let's say you two draw the upper body, and we two draw the clothes.

C1: No way.

…………

(C2 slips away and goes to play with other groups again. C1 plays with stationery. Only C3 and C4 in the group continue to work.)

C2: I'm back. What on earth is this you're drawing? It's so terrible.

Teacher-Student Conversation after Class -

Teacher: How was it today? Did you perform well?

C2: I made quite a few mistakes. 50% because of C1, 10% because of me, and the

rest because of them two. C1 was too bossy. I saw two repeated divisions of labor and wanted to change them, but he just held me down and didn't let me do it.

Teacher: Was it because you didn't communicate and discuss well?

C2: When the group was taking action, C1 didn't follow the planned division of labor at all. He was always making troubles. I didn't do very well either, but I'm quite satisfied that I kept working on it.

Teacher: Do you have anything else to say?

C1: I don't want to cooperate with C2. I feel he's so annoying. C2 is always against me, and I always have to give in to him. But I've also thought that I shouldn't have argued with C2 for such a long time.

Teacher: That makes sense. If you hadn't wasted so much time, you might have done better. It seems that mutual discussion is very important when learning in groups.

C4: I feel so annoyed. Good friends shouldn't be like this. I'm not happy. I don't like

the group members arguing. C1 keeps scribbling, and that shouldn't happen.

…………

Teacher-Student Conversation before the Second Class -

Teacher: Will you argue again this time?

C3: I didn't argue last time.

C1: No, I'll give way to C2.

C2: I'll try to be more patient with him.

C4: I'll also be patient with both of them. I'll also try to stop them from arguing.

C1: I'll discuss more with everyone.

…………

Teacher-Student Conversation after Class -

Teacher: How did you perform in today's group activity? What did you do?

C2: I outlined and was responsible for correcting the wrong parts. I didn't argue

with everyone. C1 didn't act on his own either. When they asked me to stop, I stopped. I'm now open to others' opinions.

C1: I performed well and didn't argue with C2 anymore. C2 said my blue marker wasn't good, so I used a black one instead. I learned to accept his suggestions, and we discussed together. It felt good. We can be good friends if we can be more patient. I just don't know if C2 agrees.

C2: Yes, I agree.

C3: The thing I'm most proud of today is leading everyone to complete the task quickly and well. They (C1 and C2) have changed a lot compared to last week. They don't argue so much, almost not at all. I like being friends with them and would like to be in the same group with them in the future.

C4: I felt good this week.

At the beginning of the first class, Group C behave as the teacher expected. They "slip away" from the start and have no sense of responsibility for the task. However, this time, if they don't do it themselves, no one could take over for them. So the four of them have to start working amidst arguing. Almost every sentence in their communication is filled with expressions of rejection of others, such as "Why should...", "I just want to...", "Forget it", "Too bossy", "Don't want to", "Don't be", "No way", "Don't agree", "Don't know". Moreover, everyone lacks confidence in their ability to complete the task, so they even have "no discussion" about the division of labor. Due to the lack of confidence, C2 is more willing to shift the blame for the group's failure to run smoothly onto others, believing that he is "so unlucky" and others are "terrible". There is even no way to talk about the work ideas and understanding of the content. The results of such work and the feelings during the process also make everyone uncomfortable. After class, the teacher timely guides the students to reflect, and before the teacher says anything, the children all say that they are "very annoyed" by such argues and that "it is not good". So before the second class, they decide to "be patient", "stop", and "discuss". Compared with the first time, the teaching process is much quieter. They "feel good" in this class, could "be good friends" and are "willing to be in the same group with them" because they "don't argue with everyone", "don't act on their own", "stop", "be open to others' opinions", "discuss together", and "be patient". These changes, although limited, are surprising. Students in Group C themselves feel troubled by their original behavior patterns and take the initiative to seek changes. They form their own strategies such as "be patient" and "not act on their own", and finally see the significance of the changes themselves.

(One month later, in the second theme activity, the groups are still organized as before, and the students are asked to make big toys.)

C4: What should we do? Let's discuss it together.

C2: I want to make a big house and stay inside.

C1: I don't like that. Let's make a maze instead.

C3: I don't think either of them is good. Let's make a castle.

C4: Then we need to have enough materials.

C1: Anyway, I don't agree.

C3: What should we do then?

C2: Just follow my plan.

C1: If we make his one, I won't participate.

C3: Don't be like that. Let's discuss it.

C4: Yeah, let's take a vote.

(After voting, C2 agrees with C1's opinion.)

C1: Look at my great work.

C2: Not so good. It's too rough, and it's not taped up properly.

C1: If you keep saying something bad, I won't be polite.

C2: Anyway, it's just not good.

C3: Everyone, hurry up and make it!

C4: Didn't we agree that you wouldn't argue anymore? Why did you forget again?

Let's discuss how to make the toy well.

C1: OK, I give in.

C2: I apologize too.

In the second task, C1 and C2 still want to act as they please without considering the wishes of others. However, after being reminded by their peers, they are able to follow the "vote by raising hands" agreement, and can even use communicative languages like "I give in" and "I apologize too". Although problems keep recurring, the social interaction and recognition abilities of the students in Group C have changed and grown during these adjustments.

III. Reflections on Cooperative Learning in Homogeneous Groups

(1) Students' Engagement in Homogeneous Grouping Is Good, with All Groups Developing within the Zone of Proximal Development

Judging from the interaction processes of several types of groups, although the directions and qualities of the interactions vary greatly, all students in each group are within the "system" of interaction and there is no phenomenon of being left out or excluded. Without relying on specific individuals, everyone needs to fully mobilize their own energy to complete the learning tasks. In the process, due to the homogeneity of willingness, the frequency of student-student interaction is even higher, and it is no longer concentrated on the one-way flow of information from high-level students to low-level students. Meanwhile, negative and inferiority complexes among students are better avoided.

In homogeneous grouping, group members have many similarities or likenesses, so it is easier for them to learn from and imitate each other. The role models are more exemplary, and the content they need to imitate falls within the "zone of proximal development" of each student's existing abilities, making it easy to find the entry point for efforts and enhancing the motivation for mutual learning. Moreover, this mutual learning can come from multiple aspects, such as the imitation of learning skills, the imitation of interpersonal communication methods, and the imitation of responsibility awareness and team awareness.

(2) In Homogeneous Grouping, the Cooperative Ways and Work Qualities of Different Groups Vary Significantly

All types of students in homogeneous grouping have improved and developed. In heterogeneous grouping, high-ability students often have to focus on assisting low-ability students while in homogeneous groups, such a link is omitted, and the time is allocated to the task itself, leading to high work efficiency and quality, as well as excellent and more creative action strategies during the process. In homogeneous grouping, students in the medium-ability group get the opportunity to participate actively and even try the leadership role, with good coordination in the work but only a few in-depth understandings of the content itself and excellent action strategies. For students in the low-ability group, at least in the early stage of cooperation, they spend a lot of time on mutual acceptance and team coordination, leading to low work quality and efficiency.

(3) In Homogeneous Grouping, Students in Different Ability Groups Have Different Growth Focuses

In homogeneous grouping, students develop in different ways, but the focus of development first lies in the "shortcomings" in their own knowledge and ability structures, that is, what is lacking. In order to maintain smooth cooperation, students in the high, medium, and low ability groups have different levels of concerns. First, group members need to have good social development such as identification and coordination. Second, they will then try to promote the progress of the work and formulate action steps. Third, they will exchange thinking paths and action strategies related to the learning content during cooperation. These three aspects show a progressive trend, and only when the previous level is achieved will students focus on the next level of cooperative behavior. For students in the low-ability group, they first need to "compensate" for the lacking social development before gradually focusing on the task itself.

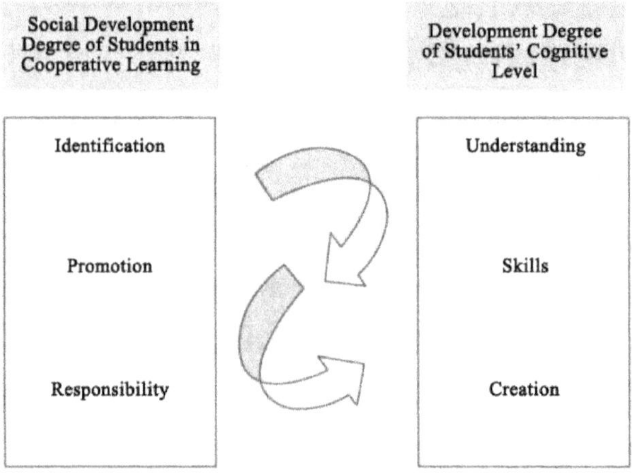

Figure 3-3 Structure Diagram of Students' Growth Focuses in Homogeneous Groups

(4) Based on the Characteristics of the Group, Teachers' Guidance Should Seize the Intervention Points

Students in homogeneous grouping are at different levels, with different learning situations and problems, so teachers should adopt different guidance strategies. High-ability students generally do not seek help from teachers, and the teachers will mostly give them advisory references when monitoring the classroom. In cooperative groups composed of students with medium academic levels and introverted personalities, students have the ability to complete learning tasks, but they may need more encouragement and support from the teacher to foster a sense of agency during group activities. In the groups of students who need further development, there may exist the most problems in cooperation such as unclear learning tasks, weak motivation, and constant conflicts among group members, and teachers need to invest more energy for such groups. In the process of guidance, teachers should not directly get to the main topic, nor should they simply criticize. Instead, they should play the role of a "part-time tour guide", intervene in a timely manner according to the progress of the task, and provide targeted guidance. Not only should they be patient and meticulous, but they should also wait patiently, helping students to actively adjust their behaviors in reflection and see the significance and their own progress in behavior improvement.

As mentioned above, since this research uses the thematic units in the *Morality and Life* course for cooperative learning research, the appropriateness of homogeneous grouping and the characteristics of students' growth are subject to the limitations of "premise problems". Therefore, willingness-based homogeneous grouping is an effective teaching organization form with the teaching goals of promoting students' social development and encouraging active participation among all students.

12. The Problem of Rationality of Mode Selection in the Teaching Reform

In 2001, the *Outline of Basic Education Curriculum Reform (for Trial Implementation)* proposed: “The current situation of overemphasizing reception learning, rote memorization, and mechanical drills in the course of curriculum implementation should be changed. It emphasized fostering active participation, inquiry, and hands-on practice. Students’ abilities of collecting and processing information, acquiring new knowledge, analyzing and solving problems, communicating and cooperating should be cultivated.” The *Outline for National Medium and Long-term Education Reform and Development (2010 - 2020)* also mentioned that it is necessary to “deepen education and teaching reform, innovate education and teaching methods, explore multiple cultivation methods, advocate heuristic, inquiry-based, discussion-based, and participatory teaching, and help students to learn how to learn.” These policy documents all have a common direction of change, emphasizing students’ autonomy in classroom teaching, cultivating children’s learning ability, practical ability and innovation ability. In these years, some schools, based on their own practical environments and actual needs, have claimed teaching reform, such as autonomous guidance learning, teaching by learning, learning before teaching, etc., which are called “modes”. Inspired by successful examples, many are adopting or developing their own models.

Ⅰ. Reform Modality and Mode Pursuits

These teaching modes centered on student subjectivity share the same historical background, and their propositions and slogans for reform also have great similarities. However, due to different reform basis and environment for different schools, the original intentions and implicit concepts of school reforms are not the same, and the reform modality is also inconsistent. For example, some classrooms emphasize students’ constructing conclusions. Teachers raise questions, and students are divided into groups to explore answers which last for a long time. The design prioritizes cultivating critical thinking and learning habits. Students do not master many conclusions but have experienced the thinking process. Based on the concepts of small class or individualization in schools, some teachers emphasize reflecting students' differences in teaching, and arrange autonomous learning and group discussion in teaching, with the aim of reflecting each student's experience and implementing differentiated instruction. Many schools adopt a structure where student-centered activities precede teacher summaries. Students learn textbooks by themselves with the help of learning guidance materials according to teachers' learning requirements, and then communicate with classmates about the problems encountered in their own learning process which could be solved under the guidance of teachers during their inspection. Finally, teachers make summaries. Some principals even stipulate that teachers' summaries should take no more than "ten minutes", or can be replaced by students' summaries. In such classrooms, the content that students learn is relatively concentrated, with a strong purpose, which enhances students' learning autonomy and effectiveness. In these reformed teaching modalities, students' high participation is a common feature, and student-centered activities occupy an absolute position regarding to teaching time. The application of ways including autonomous learning, group learning has improved teachers' teaching habits of single lecturing. Educational reform is a social practice through which social behaviors evolve and problems are understood more deeply. The several teaching modes listed above are not all the circumstances of the current reform, but they have already shown the diversity and complexity of reality. In practice, since these modes appear in the form of reform, they must be different from the traditional ones. As traditions are commonly recognized, reforms naturally have common manifestations. ①Among these reform forms, emphasizing students' dominant position in the classroom is the most common feature, which has been the consistent pursuit of educational reform since China advocated quality education at the end of the 20th century. ②Reform rationale lies in addressing current challenges and driving improvement. Through the reform of teaching forms, to a certain extent, the purpose of reforming subjects can be fulfilled, furthermore, problems and deficiencies are solved. Therefore, this is also the inherent rationality of reform.

Through attempts in reform, teachers have understood the significance of teaching in different teaching styles, and the reform has also solved practical difficulties or met value pursuits to a certain extent. Therefore, many schools began to imitate successful experiences. The common ways of learning and imitating are shown as follows. ①All teachers in the school are required to implement a unified teaching mode regardless of grades, disciplines and lesson types. ②In this mode, the sequence of teaching activities and the time of each link should be fixed. The common practice is "learning before teaching", and teachers' lectures should take as little time as possible, and even the time for teachers to lecture is stipulated. ③Many schools prefer to choose modes with "strong realistic effectiveness". Although reform modes do have something in common, behind the common points are conceptual orientations of harmony without uniformity and not exactly the same original intentions for reform. Practically effective models gain traction because they align student agency with textbook-centered knowledge acquisition. Teaching is a complex system, and a single mode cannot carry the multi-dimensional concepts of reform. Teaching reform breaks through the original single form but goes to another single form. Easy-to-implement models are often treated as universal solutions. Therefore, while we are glad that the reform modes have brought changes to practice, we also need to return to the modes themselves and reflect on what we really want to pursue and what the modes can actually achieve.

II. Questions in the Selection of Teaching Modes

(1) Whether the Mode Selection Is Consistent with the Concept

As a practical form, a mode is to turn concepts into operable procedures, allowing more people to share them and facilitating more people to learn and operate them. There should be a pursuit of modes in practice. Any mode is generated under certain concepts and has its original intention. They simplify concepts into context-specific operational steps, formalizing teaching processes. People who create modes naturally understand what their original intentions are and what their goals to be pursued are. Or in their view, the mode, the concept, and the goal are unified. However, when the mode is promoted, in the changed situation, do people who imitate the mode understand the meaning pursued by the mode? Can they achieve the consistency between the mode and the concept and between the mode and the purpose? Learning and choosing a mode is simply a visible and operable activity procedure and time, which is equivalent to stripping the original intention of teaching design, teaching goals and student needs from the mode. These fixed operational procedures do not necessarily restore the concepts and purposes pursued by the mode. Therefore, in the changing and complex teaching situations, grasping the concepts and essence behind a mode is the top priority. Otherwise, the mode will become a constraint on teaching behaviors.

(2) Whether the Mode Selection Is Narrowed to the Pursuit of "Practical Effectiveness"

In the reform, various teaching methods and teaching modes have emerged. However, in practice, the imitations of many schools are extremely convergent. Students first learn new content by themselves, then discuss the new content with their classmates, and finally, teachers organize students to practice these contents in class. Such a process positions the meaning of the classroom as understanding the content of textbooks, determining knowledge points, and consolidating knowledge points. Its teaching purpose is no different from that of traditional teaching, but in the process, students play an active role and have a high engagement. Students' subjective participation makes the classroom teaching progressive and even effective, which is the reason why many schools, principals and teachers identify with this mode. However, such teaching doesn't fully realize the original intention of teaching reform and achieve the fundamental significance of classroom reform. It is just that in this mode, the traditional and habitual values have reached a compromise with the forms of reform and practical effectiveness. This compromise reduces the risk of reform but deviates from the orientation of reform.

(3) Whether the Methods Can Correspond to the Procedures

Each method has its significance and limitations. In a unified teaching model, the teaching method is fixed and correspond one-to-one with the teaching procedure and the time sequence. For example, in a fixed sequence like self-study--discussion--practice--summary, the limitations of the methods themselves are hard to avoid. Independent study based on the learning guides gives play to students' initiative. However, the whole class is centered around the learning guides and becomes a definite task for teachers and students to complete. Although it gives purpose to the behaviors of teachers and students, it may also narrow down the content, limit thinking and affect generation. Even the widely recognized group discussion method, if placed entirely in such a sequence, will also have limitations in use. For example, the convergence of children's cognition may cause the discussion to repeat the existing level, or even lead to misinterpretation and the loss of children's potential questions. The limitation of avoidance strategies lies in their appropriate application. Depending on the objectives and content, teachers can create different student-centered learning methods for students, such as experiencing, inquiring, thinking, discussing and practicing. The communication methods between teachers and students are interactive and definitely not a simple time sequence.

(4) Whether the Main Form Necessarily Realizes the Significance of the Subject

In traditional teaching, teachers dominate classroom discourse, determining and controlling the content and rhythm of students' thinking. In the reform, with the approach of "learning before teaching", teachers' summaries must come later and not exceed the specified time, which indeed subverts teachers' control rights. But does this mean that we have directly achieved the value pursuit of teaching? The essence of subjective form resides in subject development. If the dimensions and depth of development are lacking, the change in form is not the original intention of the reform. In practice, some reformers propose that teachers should "lecture as little as possible" in class, but this does not mean "teach as little as possible". "Teaching" is not equivalent to "lecturing", and is the obligation of teachers, which can be situation creation, stimulation, guidance, evaluation, and of course, explanation. The value of students' teaching subjectivity can only be realized through teachers' continuous regulation in class.

III. Pay Attention to the Premise for Selecting Teaching Modes

John Dewey, the key figure of empiricism, once talked about the subject of teaching methods in *The Child and the Curriculum*. He believes that "the child and the curriculum are simply two limits which define a single process. Just as two points define a straight line, so the present standpoint of the child and the facts and truths of studies define instruction. It is continuous reconstruction, moving from the child's present experience out into that represented by the organized bodies of truth that we call studies."[1] Dewey put a strong emphasis on the child whose current "standpoint" is the starting point of teaching. But what determines teaching methods? It is the relationship between the child's current "standpoint" and the subject's core knowledge. The purpose and significance of teaching lie in enabling the child to move from "present experience" to "that represented by studies". The rationality of teaching needs to examine whether students' subjectivity has been brought into play in class. In addition, it also examines what kind of "facts and truths of studies" students' subjectivity in class points to and what kind of "experience represented by studies" has been realized. Firstly, the study experience here should not be just the quantity and solidity of knowledge acquisition. Second, academic experience does not emerge naturally from student subjecthood alone. "Nothingness can

---

1 Dewey, J. *The Child and the Curriculum*[M]. Translated by Lin Baoshan & Kang Chunzhi. Taipei:Wu-Nan Book Inc., 1990:112, 116.

only produce nothingness, and something cannot be created out of nothing. Immaturity can only produce immaturity. If we throw the child back to his existing self, believing it to be the best ideal, and ask him to extend outward to new truths or behaviors, this is impossible"[1]. The premise for selecting teaching modes and teaching methods is to analyze what possibilities the curriculum can bring to students. Teachers should first be clear about the possibilities of these teaching objectives and functions contained in the content. Then they should interpret, transform and organize the possibilities to form the purpose and value pursuit of teaching based on their understanding of learners, themselves, and the educational and teaching situations.

(1) Analysis of Curriculum Potential

What is the experience represented by studies? What students experience in class must not be just study knowledge, but also those curriculum elements that can promote their growth. Scholars like Schwab, Peretz put forward another proposition, that is, curriculum potential. Schwab believes that curriculum potential is the possible curriculum contained in study content that is helpful for students' growth and development. Peretz believes that curriculum potential is "all learning experiences from particular sources to achieve a broad educational goal"[2]. In practice, some teachers believe that students can understand the content of textbooks by themselves, so they really don't need to explain it. If the learning experience that students need is just superficial tasks such as "what the content is" and "how to answer" in textbooks, this assumption of teachers is reasonable. As Peretz said, teachers' daily experience easily narrows their sight of using various potentials of curriculum textbooks. Teachers are used to believing in the obvious interpretations of textbooks, especially those things they

---

1 Jiang Shanye. *Concise International Encyclopedia of Education·Curriculum*[M]. Beijing: Educational Science Publishing House, 1991:11.

2 Jiang Shanye. *Concise International Encyclopedia of Education·Curriculum*[M]. Beijing: Educational Science Publishing House, 1991:11.

are already familiar with... Therefore, it is necessary to enhance teachers' awareness of the opposite aspects of useful curriculum textbooks....[1] The concept of curriculum potential reminds teachers that teaching goals are not simply expressed in the text of textbooks and are not fixed. They need to be explored by teachers. Teaching design should consider whether students can obtain something and how to obtain it, but first of all, it should consider what to obtain. According to Schwab's view, when each study content is transformed into curriculum content, it contains three dimensions that may generate meaning, namely, theme, source and understanding[2]. The theme expressed by study content, that is, the meaning and significance mainly expressed in the content materials, is evident and readily observable. The source dimension refers to the methods and principles by which study content is generated. When study experts explore disordered study materials, they need to use specific methods and principles to make chaotic study knowledge orderly. Each study content contains certain methods and principles by which this study content is formed. The third dimension is understanding. Because study content is a complex organization composed of multiple parts, it can be understood only by using certain principles, using different thinking methods from multiple perspectives, and asking different questions. For example, when a piece of scientific material enters into the curriculum, curriculum or teaching designers can choose its theme dimension to provide learners with descriptions and explanations of related phenomena. Or they can choose a certain principle or method required to understand this material as the learning content, so that learners know how to make judgments. For example, if the source dimension of a poem is taken as the learning content, students can discover the characteristics of the poem by

---

1 Schwab, J. J. The Practical 3: Translation into Curriculum[J]. *School Review*, 1973(81):501-522.

2 Deng Zongyi. Constructing Chinese Didactics: (Re)discovering the German Didactics Tradition[J]. *Jahrbuch fur Allgemeine Didaktik (JfAD)*, 2012(1):108-128.

practicing writing and analyzing poems. This not only achieves the goal of letting students understand the characteristics of the poem, but also enables them to master the skills of analyzing and composing poems. This dimension has potential value for learners.

For this issue, some scholars believe that although German didactics has a different conceptual system, at the teaching design level, it also pays great attention to the analysis of the potential of curriculum content which has made great achievements. German didactics suggests that teaching content is the knowledge, experience and wisdom that have been specially selected and organized to achieve educational purposes, and is a medium for promoting human development, liberation and freedom. Teaching content contains educational potential that needs to be discovered and realized in teaching. "In order to be competent for this work, teachers need to analyze and interpret the meaning of these contents when conducting teaching design." As the first step of teaching design, teachers should understand the educational intention embedded in the curriculum content by curriculum designers and reflect on what considerations the designers had when selecting a certain content into the curriculum. The German scholar Klafki provides teachers with a framework for analyzing content when conducting teaching design, which is divided into five steps. ①Value of the content. What principle, method, technique or attitude does this content provide for learners? ②Significance for the present. What is the significance of the experience, knowledge, ability or skill that students can acquire? ③Significance for the future. What impact will a certain content have on students in the future? ④Content structure. How is the content structured? Is the content layered? Does it have different layers of meaning and significance? ⑤Educational representativeness. For the children of specific age stage, what special cases, phenomena, situations, experiments, persons and elements are interesting, stimulating, approachable and conceivable?[1]

(2) Studies from Different "Sources" Have Different Teaching Values

Schwab emphasized the "source" in the studies, that is, "each study content contains certain methods and principles for forming this content" as the potential that can be exploited in the curriculum. This potential is different, forming different study characteristics. This difference is both the limitation of teaching design and the possibility of teaching significance. Study courses come from one or more studies and naturally carry the inherent attributes of the studies themselves. The knowledge and experience of these studies have different production modes or different research methods when they are produced. In teaching, when understanding and interpreting these study contents, we should also follow these characteristics of thinking, expression and communication. For example, *Chinese Language* in the humanities has both aesthetic and comprehensive characteristics. So we should understand the meaning of the text, feel and express beauty in emotion intensification. The formation of morality is based on reflection of the experience or speculation. *Mathematics* is a kind of mathematical logic, a Cartesian tradition[2], and also a rigorous deduction in the mind. Natural sciences such as physics and chemistry are based on experimental induction. In the same teaching modes, it is assumed that the properties of these studies are the same, so the same expressions and ways of thinking can be adopted. If the main task of teachers and students in the *Chinese Language* class is to find the clues of the text and the words and phrases that describe the clues - even if done in an autonomous or discussion-based way - the class is essentially teaching *Chinese Language* in the same way mathematical knowledge is formed. As a result, the meaning of understanding and the aesthetic value that *Chinese Language* teaching requires have been lost. It is precisely because a thing does

---

1 Klafki, W. Didactic Analysis as the Core of Preparation of Instruction[J]. *Journal of Curriculum Studies*, 1995(1):13-30.

2 Wu Guosheng. Science and the Humanities[J]. *Social Sciences in China*, 2001(4):10-13.

not have numerous attributes that it can be what it is and possess the value of its own attributes. The teaching of each study course has its own characteristics and can also have its own functions, thus, teaching itself has become rich, complex and full of charm.

(3) Teaching Is the Unique Educational Creation of Teachers

The document carriers of the curriculum are mainly curriculum standards and textbooks. When the writers transform their understanding of the curriculum into texts and words, the meaning has already been weakened. If the teaching takes the understanding of the words in textbooks and the mastery of knowledge points as the fundamental aim, it will inevitably narrow the understanding of the curriculum again. Teaching should not and cannot be the further weakening of the textbook content. The guide in the teaching process is "present", and teachers can tap the potential of the curriculum, so those parts that are implied in textbooks and not all expressed in textbooks, those parts generated from teaching, and those parts that are intended to be expressed based on texts can all be the content of teaching. Teaching is the most active link in realizing the potential of the curriculum. Dou Guimei, a famous Chinese teacher of *Chinese Language* teaching, put forward a four-level analysis step when talking about her interpretation of textbooks during lesson preparation. Firstly, analyze what the text actually says. That is, it is necessary to make the original text clear, read it accurately, understand it thoroughly, grasp its essence, and interpret the intended meaning behind the words. As an independent reader, one should understand, imagine and analyze the text instead of simply copying others' understanding. Secondly, analyze what the text wants to say. That is to say, the form of expression for an article depends on relevant background factors. Then teachers should look up the author's life, the historical background of the writing period, relevant social thoughts, and the basic knowledge and characteristics of the literary genre itself. Thirdly, analyze what the text can say. Different people have different understandings of the same text. Different reading levels, personal experiences, mentalities, and even in different social and historical periods will have different interpretations. These interpretations from many perspectives help teachers first achieve "understanding". Fourthly, analyze what the text should say. At this point, one should adopt a teacher's perspective, "get rid of the reconstruction of the author's psychological experience", and think deeply how to transform the reading experience into something suitable for students to understand and accept. She believes that the purpose of teachers' understanding and interpretation of the text is "to understand the author better than the author does". Then the significance of curriculum fundamentally comes from teachers' own lives[1]. In these four steps, if the first three steps are teachers' interpretation, selection and organization of the curriculum potential, the fourth step is the transformation of curriculum potential by teachers on this basis. Teachers need to re-interpret, transform and organize teaching content according to their understanding of learners, themselves, and educational and teaching situations.

IV. The Way to Learn Teaching Modes Is Meaningful and Creative

The generation of modes is conditional on specific situations. Learning modes requires understanding of the value pursuit and core concepts behind them. It needs to be more "abstract" and accompanied by creative actions, rather than simply replicating procedures. This process also needs to be realized through practical attempts and reflection. For example, in practice, some practitioners in China have experienced the reform path from "links" and "modes" to "modules"[2]. At the beginning of the reform, based on students' learning needs, they put forward six teaching links that reflect students' subjectivity, that is, self-study and questioning, communication and display,

---

1 Dou Guimei. *To Be a Teacher with Professional Dignity*[M]. Guilin: Li Jiang Publishing, 2007:24.

2 Sun Chaoren & Sun Miao. Practice and Reflection on the 'Six-Module Constructivist Classroom' Based on the Principle of 'Teaching by Learning'[J]. *Journal of Shanghai Educational Research*, 2012(11):52.

interactive inquiry, intensive teaching and guidance, correction and feedback, and transfer and application. After a period of exploration, in order to avoid the rigid use of the mode, the six links are changed into six modules, realizing teachers' three-dimensional, random and combined use of each link. Trying a mode is a means for practitioners to explore the concepts behind the mode, from having unclear and new ideas to learning an operable and replicable mode. After experiencing the significance of the reform and understanding the value of teaching, practitioners break through the fixed mode and move towards rich and diversified practical styles that are not contrary to the basic principle of students' subjectivity. Therefore, the modes in the reform are temporary operational patterns for promoting concepts and are "rules" set for those who do not understand the concepts. Once the concepts are understood, practitioners need space to independently construct each rich, complex and multi-dimensional classroom. Therefore, the reform should also leave spaces for those who understand the concepts.

[Originally published in *Theory and Practice of Education* 2014(31) (Feng Qi, Lv Lijie & Yuan Qiuhong)]

13. The Tradition Moving Towards the Future: Discussion on the Development of School-based Curriculum of Traditional Culture

In March 2014, the Ministry of Education issued the *Outline for Improving the Education of Excellent Traditional Chinese Culture* (hereinafter referred to as the *Outline*), proposing that traditional culture education should be strengthened in primary and secondary school curriculum and conducted top-level design on how to promote the education of excellent traditional Chinese culture in school. In January 2017, the General Office of the Communist Party of China Central Committee and the General Office of the State Council issued the *Opinions on Implementing the Project for the Inheritance and Development of Fine Traditional Chinese Culture* (hereinafter referred to as the *Opinions*), which for the first time explained the work of inheriting and developing excellent traditional Chinese culture in the form of official documents of the central leadership, providing a channel and development path for implementing the education of excellent traditional Chinese culture. Traditional culture serves as the wellspring of national cohesion and creativity, forming a cornerstone of national and cultural confidence. School education is the main channel for cultivating talents. At present, many schools disseminate traditional culture in various ways such as national curriculum, school-based curriculum and school activities, shaping the cultural pattern, personality and temperament of a generation. In other words, the traditional culture transmitted in the curriculum determines what kind of cognitive understanding, value recognition, and cultural choice of excellent traditional Chinese culture the young students of a generation have. As part of a series of studies, this study investigates the current situation and existing problems of the school-based traditional culture curriculum nationwide, aiming to provide path thinking and practical references for the optimization of school-based traditional culture curriculum. The school-based traditional culture curriculum in this study refers to a type that is independently offered and continuously implemented by the school and take excellent traditional Chinese culture as the theme.

I. The Educational Implication and Curriculum Value of Excellent Traditional Chinese Culture

(1) The Educational Implication of the Inheritance and Development of Excellent Traditional Chinese Culture

The inheritance and development of traditional Chinese culture are not only the needs of times for enhancing China's cultural soft power and strengthening cultural confidence but also the basic requirements of the internal regulations of culture, conveying the value significance of the continuity of the ethnic humanities. The continuity of the ethnic humanities depends on the bidirectional interaction between collective culture and individual perspectives. On the one hand, nation members "rely on cultural frameworks to regulate their behaviors", achieving symbolic, identificatory, and valuative understanding of cultural subjects[1]. On the other hand, under this influence, citizens with national responsibility are cultivated, and they will expand the extension and enrich the connotation of national culture through their own qualities and abilities[2]. Education, in this bidirectional interaction, not only cultivates the growth of individuals as the core of the cultural program but also promotes the inheritance and development of culture as a tool for transforming social culture. In other words, education should not only discipline and guide individuals with national traditional culture but also cultivate the subjective initiative of talents to develop national traditional culture. In realities, students will experience the lifestyles, behavioral norms, and thinking differences brought by different cultures, and

---

1 Geertz, C. *The Interpretation of Cultures*[M]. Translated by Nari Bilige, *et al.* Shanghai: Shanghai People's Publishing House, 1999.

2 Qin Guangguang, Feng Li & Chen Pu. *A Dictionary of Cultural Studies*[M]. Beijing: China Minzu University Press, 1998.

make choices and adjustments based on their own cultural understanding, thus forming groups with behavioral convergence and heterogeneous values. Under the influence of high-quality education, the deep structure of excellent traditional Chinese culture, such as values, psychological traits, and emotional thinking, and other core elements of national identity and cohesion that constitutes national identity and cohesion[1], can enable students to understand conceptually, identify in value, and assimilate in behavior, and then achieve collective identity recognition, emotional attachment, and the enhancement of national cohesion at the spiritual level. Therefore, education is both the main way for the inheritance and development of traditional Chinese culture and can promote the continuity of the Chinese nation. In addition, it can also prompt traditional culture to move from "telling as it is" to "building the future".

(2) The Curriculum Is the Path for Cultivating People by Culture, and the School-based Curriculum Is the "Node" of Cultural Context

The curriculum is the path for cultivating people by culture. Judging from the things that students should obtain in the curriculum experience, the curriculum itself should form a unique personality structure and provide sufficient cultural resources to help students achieve internal transcendence on the basis of accepting cultural norms.[2] In terms of China's national curriculum system, courses such as *Chinese Language*, *History*, *Morality and the Rule of Law*, *Music*, *Sports* and *Art* have already systematically reflected traditional Chinese culture. However, culture is a social product integrating forms such as literature, art, science and morality. Its acquisition is not only the collection of knowledge and information but also requires accepting values in emotional resonance, understanding and identifying in cultural experience and recognition

1 Zhao Shilin. On the Essence of the Inheritance of Ethnic Cultures[J]. *Journal of Peking University (Humanities and Social Sciences)*, 2002(3):10 - 16.

2 Dewey, B. J. Democracy and Education: An Introduction to the Philosophy of Education[J]. *American Journal of Sociology*, 1916(1):40-49.

of differences. The school-based curriculum is mostly conducted based on the humanistic environment, regional resources and historical accumulation of schools and local areas with their own characteristics.[1] If the classified national curriculum clarify the core context of Chinese culture, the school-based curriculum can be the node where these contexts converge and intersect. Meanwhile, the recognition of culture involves a process from the shallower to the deeper and step by step. Without personal emotional attachment and the existence of local roots, it is difficult to maintain the recognition of the deep structure of excellent traditional Chinese culture. The school-based curriculum is gradually developed based on the utilization of various local resources, so it shows that it has unique educational value as the "node" of the cultural context.

II. Research Design and Methods

This study investigated the actual situation of the quantity, category, regional characteristics, organization form and teaching quality of school-based traditional culture curriculum, as well as the external influencing factors such as social concern, resource utilization and the teaching staff. It adopted a mixed research design by using methods such as public opinion analysis, questionnaire survey, individual interview and classroom observation. According to the total number of regional divisions in the eastern, central and western regions in China's "Seventh Five-Year Plan", stratified quota sampling was carried out to determine 45 research schools in the eastern region, 43 in the central region, and 32 in the western region respectively. From October 2018 to January 2019, two rounds of investigation and research were conducted on primary and secondary schools in 12 provinces, municipalities and autonomous regions sampled, obtaining a total of 120 school curriculum plans (or curriculum schedules), 1,542 teacher questionnaires, 6,874 questionnaires from primary school students, and

---

1 Lv Lijie & Yuan Qiuhong. The Logic of Curriculum Organization in School-based Curriculum Development[J]. *Educational Research*, 2014(9):96-103.

5,356 questionnaires from secondary school students. Meanwhile, we also interviewed 10 principals and 24 teachers respectively and conducted 16 classroom observations. From this, the implementation status of school-based traditional culture curriculum in primary and secondary schools in China was discovered and sorted out.

(1) Investigation on the Implementation Status of School-based Traditional Culture Curriculum

The research team preprocesses and integrates the collected data of the 120 school curriculum plans (or curriculum schedules) according to multiple aspects such as the proportion, offering types, organization form, and management appraisal of school-based traditional culture curriculum, and imports the detailed classification level data into the sunburstR package (http://cran.r-project.org/package=sunburstR) to draw a sunburst diagram. The current situation of other aspects of school-based curriculum is calculated using the built-in statistical function commands of the R language and describes statistically in the form of average, percentage, etc.

(2) Description of the Group Status of Teachers' and Students' Attitudes

To observe the actual modality of students and teachers in the actual research, this study conducts scale development and design on teachers' attitudes and students' attitudes (including students' satisfaction with school-based traditional culture curriculum and traditional cultural identity) from the 120 schools in the first-round research, and then conducts the second-round research. The scale design for teachers' attitudes is theoretically based on the definition of attitude by Katz *et al.* in 1959, that is, attitude is an organized set of cognition, emotion and behavioral tendency held by an individual towards a specific object (person, event, thing). Based on this, attitude can be divided into three main levels, namely cognition, emotion and behavioral intention[1]. The student satisfaction borrows from the customer satisfaction index model based on causal relationship launched by Dr. Fornell of the National Quality Research Center of the University of Michigan Business School, forming a student satisfaction theoretical framework for school-based traditional culture curriculum. It is mainly divided into three aspects including student expectation, perceived quality, value perception and student loyalty[2]. The scale for students' cultural identity refers to the psychological level structure of ethnic cultural identity, including three dimensions, that is, cultural symbol identity, cultural identity recognition and value culture identity[3].

All questionnaires used a 5-point Likert scale for measurements. Among them, the teacher attitude scale and the student curriculum satisfaction scale are self-report scales, and the student cultural identity scale is a situational judgment test scale. The researchers calculate the Cronbach's Alpha reliability coefficient of each scale by using the custom function of the R language. As can be seen from Table 3-2, the Cronbach's Alpha reliability coefficients are all above 0.75, indicating good consistency. In order to test the validity of the three scales, first, the KMO program in the additional psych package (https://cran.r-project.org/web/packages/psych/) is used to calculate the KMO values of each scale. It can be seen that the KMO values of three scales are all above 0.8, which is suitable for exploratory factor analysis. In addition, orthogonal rotation based on the maximum variance method is carried out through the *factanal* function, the *factor. analysis* function within the R language, and the *fa* function in the

---

1 Li Jie. Research on the Current Situation and Transformation of University Students' Attitudes Toward Life[M]. Shanghai: Shanghai People's Publishing House, 2015.

2 Liu, R, & Jung, L.The Commuter Student and Student Satisfaction[J]. *Research in Higher Education*,
1980(3):215-226.

3 Wang Pei & Hu Fawen. National Cultural Identity: Implications and Structures[J]. *Journal of Shanghai Normal University (Philosophy & Social Sciences Edition)*, 2011(1):101-107.

additional psych package. After analysis, it is found that the standardized factor loadings of three scales are all between 0.568 and 0.871, and the total explained variance exceeds 75%, as shown specifically in Table 1. To sum up, the scales in the second round have good validity. On the basis of confirming that the scales had good reliability and validity, the R language is used to conduct cluster analysis on various groups according to the dimensions at all levels of the research. Moreover, the additional R package pheatmap is used to draw a "heatmap" to describe the group status of teacher attitudes, student course satisfaction and traditional cultural identity (https://cran.r-project.org/web/packages/pheatmap/index.html).

Table 3-2 Reliability and Validity Test Statistics for Each Scale

Scale Name	Educational Stage	Cronbach's Alpha	KMO Value	Total Explained Variance
Teachers' Attitude	All	0.940	0.961	82.836%
Student Curriculum Satisfaction	Primary School	0.922	0.945	86.497%
	Secondary School	0.833	0.901	84.742%
Student Cultural Identity	Primary School	0.804	0.869	78.839%
	Secondary School	0.777	0.827	76.438%

(3) Model Construction of Curriculum Satisfaction and Cultural Identity

Judging from the things that students should obtain in the curriculum experience, the curriculum itself should form a unique personality structure and provide sufficient cultural resources to help students achieve internal transcendence on the basis of accepting cultural norms. Thus, the curriculum serves as a pathway for cultural cultivation, and what students obtain in school-based traditional culture curriculum should be the generation of the identity of excellent traditional Chinese culture. In order to explore the relationship between the two, this study adopts the Structural Equation Model (SEM) of Amos 21.0 software to verify the model relationship between students' satisfaction with school-based traditional culture curriculum and cultural identity generation. SEM is an important model construction method that integrates multiple data analysis methods such as path analysis and confirmatory factor analysis.[1] The study uses the Maximum Likelihood (ML) method for model estimation. After several cycles of model prediction, operation and adjustment, a model is obtained. With $X^2/df = 3.12 < 5$, $GFI = 0.957 > 0.90$, $CFI = 0.931 > 0.90$, $RMSEA = 0.067 < 0.08$, this model demonstrates good fit indices. It is hoped that the construction and interpretation of this model can illustrate the role of school-based traditional culture curriculum in cultivating students' cultural identity. In addition, it puts forward more reasonable and effective suggestions for the improvement of school-based traditional culture curriculum aiming at enhancing students' identity of excellent traditional Chinese culture.

(4) Public Sentiment and Spatial Autocorrelation Analysis of Traditional Culture Education

The social concern in the external atmosphere does not directly affect the specific implementation of school-based traditional culture curriculum. However, it imperceptibly influences every student, teacher, principal and other curriculum designers and implementers, and will affect the practice of traditional culture education, and then change students' cultural identity. It can be seen that public sentiment toward traditional culture education is critical to the implementation of school-based curriculum and the generation of students' cultural identity. Therefore, the researchers select news reports on traditional culture education from mainstream media such as People's Daily Online, Xinhuanet and Sina, as well as education websites of various provinces and municipalities from 2014 to 2018, and conduct statistical analysis on them to judge the public sentiment on traditional culture education across the country.

---

1 Guo Congbin & Min Weifang. Education: Establishing Rational and Intergenerational Mobility Mechanism--The Application of Structural Equation Model in the Research on the Relationship between Education and Intergenerational Mobility[J]. *Educational Research*, 2009(10):5-12.

In addition, in order to more clearly reflect the public sentiment level of traditional culture education in various provinces and municipalities, the researchers import all the reports into NVivo11 software, and carry out free node coding on the educational carriers (such as Confucius, Kunqu Opera, shadow puppetry, Chinese classics, etc.) and cultivation paths (such as national curriculum infiltration, study tours, etc.) reported by traditional culture education news in various provinces and municipalities. As to the competitiveness of public sentiment on traditional culture education in various provinces and municipalities, the data processing method in scientific research management[1] is referred to formulate Traditional Culture Education Public-sentiment Competitiveness Index (TCEPCI), that is, $TCEPCI_{\text{a province}} =$

$$\sqrt{\frac{\text{Number of Traditional Culture Educational Carrier in a Province}}{\text{Average Number of Traditional Culture Educational Carriers across 31 Provinces}} \times \frac{\text{Number of Traditional Culture Cultivation Path in a Province}}{\text{Average Number of Traditional Culture Cultivation Path across 31 Provinces}}}$$

The diversification of educational carriers and cultivation paths of traditional culture in various provinces and municipalities makes it difficult to reasonably quantify the public sentiment power of traditional culture education in various provinces and municipalities. This formula can objectively obtain the index situation of each province and municipality through the ratio of a certain province and municipality to the average value. All the above calculations are completed using the R language. Then this study imports the TCEPCI index into the Getis-Ord General G module in ArcGIS software for global spatial autocorrelation analysis. In the global autocorrelation analysis using the G-index, a statistically significant result ($P \leqslant 0.05$) with a positive Z-value indicates that the research competitiveness of Chinese university counselors exhibits spatial clustering effects in its distribution. When the ratio of the observed G-index to the expected G-index is greater than 1, it indicates that the data are

1 Ma Tingcan, Cao Mukun & Wang Guifang. Analysis of the Regional Competitiveness of Basic Research in China Based on the National Natural Science Foundation of China[J]. *Chinese Science Bulletin*, 2011(36).

clustered at high values. If the ratio is less than 1, it indicates that the data are clustered at low values.[1] However, in the study, if the ratio is equal to 1, it indicates that there are both high-value clustering and low-value clustering in the regional space, and further local spatial autocorrelation calculations are needed for judgement. The researchers use LISA to evaluate the local spatial autocorrelation intensity of public sentiment competitiveness on traditional culture education. Local spatial autocorrelation analysis is carried out by using the Local Indicators of Spatial Association (LISA) module: the number of data simulation calculations is set to 999 times, and the areas and types where the clustering effect occur are displayed in the form of pictures to predict the trend of public sentiment on traditional culture education in various provinces and municipalities.

III. Research Results and Analysis

(1) Current Status of School-based Traditional Culture Curriculum Implementation

1. School-based Traditional Culture Curricula are Rich and Diverse in Categories, and There are Deviations in Content Recognition in Some Individual Schools

Among the 120 schools in 12 provinces and municipalities surveyed, 107 schools offer the school-based curriculum, and 92 of them have school-based traditional culture curriculum. A total of 321 school-based traditional culture curricula have been collected. It can be said that there are a large number of school-based traditional culture curricula offered across the country occupying a large proportion at present. They are divided and classified into three major types, “Taoist Studies”, “Practical Arts” and comprehensive. Among them, the “Taoist Studies” curriculum refers to that with a high degree of abstraction in

---

1 Getis, A. & Ord, J. K. The Analysis of Spatial Association by Use of Distance Statistics[J]. *Geographical Analysis,* 1992(3):189-206.

cultural content and a distinct and systematic ideological system, further being divided into three sub-categories: history, classical texts and moral education. The "Practical Arts" curriculum refers to that related to lifestyles and ways of leisure with operational and folk content. According to specific content, it can be further divided into 21 subcategories such as tea art, etiquette, and the 'Four Arts' (qin, chess, calligraphy and painting) as shown specifically in Figure 3-4. The comprehensive type refers to the theme curriculum, which blend the contents of "Taoist Studies" and "Practical Arts" into a unity through themes and integrate students' learning methods such as cognition, experience and inquiry. Statistical results show that there are 78 curricula of the "Taoist Studies", 245 curricula of the "Practical Arts" and 7 curricula of the comprehensive type. These curricula convey and promote the traditional Chinese culture from multiple aspects such as ideology, literature, etiquette and living customs, showing distinct educational values. However, through the analysis of school curriculum plans or schedules, some phenomena are found as follows. Some schools require students to recite too many ancient texts. For example, third-grade students are required to recite the entire contents of *Canons for Disciples*, *Three Word Primer*, *One Thousand Words*, *The Ideal of Learning*, *The Doctrine of Mean* and *Mencius*. Some other schools propose to "attach importance to the Doctrine of Mean in classical culture, and to integrate it into the classroom in an unbiased and all-round way, so that the classical culture that has been put on the shelf can take root". In addition, some schools organize students' experience activities such as bowing in front of the statue of Confucius and tying ideal ribbons on the Zhuangyuan Bridge before the senior high school and college entrance examinations to pray for good grades. Cultural inheritance is the process of selecting traditional and existing cultures, and cultural selection is the process of establishing the knowledge and values that are most suitable for social development.

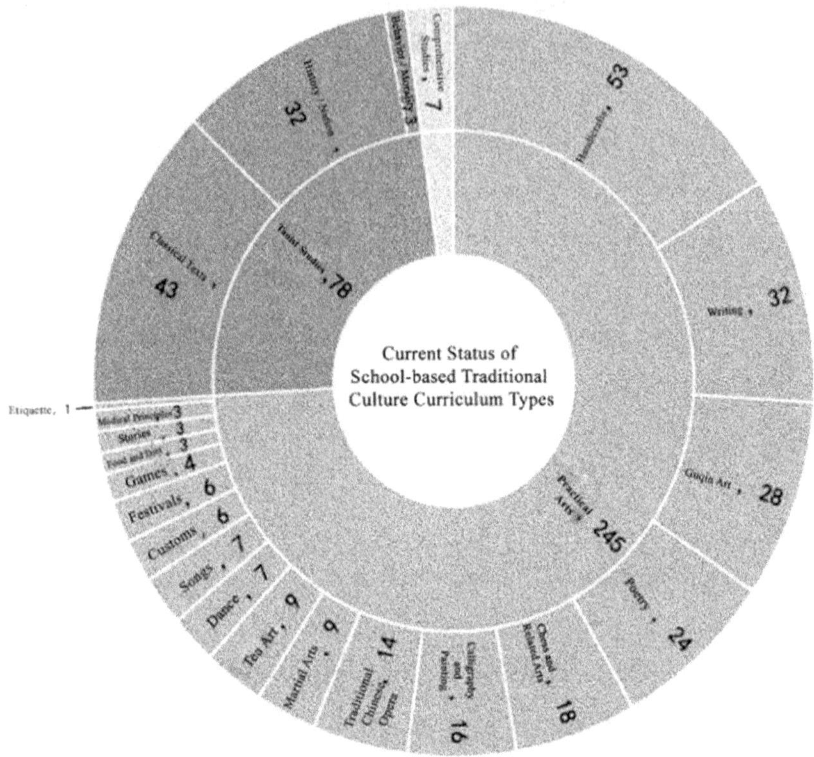

Figure 3-4 Sunburst Diagram of the Current Status of School-based Traditional Culture Curriculum Types

Curriculum design is the process of cultural selection, and the curriculum shapes students' understanding of traditional culture. Traditional culture realizes inheritance and continuation through school education, especially school curriculum, which is also a process of selecting traditional culture. What is retained and continued in school curriculum and what kinds of traditional culture should be developed together constitutes people's understanding of traditional culture in future. In this sense, school curriculum is the processes of understanding, selecting, and restructuring traditional culture, and the curriculum is the transformation of culture. Therefore, it is necessary for us to explore and name the common value of traditional culture curriculum, and to sort out, identify and grasp the unity in the values and goals of traditional culture curriculum among the richness and diversity of curriculum forms such as content area, literacy function, cultural background and historical origin, thus establishing a "diversity in unity" ideological orientation for such curriculum.

2. The Implementation of School-based Traditional Culture Curriculum Relies on Local Resources, but There Are Still Overall Deficiencies in Class Hours and Methods

In the curriculum implementation, all regions make full use of the advantages of local cultural resources and offer school-based traditional culture curriculum with regional characteristics, such as the school-based curriculum of *Entering the Old Summer Palace* in Haidian District, Beijing, the *Shadow Puppetry* in Gansu, *Entering Confucius* in Linyi, Shandong, the *Waist Drum* curriculum in Shaanxi, and the *Bamboo Carving* curriculum in Changzhou, Jiangsu. These curricula make use of local resources, consider students' living environments, and play their unique and flexible educational roles. In the survey, we also found that school-based traditional culture curriculum has the implementation difficulties common to all types of school-based curricula, that is, the problem of class hour guarantee. Over 80% of primary schools offer 12 academic hours per year for these curricula, whereas most secondary schools provide only 4 hours annually. The reason is that the class hours in secondary schools are very "tight", and students state that school-based curriculum is often replaced by some subjects such as mathematics and physics. In addition, in terms of the implementation methods, 53.66% of primary and secondary schools only implement the curriculum in the classroom. Only 1% of students have been to communities, memorial halls, folk custom museums, museums, and Confucian academies more than four times in school-based curriculum. The content of traditional culture has been presented systematically in national curriculum, especially in subjects such as *Chinese Language*, *History*, *Morality and the Rule of Law*, *Music*, *Sports* and *Art*. What is the relationship between the content of traditional culture in school-based curriculum and that in national curriculum? If school-based curriculum is just the supplement and expansion of the national curriculum content, to what extent is an increase in quantity appropriate? If it is considered that the more the better, the vastness and richness of Chinese culture will make the curriculum capacity unlimited. Especially if the supplementary part of school-based curriculum has nothing to do with the senior high school and the college entrance examination, it will naturally be regarded as a schoolwork burden by teachers and students and become a curriculum that neither teachers nor students are willing to truly implement. Therefore, the traditional cultural content in school-based curriculum should not be measured by the volume of knowledge or information imparted. Rather, we should perceive and practice culture in a comprehensive, experiential and operational way, that is, understand culture by integrating existing information and knowledge, and practice the expectations and curiosities on culture. We can also let students perceive the existence of traditional culture in the created situations and environments.

(2) Group Description of the Subjects of School-based Traditional Culture Curriculum

Teacher-student group dynamics were visualized using K-means heatmap clustering with average distance algorithms. This algorithm is calculated based on the average distance from the central value of a certain dimension. The clustered groups have no difference in good or bad. Within each cluster zone, every grid cell represents a teacher's or student's standardized score relative to the dimensional mean, with darker color intensity indicating higher scores while lighter shades correspond to lower values[1]. Each line represents the score situation of the same teacher or student in different dimensions, and the tree diagram on the left represents the clustering results of each teacher or student.

1. Cluster Analysis of Teachers' Attitudes towards School-based

---

1 Yang Man, Lv Lijie & Ding Yiran. The Investigation and Promotion Strategies of the Identity of Chinese Excellent Traditional Culture of Contemporary Pupils[J]. *China Educational Technology*, 2019(6):44-51.

Curriculum of Traditional Culture

The investigation and measurement of teachers' attitudes towards traditional culture education are mainly carried out from three aspects including cognition, emotion and behavior. Generally speaking, teachers highly recognize traditional culture education in emotion and strive to practice it in behavior, but their overall cognition of traditional culture education is slightly weak. In actual interviews, it is mainly manifested that teachers recognize the necessity and urgency of offering school-based traditional culture curriculum, and 91.77% of teachers are willing to practice the concept of traditional culture for life. However, there are only a few full-time teachers or only part-time teachers of school-based traditional culture curriculum in a school, and most of them have insufficient mastery of relevant knowledge and the spiritual essence of traditional culture. To sum up, the current teacher group shows a good trend of quickly responding to the *Outline*, but is restricted by the insufficient full-time faculty, inadequate in-service training, and lack of external support, reflecting their inability to cope with the situation. According to their specific differences in various aspects such as cognition, emotion and behavior, they can be divided into "mediocre teachers", "active teachers", "excellent teachers", "intentional teachers", and "executive teachers" (as shown specifically in Figure 3-5).

"Mediocre teachers" perform mediocrely in the three aspects of cognition, emotion, and behavior towards school-based traditional culture curriculum, mostly showing a muddling-through practice modality, accounting for about 8.33% of the whole. "Excellent teachers" perform well in all three aspects. "Active teachers" account for 23.56% of the total number of teachers. They perform well in emotion and behavior, but are relatively weaker in cognition. Most of these teachers are willing to teach relevant content of traditional culture, but are often unable to truly deepen their understanding of traditional culture due to practical obstacles. Their differences from "intentional teachers" are that they not only identify with the traditional culture emotionally but also practice it in actual education. In addition, about 17.38% of teachers are "executive teachers", who often only strive to do well among requirements from school policies or mandatory orders in practice modality and do not fully recognize or accept the practice of school-based traditional culture curriculum from their hearts.

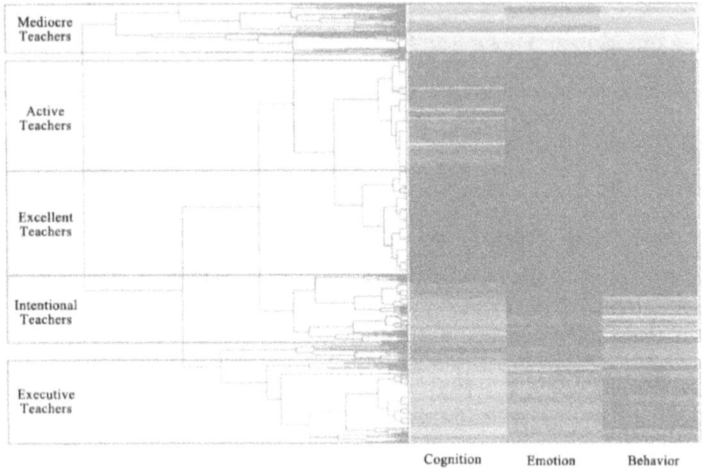

Figure 3-5 Group Clustering of Teachers' Attitudes Towards Traditional Culture School-based Curriculum

2. Cluster Analysis of Students' Satisfaction with School-based Curriculum

Judging from the overall situation of students' satisfaction with school-based traditional culture curriculum at present, students have relatively high expectations. However, their ability to perceive teaching content and methods remains relatively underdeveloped, which has also led to different performances in value perception (learning gain) and student loyalty later. This also reminds us that traditional Chinese culture is still the core value pursued by students in their learning and life today. School-based curriculum is not simply "telling" information, "preaching" values, or "implanting" mysterious traditional cultural knowledge. Instead, they let students learn how to make choices in a multicultural context, discover beauty and gain beliefs in familiar cultural elements.

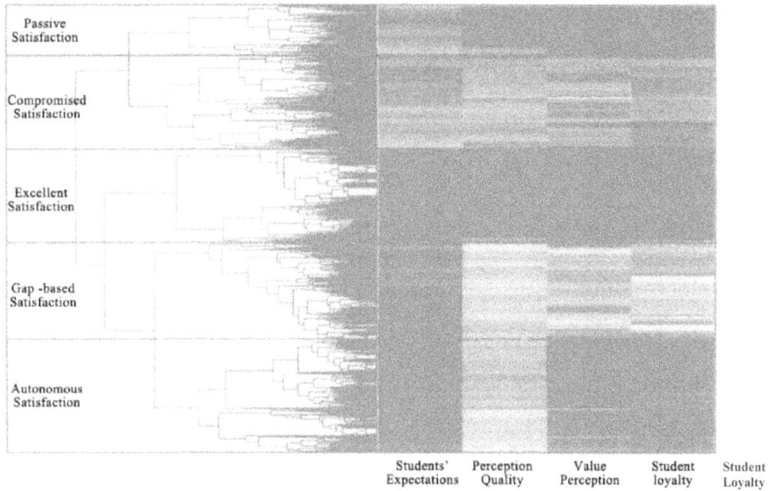

Figure 3-6 Group Clustering of Primary and Secondary School Students' Satisfaction with School-based Traditional Culture Curriculum

According to the specific differences of students in the four dimensions of curriculum satisfaction, students can be divided into five types including "passive satisfaction", "compromised satisfaction", "excellent satisfaction", "gap-based satisfaction" and "autonomous satisfaction" (as shown specifically in Figure 3-6). The proportion of students with "passive satisfaction" is relatively low, accounting for 9.39%. Although their initial expectations towards school-based traditional culture curriculum are moderate, the teachers' well-designed curriculum implementation with appropriate methods result in advanced perceived quality, value perception and student loyalty. "Compromised satisfaction" shows average performance in all four dimensions and presents a low equilibrium modality for school-based traditional culture curriculum. The two types of "excellent satisfaction" and "gap-based satisfaction" are in opposite situations. The former means that students' relatively high expectations are met, and thus they are quite satisfied in all aspects. The latter means that students' expectations are not met, resulting in a huge gap between expectations and gains, which diminishes students' satisfaction with the curriculum and will not generate loyalty to the curriculum. Both of these two types account for about 20% of the total. In addition, there is another type of "autonomous satisfaction". Students with this type have high expectations. Although they do not feel good quality in the curriculum implementation, their autonomous learning and research have also led to satisfactory curriculum outcomes.

3. Cluster Analysis of Students' Cultural Identity

Student cultural identity formation typically follows a spiral progression from the apparent perception of cultural carriers to the internalized comprehension of cultural spirit. It is not only affected by school education but also by factors such as family and society. Judging from the overall situation of primary and secondary school students' traditional cultural identity at present, the differences are obvious. There are significant differences among various groups, and the convergence characteristics within each group are distinct. It is precisely because when individuals accept the implicit norms of national cultural concepts, they will not only understand and identify with group paradigms but also shape individual differences in cultural understanding based on their own life experiences and growth experiences. It can be seen that individuals both generate "identity" that is the same as or similar to that of the ethnic group and obtained "heterogeneity" with different personal understandings[1]. Based on the performance differences in the three dimensions of cultural symbol identity, cultural identity recognition and value culture identity, the realistic groups can be divided into five types, that is, "deep-level identity", "equal identity", "passive identity", "cognitive identity" and "apparent identity" (as shown specifically in Figure 3-7).

---

1 Han Zhen. Characteristics of Cultural Identity of Oversea Chinese in the Era of Globalization[J]. *Academics,* 2009(2):25-32.

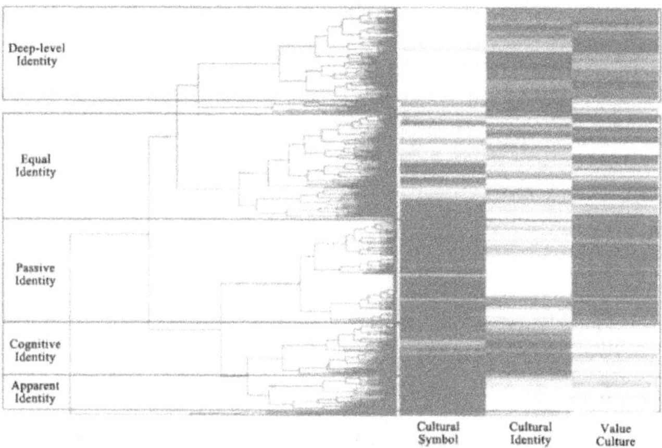

Figure 3-7 Group Clustering of Traditional Cultural Identity of Primary and Secondary School Students

Among them, "deep-level identity" and "apparent identity" show opposite performances in cultural symbol identity. Perhaps students can't remember the meaning of certain concrete cultural symbols, but they have already understood and comprehended the essence of traditional Chinese culture through previous learning and permeation. This type of students is more common in the senior grades of secondary school and accounts for 23.48% of all students. Students with "equal identity" perform mediocrely in all three dimensions and have a vague and outlining understanding and recognition about traditional Chinese culture. Students with "passive identity" have formed an understanding and recognition on representative symbols and basic concepts in culture after being passively influenced by all aspects of traditional culture education. However, they haven't really transformed it into emotional dependence and subjective identity recognition, so they perform relatively low in cultural identity. In addition, there is another type called "cognitive identity", which accounts for about 10% of the total. Students of this type should have achieved good performance in the recognition of cultural symbols and cultural identity after a period of learning, but they haven't yet obtained a deep identity for the spiritual value in traditional culture. For this reason, this type is more common among students in lower grades.

(3) Model Construction of the Relationship between Students' Curriculum Satisfaction and Traditional Cultural Identity

In the model of satisfaction with school-based traditional culture curriculum and students' cultural identity (as shown in Figure 3-8), the average variance extracted (AVE) values of latent variables generated by each observed variable are calculated to be greater than 0.5, and each parameter of the model is also significant at the level of $P \leq 0.05$ (except for the correlation between student expectations and value perception). It can be judged that there is a good internal logic among the various dimensions of the model construction. From the model diagram and the general situation of correlation coefficients, it can be found that the satisfaction with school-based traditional culture curriculum convey enhancement of students' cultural identity through the implementation of school-based traditional culture curriculum. Admittedly, the generation of students' identity of excellent traditional Chinese culture is certainly not limited to the implementation of school-based curriculum. It also depends on the permeation of national curriculum in school education, as well as the joint educational force formed by social education and family education. However, the construction of this model illustrates that school-based traditional culture curriculum is an appropriate and effective path to enhance students' cultural identity.

From the relationship construction of curriculum satisfaction on the left side of the model, it can be found that students' perception of the teaching methods and teaching content of school-based traditional culture curriculum determines students' learning gains, that is, perceived quality has a decisive effect on value perception, with a direct effect of 0.62. And the level of students' value perception will play a decisive role in their curriculum loyalty, with a direct effect of 0.69. In addition, student expectation exerts a certain yet relatively low influence on perceived quality, value perception and student loyalty, especially in the aspect of value perception (the direct effect = 0.28). Thus, although it is found in the survey that most students have expectations for the content of traditional culture, their own perception and gains in traditional culture curriculum are the important reasons that truly affect their curriculum satisfaction. This point indicates that in the current design and implementation of school-based traditional culture curriculum, it is necessary to promote the embodiment and diversity of teaching methods and the appropriateness and timeliness of teaching content, fully consider students' own experiences and roots. In addition, we should improve the school-based traditional culture curriculum in a timely manner to enhance students' perceived quality on such curriculum, and then promote students' value perception so as to improve students' satisfaction with such curriculum.

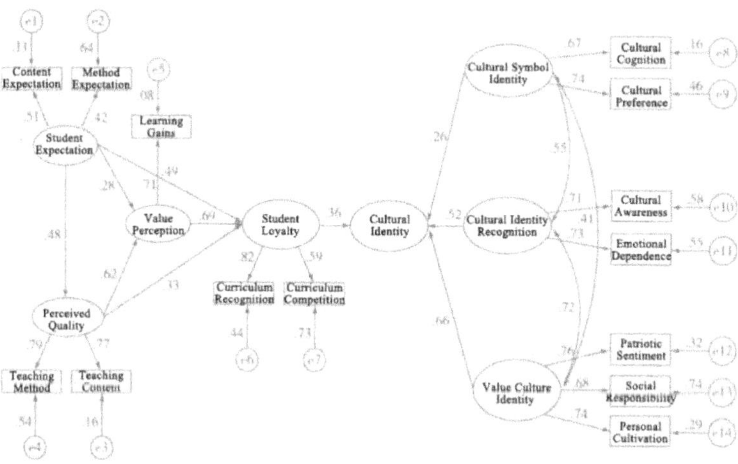

Figure 3-8 Model Construction Diagram of Primary and Secondary School Students' Curriculum Satisfaction and Cultural Identity

In addition, from the cultural identity model on the right side of the model construction, we can clearly find that the three dimensions having correlation with generation of students' cultural identity from the highest to lowest are value culture identity, cultural identity recognition and cultural symbol identity. Meanwhile, the correlation coefficients among the three are 0.55 between cultural identity recognition and cultural symbol identity, 0.72 between cultural identity recognition and value culture identity, and 0.41 between cultural symbol identity and value culture identity. It can be seen that the generation of students' cultural identity tested in practice is consistent with the relevant theoretical assumptions. The generation of cultural identity is not achieved overnight. Instead, it generates awareness and dependence on their own cultural environment through students' cognition and preference for cultural symbols. It develops identity recognition and attachment to excellent traditional Chinese culture through self-promotion constantly in the recognition of differences in multiculturalism. On this basis, students realize the recognition of the spiritual essence of the Chinese nation's culture, that is, understand the value culture of "emphasizing benevolence, valuing the people, keeping integrity, advocating justice, respecting harmony, and seeking common ground" in excellent traditional Chinese culture. To sum up, the generation of cultural identity is a process of clustering layer by layer and gradual improvement. This requires us to promote its vertical coherence in curriculum design and implementation around the requirements of the *Outline*, and gradually promote students to rise from the symbolic recognition of the artifacts with traditional culture to the conceptual understanding at the spiritual level.

(4) Dynamic Changes of the Public Sentiment on School Traditional Culture Education

We sort out and analyze 1,684 valid news reports on traditional culture education policies and traditional culture-related activities carried out by basic education schools in various provinces and municipalities across the country from 2014 to 2018. In terms of the quantity, the number of reports related to traditional culture education from 2014 to 2018 was 119, 146, 263, 432, and 724 respectively. It can be seen that since the Ministry of Education issued the *Outline* in 2014, the number of public sentiment reports has generally shown an upward trend year by year, and since 2017, the upward trend has noticeably accelerated. The reason why 2017 became a special time node is mainly due to the promulgation of the *Opinions* document. In order to thoroughly implement the basic ideas of the *Opinions*, various provinces and municipalities have successively strengthened their concern and emphasis on the education of excellent traditional Chinese culture, and vigorously enhanced the publicity, providing guidance from various aspects such as policy interpretation, specific requirements, tasks and targets, and practical strategies. This also fully illustrates that adhering to the policy orientation is the basic feature of practicing traditional culture education in various regions and that the leading role of policies is actively played during the implementation of traditional culture education in various regions.

Through quantitative calculation, it can be found that provinces such as Chongqing (3.949), Sichuan (3.466), Shandong (3.370), Henan (3.171) and Anhui (2.898) have relatively high TCEPCI levels and have good competitiveness in the public sentiment on traditional culture education. Among them, provinces such as Shandong, Henan, and Anhui have shown extremely strong advantages in the diversity of educational carriers by virtue of the development and utilization of their own characteristic intangible cultural heritage resources, while Chongqing and Sichuan have exerted efforts in the diversity of educational paths and possess a relatively high level of competitiveness. In addition, from the overall measurement results, it can be found that the current competitiveness of the public sentiment on traditional culture education in China has already shown a spatial distribution pattern with large differences. Then, is there "knowledge spillover" of cross-reference in terms of educational methods and resource exploration among adjacent provinces, which has generated a spatial agglomeration effect? According to the calculation by ArcGIS, global autocorrelation Z-value is 3.228, and the P-value is $0.001 \leq 0.001$.It indicates that an obvious spatial agglomeration situation has occurred in the competitiveness of the public sentiment on traditional culture education in China. The ratio of the observed G-index to the expected G-index is 1. It can be seen that there is both high-value agglomeration among provinces with strong competitiveness and low-value agglomeration among provinces with weak competitiveness. Subsequently, the local spatial autocorrelation test is carried out by using the TCEPCI value. The study finds that in the nearby areas of Henan, Anhui and Zhejiang in China (that is, the Central Plains region and the Yangtze River Delta region), a high-high agglomeration effect has occurred, in Xinjiang, Tibet and their nearby areas, a low-low agglomeration effect has emerged, and in Guizhou Province and its nearby areas, a low-high agglomeration effect has occurred.

The public sentiment reports on traditional culture education are often the process of news propaganda through the improvement of practices. Most of them contain information on relatively excellent or unique educational carriers and methods of traditional culture education, and they can have a reaction on practice to nourish and edify the practice, reflection and improvement of the front-line traditional culture education. With the occurrence of the spatial agglomeration effect, the traditional culture educational carriers and paths concentrated in the high-high agglomeration areas can be publicized, promoted, and influence each other. Under the influence of this knowledge spillover effect, the theoretical research and practical adjustment of traditional culture education will continue to be injected, thus continuing to seize the "high ground" and "first chance " in traditional culture education. In addition, a "free rider effect"[1] can emerge in the low-high agglomeration area where Guizhou is situated, with the knowledge accumulation, exchange and sharing, and outcome spillover of the surrounding provinces with strong public sentiment power on traditional culture education in this area. It can be predicted that in the near future, the public sentiment power on traditional culture in this area will also increase to a certain extent, which will promote the development of traditional culture education.

IV. Discussion: Focus for Improving the Quality of School-based Traditional Culture Curriculum

The curriculum value lies in shaping students' body and mind. The value of school-based traditional culture curriculum lies in enabling students to

---

1 Sun Yangchun & Zhu Lianhua. "Spatial Spillover" and Dilemmas in Local Higher Education Returns[J]. *Higher Education Exploration*, 2016(10):52-55.

understand and comprehend excellent traditional Chinese culture with the help of rich curriculum resources, to perceive the uniqueness of their own culture and the bloodline connection with the life of the nation, which can help to form a self-cultural awareness, and then gradually form a cultural identity. To improve the quality of such curriculum and form students' cultural identity, the following aspects need to be considered.

(1) Define the Appropriate Curriculum Form of School-based Traditional Culture Curriculum

Traditional culture education realizes the educational function through various forms such as national curriculum, school-based curriculum and school education activities. We need to think about what the function of school-based curriculum is and what kind of curriculum form it should have. National curriculum sort out and present traditional culture through courses such as *Chinese Language*, *History* and *Art*, forming a content system of traditional culture in different fields, which has the characteristics of systematization and structuring. The function of school-based curriculum is to continue these contents or make these contents three-dimensional and "come alive". Therefore, school-based traditional culture curriculum should present integrated, characteristic and diversified forms. School-based traditional culture curriculum should not only supplement the traditional culture in national curriculum in quantity. Therefore, it is not that the larger the content volume the better, nor that the more "traditional" it is, the more correct it is. Its fundamental purpose is to shape the basic cultural structure of students on the premise that students accept it. It is necessary to experience the artifacts, skills, customs and diet in traditional culture at the "Practical Arts" level. The cultural system, which is different from the knowledge system, needs to be concretized into stories, skills, knowledge and artifacts first, and then abstracted into the emotional system and value system behind them. The "Taoist Studies" without "Practical Arts" is too abstract and tends to be preachy. Of course, a culture with only "Practical Arts" lacks the core essence and only inherits traditions without real culture. "Practical

Arts" is the basis for experiencing "Taoist Studies", and "Taoist Studies" is the aim of education. Meanwhile, the forms of traditional culture in school-based curriculum can be diverse. Diverse cultural forms need to seek the same cultural charm, and requires teachers to lead students to perceive this charm in the experiences related to artifacts, skills, customs and diet. On the one hand, this charm can be the "spirit" of the greater self with a sense of patriotism and responsibility. On the other hand, it can also be the "flavor" of the smaller self with gentleness, harmony, nature, wisdom and courtesy in viewing nature, society and others. Seeking common ground while reserving differences helps to form a rich, diverse, unified and coordinated educational ecology of traditional culture education.

(2) Further Clarify the Rights, Responsibilities and Functions of Local Curriculum Management

In 2001, the Ministry of Education issued the *Outline of Basic Education Curriculum Reform (for Trial Implementation)*, which further clarified the national, local and school curriculum management levels. At present, regional practices regarding local curriculum management responsibilities and authorities remain inconsistent. Some regions mainly convey and publicize the national curriculum policies and related documents, while some other regions directly develop local curriculum and textbooks and require schools to implement them. Simply conveying and publicizing national policies can't fulfill its management function, and the development of local curriculum and textbooks without the participation of schools and teachers may not be able to give play to the regional advantages of curriculum implementation and improve teachers' curriculum implementation ability. To promote the development of school-based curriculum, including those of traditional culture, it is necessary to further clarify the rights, responsibilities and functions of local curriculum management. Firstly, local curriculum management should perform the function of formulating local curriculum plans. Local curriculum is not simply to convey national requirements but to combine national requirements with the needs and goals of local curriculum development to generate local curriculum plans. Secondly, local curriculum should be responsible for the supervision of the basic standards of national curriculum and supervise the implementation of national curriculum. Thirdly, regional curriculum resources need to be coordinated. For school-based traditional culture curriculum, this function is even more important. Coordinating with local cultural departments, cultural celebrities, and media organizations, introducing local traditional culture resources, recommending typical case schools and establishing regional traditional culture publicity platform will significantly contribute to the development of school curriculum. Finally, professional guidance should be provided for schools and teachers, including helping schools and teachers identify and select traditional culture, providing curriculum development techniques, and grasping the methods of curriculum implementation.

(3) Traditional Culture in Curriculum Needs to be Integrated into the Contemporary Ethical Universals and Aesthetic Universals

The forming process of Chinese traditional culture is long with diverse types and abundant contents, and mainstream culture, folk culture and regional culture are integrated. What content can and deserves to be incorporated into the curriculum system is a premise question that needs to be considered to ensure the quality of such school-based curriculum. Such cultural screening work is a systematic project for the whole society and cannot be undertaken by a certain school. However, as an institution representing the country to cultivate teenagers, what a school transmits must have basic value norms and meet the standards of morality, ethics, and civilization. As scholars of the social curriculum school believe, the school curriculum serves as vehicles for cultural reproduction and should guide societal cultural development[1]. Traditional

---

1 Apple. M. W. *Ideology and Curriculum*[M]. Translated by Huang Zhongjing. Shanghai: East China Normal University Press, 2001:37-41.

culture curriculum originates from traditional culture, but at the same time, the curriculum is also actively screening and selecting traditional culture. The traditional culture in curriculum constructs young people's cognition of traditional culture, shapes and depicts the public image of traditional culture. The "reproduction" nature of traditional culture curriculum in cultural transmission requires us to treat the cultural selection in curriculum with caution. Traditional culture is not a propaganda tool or a disciplinary rod. What it conveys should be something desirable, something that makes the young people proud, willing to believe in and pass down. Traditional culture is not a static concept, but rather exists in a dynamic process of evolution and development. The culture of each era is a continuation of the cultures that came before it, and each era has its own innovative cultural essence. The so-called traditional culture is the tradition that has been screened, integrated and transformed by the times. "Our doubt, interest, censure and dispute about tradition are all due to our confusion and expectations for the present and the future... The secret that traditions can become the traditions of each generation and hold different meanings for successive generations lies in the fact that the tradition allows each era to extend it with its own understanding and interpretation, much like the rebirth of the phoenix from the ashes."[1] Traditional culture curriculum is the process of interpreting and extending traditional culture. It is necessary to use the mainstream forms of interpersonal communication, psychological contracts and aesthetic standards in modern life to screen the expressions in ethical systems such as "filial piety and fraternal duty, respect for seniority, and reverence for teachers". It is also necessary to use the modern national form and value beliefs to transform the connotations of "benevolence, people-oriented, integrity, justice, harmony, and common ground".

(4) Traditional Culture in Curriculum Should Form an Individual

---

1 Yin Ding. *The Fate of Understanding*[M]. Beijing: SDX Joint Publishing Company, 1998.

Cultural Schema with World Civilizations

School education fulfills the educational function through the curriculum. The curriculum system constructs students' knowledge system and value system, which also deeply influences students' cultural system. Cultural identity begins with recognizing cultural differences. After understanding the differences between one's own ethnic culture and other ethnic cultures, one forms a cognition of the uniqueness of one's own culture, and then it is possible to form an identity. School curriculum structures do not exclude and even pay equal attention to other cultural forms and civilized ways, which gives students a broader cultural cognition. International understanding and global competence are essential competencies for students' survival and development in the future. Understanding other cultures and experiencing the new and unknown are an inescapable part of students' life today. Through various media, personal experiences and the spread of experience, today's students are living in an environment surrounded by multicultural information. As far as the development of ethnic culture and group culture is concerned, the intermingling and rivalry between cultural identity and cultural change are precisely the inevitable paths for cultural self-reflection, self-renewal, creation, and development. As for individual culture, individuals, with their own cultural belonging awareness, communicate and develop in various cultural circles around the world and also need to have an identity with other cultural elements. The traditional culture in the school curriculum structure needs to coexist with an international perspective, but it is necessary to integrate the needs of different cultures within the psychological structure of identification with one's own ethnic culture. It is difficult to have a fixed and unified psychological schema for this integration. The curriculum only provide the elements for forming a psychological schema, but each person's cultural psychological structure needs to be completed respectively through their own experiences in diverse, differentiated, and changing school and social life.

[Originally published in *Educational Research* 2019(9) (Lv Lijie & Ding Yiran)]

14. On Evaluation Dimension Construction of Curriculum Development Quality in Basic Education Based on Education Equity

Measuring a nation's educational quality requires looking beyond student academic performance. The quality of the educational process is also an important connotation of educational quality. Curriculum is the main way for basic education to cultivate talents and bears the expectations of the national education policy and the cultivation goals of each educational stage. The development status of the basic education curriculum is an important indicator reflecting the educational quality of a country. Since the promulgation of the *Outline of Basic Education Curriculum Reform (for Trial Implementation)* in 2001, in important national education reform documents such as *Outline of Educational Planning*, *Opinions of the Ministry of Education on Deepening the Comprehensive Reform in the Education Field in 2013*, and *Opinions of the Ministry of Education on Comprehensively Deepening Curriculum Reform and Implementing the Fundamental Task of Fostering Virtue in Education*, China has always regarded the basic education curriculum as an important issue in the basic education reform. The quality of the basic education curriculum development requires continuous attention and research.

I. The Development of the Basic Education Curriculum Is an Important Dimension for Measuring the Equity of Educational Quality

Educational equity is an important foundation of social equity. Equity is the primary measure for pursuing social justice, emphasizing unified standards for all, without favoritism or discrimination. Equity is not simply a matter of quantity, and it refers to the relationship among social members. It is the internal balance of rights, responsibilities and interests among social members in terms of starting point, process, and result on the basis of equality of human nature, so that everyone gets what they deserve and can coexist harmoniously. The report of the 17th National Congress of the Communist Party of China listed education as an important task for improving people's livelihood and realizing social equity, proposing that "education is the cornerstone of national rejuvenation, and educational equity is an important foundation for social equity". The *Outline of Educational Planning* more explicitly identifies the promotion of educational equity as one of the strategic priorities for educational development, and proposes that "promoting equity should be a basic national education policy" and "improving quality should be the core task of educational reform and development." That is to say, promoting educational equity and enhancing educational quality are core goals of China's basic education development. What is educational equity? Chinese scholars generally agree that educational equity can be divided into starting equity, process equity and result equity. Looking at a series of education policies in China in recent years, great emphasis has been placed on providing every child with an equal opportunity to receive education. Receiving education is a necessary prerequisite for children in modern society to acquire survival abilities, integrate into society, and get a happy life. Therefore, providing every child with an equal opportunity to receive education is a fundamental action in the pursuit of social fairness and justice, and it is also the core content of starting equity within the educational equity system.

Quality-oriented equity is the in-depth pursuit of educational equity. Ensuring the equality of children's educational opportunities is the primary stage of achieving educational equity. Some scholars believe that for basic education at the present stage, the contradiction between social demand and educational supply is changing from the shortage contradiction in the total supply to the structural contradiction caused by the insufficient supply of high-quality education. Pursuing quality-oriented educational equity is the internal requirement for basic education development in an era following the full accomplishment of universal nine-year compulsory education.[1] What is quality-oriented educational equity? Many countries in the world, especially after the 1960s, have gone through a similar exploration path of educational equity. Correspondingly, the international community's understanding of educational equity has also changed. Initially, the focus was on equity at the starting point of education, namely the equality of the right and opportunity to receive education. Later, attention shifted to equity in educational outcomes. The focus then moved from narrow equality in academic performance to the growth rate of educational outcomes. Finally, attention expanded from direct educational outcomes to the indirect influence of the educational process. That is to say, the current understanding of educational equity is that it is necessary to provide children with not only fair educational opportunities and rights, but also equally high-quality educational processes, thereby achieving equally high-quality educational outcomes. What are fair educational results? Chinese scholars generally agree that the same and equal educational results do not exist and are unnecessary. Standard can be set for educational result, and once the standard is met, that is, the quality is qualified, then the equity in educational results is realized. What is more difficult to examine and more meaningful than result equity is the quality of the educational process. The quality of the educational process directly affects the quality of educational results, and meanwhile, has a more profound and latent and lagging influence on children's development. The quality of the educational process refers to the quality of the internal educational mechanisms, the educational environment, and the processes of teaching and learning within the education system. This quality must meet certain standards, but more importantly, it needs to respect differences, reflect individuality, and provide students with choices, thereby maximizing the full development of students with different potentials. How to examine the quality of the educational

---

1 Tan Songhua & Wang Jian. Pursuing Quality-oriented Educational Equity[J]. *People's Education*, 2011(18):5-9.

process? In educational evaluation reports, educational investment in the educational process is often used as an indicator, such as examining funds, school building facilities, teachers' educational background, and professional title situations. These indicators are not the educational process itself, which is precisely difficult to examine, so some substitute indicators are used for "convenient examination". The consensus among scholars is that these indicators are elements participating in the educational process and are necessary conditions but not necessarily sufficient conditions for realizing process equity and quality improvement.

The quality of school curriculum development is an important measure for judging the quality of the educational process. As the carrier of education, the curriculum also bears the educational purpose of the country, through which the school's educational philosophy should also be reflected on students. What kind of students do schools aim to cultivate, and how? What do teachers want to teach, and what can they actually teach? What have teachers taught? What do they use to teach? How do they teach? What have students learned? How is the learning process? How do they feel? All these constitute the curriculum. Some people regard the curriculum as extensive and intangible, omnipresent in the educational process, as the educational life itself, and as everything that triggers changes in students' experience. Some people want to track it and fix it as expected goals or results, or even as a content system that influences students. The operation process of the school curriculum is the core part of the educational process. The quality of the school curriculum development is an important symbol of the quality of the school educational process.

II. Evaluation Orientation for School Curriculum Development Quality Based on Equity

(1) The Connotation of Curriculum Development

There are multiple interpretations of curriculum development. Firstly, curriculum development can be regarded as the history of curriculum evolution, examining its changes in different periods and the orientations and characteristics it exhibits. Secondly, curriculum development can be regarded as the longitudinal stages of the curriculum development process, which necessarily includes curriculum promotion links such as research and formulation, promotion and interpretation, implementation and adjustment, creation and feedback, etc. It is the evolutionary growth process of the curriculum and the interaction and negotiation in the process. The curriculum development mentioned in this article actually refers to the development of the curriculum, which is the performance status of the curriculum at different levels in a certain period, including both factual components and value judgment. "Curriculum is not the product of speculation but the result of action"[1]. The curriculum needs to be tracked in actions at different levels. Some scholars believe that "among numerous meanings of quality, two are crucial for quality management. One is that product characteristics can meet customer requirements and thus satisfy customers, and the other is the absence of deficiencies."[2] If we understand "the absence of deficiencies" as meeting standards, then the quality of a product is that whether the product can achieve the purpose of production, meet the needs of users, and make all indexes up to various standards. Similarly, the quality of the curriculum is that whether the curriculum can achieve the educational purpose, meet the needs of students, and be up to national standards. The curriculum is not only a "product" provided for students' development, but also an important resource invested in the educational process and should also conform to the principle of social fairness. The famous three principles of social fairness proposed by sociologist Rawls, on the basis of taking equality as the first principle, also emphasize respect for

---

1 Hwang Jenq-Jye. *Curriculum Design*[M]. Taipei: Tung Hua Book Co., Ltd., 2002:85.

2 Research Team on Education Quality Standards of China National Academy of Educational Sciences. National Standards of Educational Quality and Their Establishment[J]. *Educational Research*, 2013(6).

differences and compensation for shortages. From the perspective of equity, when looking at the quality of curriculum development, the first thing is to explain the issue of "equality". Just like the educational process and results, the ways and results of curriculum implementation cannot achieve equality and sameness among different regions, different schools, and different students. Drawing on the examination methods of educational results and the definition of quality itself, the equality of curriculum development can also be understood as that the curriculum implemented in different schools and different classrooms have reached or executed the standards and, on the basis of executing the standards, respected the differences of students and adapted to conditions such as the environment and resources.

In recent years, many of China's education policy documents are closely related to primary and secondary school curriculum issues. These policies contain the ideal concepts of curriculum development and the key points of behavior that primary and secondary school principals and teachers should have. The following is an analysis of the key points of curriculum development contained in policy documents based on the *Outline of Basic Education Curriculum Reform (for Trial Implementation)*, *Outline of Educational Planning*, *Decision of the Third Plenary Session of the 18th Central Committee of the Communist Party of China on Some Major Issues Concerning Comprehensively Deepening the Reform*, *Opinions of the Ministry of Education on Deepening the Comprehensive Reform in the Education Field in 2013*, and *Opinions of the Ministry of Education on Comprehensively Deepening Curriculum Reform and Implementing the Fundamental Task of Fostering Virtue in Education*. (See Table 3-3)

Table 3-3 Key Points of Curriculum Development in Documents

Level	Core Content Summary	Value Points
Principles and Orientations of School Education	Educational equity, Balanced allocation of resources, Elimination of dropouts, Reduction of homework burden, Socialist Core Value System, Adhering to competency-based principle, Adhering to all-round development, Fostering virtue in education, Quality inspection	Educational equity, Fostering virtue in education
School System	Compulsory education with small class teaching, Comprehensive quality evaluation, Senior high school student development guidance, Diversified development of senior high school	Balance of compulsory education, Senior high school selectivity
Curriculum Arrangement	National curriculum standards, Development of local and school curriculum; Scientifically design the curriculum difficulty, ensuring the availability of teachers for music, physical education and art, and fully implementing and delivering the prescribed curriculum; In senior high school, the study of various courses such as arts and sciences prescribed by the country have been fully completed; Offer elective courses, and actively carry out research-based learning, community service, and social practice.	Implement national curriculum, Develop local and school-based curriculum
Teaching	Optimize the knowledge structure, enrich social practice, strengthen ability training, cultivate independence and autonomy, and lead questioning, investigation and inquiry; Respect for personality, focus on differences, create educational environment, The attitude and ability to use knowledge, All-round development; Apply information technology; Reduce the amount of homework and the number of exams, cultivate students' learning interest and hobbies, strictly implement the curriculum plan, and forbid to increase class hours and difficulty; Develop moral education resources in various subjects.	Reform teaching concepts, Reform teaching methods

Level	Core Content Summary	Value Points
Evaluation	Reform of the examination and admissions system; Academic proficiency test; Quality evaluation; Comprehensively implement the senior high school academic proficiency test and comprehensive quality evaluation.	Reform the evaluation method
Student Competencies	Cultivate students' competencies including innovative spirit, practical ability, scientific and humanistic competence, environmental awareness, aesthetic taste, active learning attitude, basic knowledge, basic skills, ability to collect and process information, ability to acquire new knowledge, ability to analyze and solve problems, ability to communicate and cooperate.	Pay attention to students' core competence
Resource	Textbook diversification, Development of curriculum resources, Teacher training, Expert guidance, Home-school cooperation.	Textbook construction, Enhance teachers' professional ability

The value points in curriculum policies are the requirements of the country on the curriculum of basic education schools, and the principled standards for examining curriculum quality. Among them, pursuing educational equity, balancing the allocation of educational resources, and adhering to fostering virtue in education are the principles and orientations of curriculum development. Compulsory education emphasizes the comprehensive and balanced development of students. The selectivity of courses for students is emphasized in the senior high school stage, which is the institutional guarantee provided for curriculum development. In addition, in terms of school curriculum arrangement, it is essential to strictly implement the national curriculum while developing local and school-based curriculum. In classroom teaching, it is necessary to reform teaching concepts, teaching objectives, and teaching methods in order to improve students' comprehensive competencies. Reforming the examination evaluation system, strengthening textbook construction, and enhancing teachers' professional abilities are the behavioral requirements that schools, teachers and curriculum administrators should implement in curriculum development.

(2) Evaluation Orientation of Curriculum Quality

Based on the perspective of equity and according to the policy analysis, we evaluate the orientation of curriculum quality and express them as the following points.

1. Conform to Educational Objectives

The curriculum should reflect the spirit of the times and align with national educational requirements and expectations. Currently, fostering virtue in education through the school curriculum system and promoting the socialist core values are the core tasks that the curriculum should undertake. In addition, the curriculum should also reflect the main characteristics of education in each educational stage at present. For example, the compulsory education stage emphasizes balance, and the senior high school stage emphasizes selectivity. Receiving compulsory education is the responsibility of every social member and the main way of socialization. At the compulsory education stage, the focus is on children who have just started receiving education. Therefore, the curriculum in the compulsory education stage points to the comprehensive and basic competencies of people. Comprehensiveness, integration and balance are the characteristics of the curriculum in this period. While in senior high school, the education is not only the cultivation of the general competencies of ordinary citizens but also the preparation for specialized university education. In addition, the minds of students in this period gradually mature, and their intellectual and ability tendencies gradually stabilize. Therefore, the curriculum needs a certain degree of elasticity to adapt to the differentiated demand of students' development.

2. Implement Curriculum Plan and Standard

The national curriculum plan presets the goals and overall structure of school curriculum in the basic education stage. The curriculum standards of various subjects are the decomposition of the curriculum plan, which not only reflect the logic of subject knowledge but also permeate value and attitude. The curriculum plan and standard are the carriers for the specific implementation of the national education policy, and implementing the curriculum plan and standard is to practice the national education policy. As mentioned before, to measure whether society and school provide equal educational opportunities for students, we need to judge not only whether students have the opportunities to go to school but also whether students obtain equal educational content in school. Whether the school implement the curriculum plan and standard indicates whether it provides students with a deeper level of equal educational opportunities. Education is a complex process, and it is difficult to comprehensively measure educational quality at a certain time node with a certain fixed measurement tool. To some extent, the educational process is the result. After students experience the educational process, there will inevitably be changes on their experiences.

3. Respect Student Differences

Equitable education does not simply treat all students in the same way but provides appropriate education for them. On behalf of the country, schools and teachers provide students with the curriculum and should also take into account the differences in student characteristics. To some extent, it reflects the differences in the environmental culture, levels, interest and needs of students. The school curriculum system should provide students with certain opportunities to choose different curricula or create different learning methods for different students. In particular, it should provide assistance and compensation for schools and students with insufficient abilities and conditions.

4. Educational Process Satisfaction

The curriculum development quality is also manifested in the educational process, especially in the safety, civilization, health and moderation in the curriculum implementation process. The quality of physical products is not only manifested in their usability but also needs to meet the needs of users for comfort, safety, and even beauty during use. The using process of the curriculum is the educational process, which permeates the entire process of students' growth and teachers' career, enduring in duration and profound in impact. These process qualities can be evaluated through the attitudes and feelings of the curriculum users, mainly students and teachers, that is, reflected in the satisfaction of the curriculum users. For example, students can feel the appropriateness of the difficulty and quantity of the curriculum, the emotional experience of teachers and students in classroom teaching is civilized and pleasant, and students and parents recognize the meaning and value of the curriculum.

III. Levels and Key Points of Evaluating the School Curriculum Development Quality

(1) Curriculum Performance Level

Evaluating the school curriculum development quality requires dividing the performance levels of the curriculum itself. In terms of the curriculum level, curriculum scholars such as Goodlad, Posner, and Brophy have made conceptual divisions. For example, Goodlad divides the curriculum into the ideological curriculum, the formal curriculum, the perceived curriculum, the operational curriculum and the experiential curriculum.[1] Posner believes that the curriculum can be divided into official curriculum, operational curriculum, hidden curriculum, null curriculum, and extra curriculum. Among them, there is a "curriculum parallelism" problem in the operational curriculum, that is, three curriculum, namely the official curriculum, the taught curriculum, and the tested curriculum (the curriculum obtained by students), coexist but are often

1 Goodlad, J. I. *Curriculum Inquiry: The Study of Curriculum Practice*[M]. New York: McGraw-Hill, 1979.

inconsistent.[1] Brophy makes a more detailed hierarchical division of the operational curriculum: the formal curriculum, the curriculum interpreted by principals or teacher committee, the unofficial but formal curriculum operated by the school, the curriculum of teacher's belief, the curriculum planned by teachers, the operational curriculum by teachers, and the curriculum experienced by students.[2] All seven curriculum levels of Brophy's are the curriculum that actually occur in practice, involving multiple forms of existence such as texts, beliefs and actions, as well as multiple curriculum subjects such as the official, school, teacher and student. They represent the paths and changes in the transmission and flow of the curriculum more clearly and detailedly. According to the division of curriculum levels, in the context of China's curriculum system, school curriculum refers to the curriculum operation process that occurs in schools after the national curriculum plan and curriculum standard are released, including the curriculum planning set by schools, the types of courses offered by the school, the curriculum understood and planned by teachers, the curriculum implemented by teachers, and the curriculum obtained and tested by students. In addition, the curriculum development status can also be regarded as the implementation process of public policy. For the evaluation of public policy implementation, in addition to the implementation of the policy itself, the influencing factors of policy implementation will be generally evaluated, including the policy subject, the policy object group, policy resources and the means of policy implementation. The evaluation of policy implementation mainly focuses on whether the policy implementation achieves the expected goals, what effects it has, and what the future trend of the policy is. The evaluation of public policy implementation constitutes a dual judgment with the

---

1 Posner, G. J. *Analyzing the Curriculum*[M]. Translated by Qiu Guangpeng, Han Miaomiao & Zhang Xianrong. Shanghai: East China Normal University Press, 2007.

2 Brophy, J. E. How Teachers Influence What Is Taught and Learned in Classroom[J]. *The Elementary School Journal*, 1982(4).

policy itself as the independent variable - namely factual judgment and value judgment.[1] The judgment of curriculum development also needs to be made from the two dimensions of factual judgment and value judgment. (See Table 3-4)

Table 3-4 Curriculum Level

<table>
<tr><th colspan="2">Curriculum Level
Curriculum Subject</th><th>Goodlad</th><th>Brophy</th><th colspan="2">Posner</th></tr>
<tr><td colspan="2"></td><td>Ideological Curriculum</td><td>/</td><td colspan="2">/</td></tr>
<tr><td rowspan="9">The Curriculum That Actually Occur</td><td rowspan="2">Official</td><td>Formal Curriculum</td><td>Formal Curriculum</td><td colspan="2">Official Curriculum</td></tr>
<tr><td>/</td><td>The Curriculum Interpreted by Official Interpreter</td><td>/</td><td rowspan="6">Operational Curriculum</td></tr>
<tr><td>School</td><td>/</td><td>Curriculum Arranged by School</td><td>/</td></tr>
<tr><td rowspan="3">Teacher</td><td>Perceived Curriculum</td><td>The Curriculum of Teachers' Belief</td><td>/</td></tr>
<tr><td>/</td><td>The Curriculum Planned by Teachers</td><td>/</td></tr>
<tr><td>Operational Curriculum</td><td>The Operational Curriculum by Teachers</td><td>Taught Curriculum</td></tr>
<tr><td>Student</td><td>Experiential Curriculum</td><td>The Curriculum Obtained by Students</td><td>Tested Curriculum</td></tr>
<tr><td rowspan="2">Curriculum Stakeholders</td><td>/</td><td>/</td><td colspan="2">Hidden curriculum</td></tr>
<tr><td>/</td><td>/</td><td colspan="2">Extra Curriculum</td></tr>
<tr><td colspan="2"></td><td>/</td><td>/</td><td colspan="2">Null Curriculum</td></tr>
</table>

1 Xie Ming. *Introduction to Public Policy*[M]. Beijing: China Renmin University Press, 2012.

(2) Key Points in Large-scale Curriculum Development Surveys

Many large-scale curriculum development surveys have similar key points for evaluation. After the new curriculum reform in 2001, large-scale curriculum implementation surveys were organized in China. The key points that these surveys focused on mainly included the implementation of the reform work, the attitudes of teachers and principals towards the reform, and the factors affecting curriculum implementation.[1] In addition, along with educational reforms, the United States, Japan, and the United Kingdom also conducted large-scale surveys on curriculum development. For example, in the United States, there was a survey on the consistency between classroom teaching and curriculum standards. Improving the educational quality of basic education has always been a focus problem for successive U.S. governments. In August 1989, at the National Governors' joint meeting held in Virginia, the governors of all 50 U.S. states jointly called on the federal government to develop national educational goals and implement uniform curriculum standards nationwide in key subjects of primary and secondary education to ensure that all students have access to education of the same quality. This proposal was supported by then American President George H. W. Bush. In 1992, the federal government formed the National Council on Education Standards and Testing and established the project research and development units for curriculum standards in five subjects, including *English*, *Mathematics*, *Science*, *History* and *Geography*, and began to draft curriculum standards for various subjects.[2] In 2002, the United States promulgated the *No Child Left Behind Act*, which proposed severe penalties for schools that failed to meet the standards. To test whether school education have

---

1 Ma Yunpeng & Tang Lifang. The Implementation Situation and Countermeasure of New Curriculum[J]. *Journal of Northeast Normal University (Philosophy and Social Sciences)*, 2002(5):124-129.

2 Lv Lijie. *The Process of National Curriculum Design*[M]. Beijing: Educational Science Publishing House, 2008.

met the standards and understand the situation and level of classroom teaching, the Wisconsin Center for Education Research and the Council of Chief State School Officers in the United States cooperated to develop a survey tool for collecting classroom teaching situations in primary and secondary schools on a large sample, namely the Survey of Enacted Curriculum (SEC for short). This survey mainly detected the consistency between the content of teachers' classroom teaching and curriculum standards[1]. The main approach was to divide the ideal teaching content into two dimensions including learning content topics and cognitive requirements through analyzing the content of curriculum standards and textbooks. Subsequently, the time allocated by teachers to each theme in their classroom teaching and the corresponding cognitive requirements were compared to detect the quality of the teaching process. This detection plan has been used in the United States for 15 years and has been promoted and used in more than 30 states. In recent years, the United Kingdom also had a review and improvement action on the quality of large-scale curriculum development. To cooperate with the revision of the national curriculum, in 2011, the Department for Education of the United Kingdom conducted a large-scale survey and review on the curriculum development situation in primary and secondary schools across the country. Through official websites, mass media, etc., the Department for Education distributed questionnaires to teachers, principals, parents, students, and individuals, groups and representatives of higher education departments in society to understand the attitudes of people involved towards the current national curriculum and the implementation of the curriculum. This survey included multiple functions such as review, survey and publicity. The main questions investigated in the questionnaire included whether the current curriculum in schools enhanced, developed, and cultivated students'

---

1 Chen Shuqing, Wang Xiuhong & Luan Huimin. The Construction and Enlightenment of Survey of Enacted Curriculum in American Basic Education[J]. *Journal of Northeast Normal University (Philosophy and Social Sciences)*, 2015(3).

understanding of various subjects, whether the curriculum promoted students' overall grasp of key knowledge in various subjects; whether the curricula offered by each school covered the four key subjects of *English*, *Mathematics*, *Science* and *Sports* in the national curriculum; how teachers constructed the curriculum and conducted teaching, whether the national curriculum was operating efficiently, and whether the curricula offered by schools to students were the best education in the world. Through the survey, the Department for Education hoped to grant teachers more freedom to give full play to their professional knowledge. The information obtained from the survey was also used to feed back and improve the national curriculum standards, and at the same time, it enabled parents to understand what their children should learn in school education, so as to better provide their children's education with support and help. In addition, in the context of curriculum reform, Japan monitored the change process through education background monitoring and analysis, teaching condition investigation and analysis. In 1996, the Central Council for Education of Japan submitted the first consultation report to the Minister of Education, Culture, Sports, Science and Technology, titled *The Model for Japanese Education from the prospective of the 21st Century*, which established the core proposition of curriculum reform, that is, enabling children to have the ability to survive, to carry out independent, autonomous, and individualized learning in a relaxed and comfortable environment. In 2002, primary and secondary schools in Japan began to implement the new *Courses of Study*. Under the guidance of the *Courses of Study*, "the educational content was strictly selected", a large number of curriculum contents were deleted, the difficulty was reduced, and the class hours were reduced. Senior high schools also reduced the class hours of compulsory courses and lowered the credit requirements for senior high school graduation. These reform measures triggered social doubts on whether the reform had led to a decline in students' academic abilities. In 2008, the Ministry of Education, Culture, Sports, Science and Technology promulgated the newly revised *Courses of Study*. On the basis of continuing to cultivate the ability to survive, it again attached importance to basic subjects and basic knowledge, extended the total class hours of primary and secondary school curricula and the class hours of subject curricula, and added some curriculum contents. Regarding the *Courses of Study* at different stages, the National Institute for Educational Policy Research conducted surveys on the implementation of primary and secondary school curriculum year by year.[1] Each year's survey was mainly divided into two parts: one was the passing rate of academic tests on core subjects for primary and secondary school students, and the other one was the survey on curriculum implementation for teachers and students. Among them, the subject tests were mainly conducted in 12 subjects, including *Japanese*, *Social Studies*, *Arithmetic* and *Science* for students in 5th and 6th grade of primary schools, *Japanese*, *Social Studies*, *Mathematic*s, *Science* and *English* for students in 1st grade to 3rd grade of junior high schools, and *Japanese*, *Mathematics*, *Physics*, *Geography* and *History* for senior high school students in 3rd grade. Each subject was tested according to the core "content areas" in its own *Courses of Study*, with results compared to previous years' performance. The annual passing rates and changes of different content areas were analyzed to serve as one of the key metrics for evaluating student academic abilities and teaching situations. The curriculum implementation questionnaire mainly focused on the teaching time situation in primary and junior high schools, the class hours of the integrated learning time curriculum, and the offering and implementation of elective courses in junior high schools, etc. In addition, Japan's curriculum implementation survey attached great importance to understanding the implementation of individual learning guidance for students. The survey for senior high schools focused on issues such as the graduation credits, teaching time, preparatory curriculum offered, and the offering time of various subjects in regular senior high schools,

---

1 National Institute for Educational Policy Research of the Ministry of Education, Culture, Sports, Science and Technology. Survey on the Implementation of the National Curriculum in Elementary, Lower Secondary and Upper Secondary Schools [EB/OL]. [2015-11-01]. http://www.Mext.go.jp/b_menu/shingi/chukyo/chukyo3/004siryo/06080913/010/012.htm.

vocational high schools and comprehensive high schools. These surveys were highly targeted, focusing on the controversial points of Japan's curriculum reform. By systematically collecting data, they provide policy bases for curriculum improvement and a new round of adjustment.

Overall, the common original intention of these large-scale curriculum development surveys is to understand the situation of the curriculum implementation process so that the quality of education and teaching can be monitored and guaranteed. The main basis for judging the quality of teaching is the national curriculum standard. The key points for evaluation are mainly whether the school curriculum arrangements are consistent with the core contents of the curriculum plan and curriculum standard, as well as the performance and attitude of students in the curriculum implementation process, so as to verify whether school education, especially classroom teaching, adheres to the concepts of educational reform and meets the basic educational quality standard. Due to the relative independence of the teaching process of teachers and the large number of classrooms, these surveys are conducted in different ways respectively.

IV. Evaluation Dimension Construction of Curriculum Development Quality in Basic Education

Referring to the division of curriculum development level theories and based on the actual situation of school curriculum in China, first-level and second-level indicators for examining the development of basic education school curriculum are established to describe the process and stages of school curriculum development. Based on the analysis of curriculum development quality orientation, curriculum development levels, and key points, the levels, dimensions and elements for evaluating the quality of basic education curriculum development are established. (See Table 3-5)

Table 3-5 Evaluation Dimensions for Curriculum Development Quality in Basic Education

First Level Indicators	Second Level Indicators	First Level Indicators	Second Level Indicators
1. School Curriculum Plan	1.1 School Curriculum Planning	3. Student Experience Curriculum	3.1 Curriculum Acquired by Student
	1.2 National Curriculum Offering		3.2 Students' Curriculum Engagement
	1.3 (Local) School-based Curriculum Development		
2. Teachers' Curriculum	2.1 Teachers' Curriculum Beliefs	4. Influencing Factors	4.1 Curriculum Subject: Principal and Teacher
	2.2 Teacher-planned Curriculum		4.2 Target Group: Student
	2.3 Teacher-implemented Curriculum		4.3 Curriculum Resource: Textbook and School Physical Resource
			4.4 Promotion Method: Supporting System, Teacher Training, Academic Research

Under the curriculum indicators, key elements for evaluating curriculum development are constructed and categorized into evaluation dimensions, including implementation plan and standard, curriculum development level, user satisfaction, user cost, and safeguard measure.

(1) Implement the Curriculum Plan and Standard

The implementation of national curriculum plan and standard by school and teacher constitutes the baseline for ensuring the quality of the educational process. Whether or not the national curriculum is implemented serves as a deeper procedural indicator for evaluating whether educational entities provide students with equitable learning opportunities. Key observable elements include: supporting curriculum systems, the implementation status of national curriculum, student mastery of national curriculum, quantity of locally developed school-based curriculum, the consistency between teacher's teaching design with curriculum standard and the consistency between classroom teaching methods/organization form and curriculum philosophies. The above elements are the basis to measure whether the school and teacher have provided students with curriculum based on the policy and standard. Meeting these criteria indicates that students receive equitable educational content in the educational process.

(2) Curriculum Development Level

In this dimension system, the curriculum development level is described through extent of implementation and the extent of differentiation responsiveness. Firstly, extent of implementation includes rationality and systematicity of the school curriculum system, principals' awareness of curriculum planning, principals' curriculum attitudes, teachers' beliefs in curriculum goal and teaching method, general method and organization form of teachers' classroom teaching, teachers' utilization of textbook, and teachers' emotional engagement in curriculum delivery. These indicators can be incorporated into multiple curriculum implementation level models such as Hall's "Concerns-Based Adoption Model"[1] for more systematic and specialized research. Secondly, evaluation factors of difference observation extent include selectivity of elective courses in senior high school, (local) school-based curriculum theme, the value recognition of (local) school-based curriculum, diversity of teachers' teaching approaches in different classes, selectivity of textbooks, and other consciousness and practices which reflect the differentiation responsiveness to students from the school and teacher during the curriculum development process.

---

1 Hall, G, E., & Hord, S. M. Change in Schools: Facilitating the Process[R]. New York: State University of New York Press, 1987:84.

(3) User Satisfaction

User satisfaction refers to the satisfaction of principals, teachers, students, and parents regarding the curriculum. Key elements include principals' attitudes toward national and school-based curriculum, value dimension and difficulty of national curriculum, teachers' recognition of current curriculum, students' feeling about the classroom, students' interest and demand for curriculum, and parents' satisfaction with the curriculum.

(4) User Cost

User cost refers to the student and teacher engagement consumed in the process of curriculum development, and key elements include students' time engagement to curriculum, students' method (e.g., tutoring) engagement to curriculum, students' emotion engagement to curriculum, teachers' time and workload engagement to curriculum, teachers' emotion engagement to curriculum, and teachers' training frequency.

(5) Supporting Measure

Supporting measure mainly refers to the curriculum promotion method and the essential resources required for curriculum development. The curriculum promotion method includes supporting policy and system related to curriculum development, such as whether the examination evaluation system is consistent with the requirements of curriculum development, whether teacher training can effectively enhance teachers' professional capabilities, and whether curriculum's academic research promotes the curriculum development. The essential resources for curriculum development include the textbook quality, and whether the school's financial resources and buildings, campus, and equipment can meet the curriculum development need.

By evaluating these elements, it is expected to assess the performance of the curriculum at different levels in the school education process and the resulting impacts. This serves to illustrate the internal operating condition of school education during the education development, in addition, presents the quality of the educational development process from one perspective. Although the school education process is relatively independent, the vast number of basic education schools necessitates transforming these elements into large-scale survey instruments. Through the analysis and comparison of big data, the modality of the educational process can be described and explained.

[Originally published in *Educational Research* 2016(8) (Lv Lijie & Ma Yunpeng)]

Topic Four: Teachers and the Curriculum

15. Characteristics and Limitations of Teachers' Collective Curriculum Decision-making

I. Teachers' Curriculum Decision-making

What is curriculum decision-making? *The Concise International Encyclopedia of Education* defines it as "a judgment on the aims and means of education or socialization, often adopted within the scope of schools and centered on the teaching syllabus". Among them, "judgment" is "the result of some conscious thinking, representing an intention to act in a particular way or produce an expected result".[1] In other words, curriculum decision-making is an intentional judgment process for curriculum issues, involving deliberation and choices. The subjects who make curriculum decisions can be an individual, several people, or a group. Smith posits that curriculum decision-making takes place within each teacher's "operational space," defined as the perceived boundary of freedom.[2] Teachers make curriculum decisions every day. Each teacher has a different understanding of curriculum standard, textbook, student and other issues, and the limits of their own control over the curriculum are also different. After the new curriculum reform, the curriculum rights of teachers in China have also changed, the "freedom limits" for teachers in curriculum decisions have naturally increased, and the issues in teachers' "operational space" and "judgment" deserve our joint reflection.

(1) Levels and Types of Teachers' Curriculum Decision-making

Since the curriculum itself has several levels, curriculum decision-making also occurs at multiple levels. Goodlad once divided curriculum decision-

---

1 Jiang Shanye. *Concise International Encyclopedia of Education·Curriculum*[M]. Beijing: Educational Science Publishing House, 1991.

2 Smith, D. L. On the Concept of Perceived Curriculum Decision-making Space[J]. *Curriculum Perspeclives*,1983(1):21-30.

making into four levels: the societal level, the institutional level, the instructional level and the experiential level. Eisner pointed out that any curriculum planning must make decisions at five levels: the priority of objectives, curriculum content, learning opportunities, the presentation of the curriculum and the ways students respond, and the evaluation process.[1] In comparison, Klein's supplement in 1991 was more specific. He divided curriculum decision-making into two areas: one is the level at which curriculum decision-making occurs, and the other is the main issues of curriculum decision-making. Among them, the level of curriculum decision-making followed Goodlad's idea and was specifically divided into seven possible levels: academic, societal, formal, institution, instruction, operation and experiential. This order is arranged according to the distance to students and the main focuses of curriculum decision-making. Curriculum decision-making at different levels are concerned with nine elements: objectives, content, materials and resources, learners' learning activities, teaching-learning strategies, evaluation methods, learners' grouping, time and space or environment. In Klein's view, the above seven levels and nine elements form a two-way matrix of curriculum decision-making.[2] Teachers, as curriculum decision-makers, can be manifested in several levels. For example, as parents, their attitudes affect curriculum decision-making at the "societal" level, or as participants in national or regional curriculum development, they affect the curriculum design at the "formal" level. However, if teachers are only limited to the role of teachers, their primary influence on curriculum decision-making occurs at the "institution," "instruction," and "operation" levels.

Calderhead divided teachers' decision-making into three types based on the characteristics of people's daily decision-making: the first type involves a lot of

---

1 Zhou Shuqing. *Curriculum Development and Teacher Professionalism*[M]. Taipei: Higher Education Publishing Co., Ltd., 2004.

2 Klein, M. F. A Conceptual Framework for Curriculum Decision Making[J]. *The Politics of Curriculum Decision-making*. Albany: State University of New York, 1991.

thinking, identifying feasible options, evaluating possible results, known as reflective decision-making. The second type is that made in an instant, which are immediate decisions to unexpected events. The third type of decision-making is made frequently, which occurs so often that it has become automated and routine, known as routine decision-making. If classroom problems are not expected, teachers need to make immediate decisions, and if they occur frequently, teachers only need to make routine decisions.[1]

(2) Changes in the Research Focus of Teachers' Curriculum Decision-making

1. The Relationship between Teachers' Decision-making and Students' Learning Outcomes

These researches emerged before the 1970s. Under the influence of positivism, behaviorism and other methodologies, in order to prove the professionalism of teachers' work, researchers used correlation analysis, experiments and other research methods to prove the relationship between teachers' behavior and students' academic performance. At that time, the assumption of the researchers was that teachers' behavior, as a stimulus, would inevitably bring about changes in students' cognitive and understanding processes.

2. How Teachers Make Decisions

With the development of cognitive psychology, after the 1970s, researchers were no longer satisfied with simplifying classroom teaching into a technical operation process and began to focus on the reasons for teachers' behaviors, that is, what was the thought process of teachers. Consequently, how teachers made decisions became the focus of research. Researchers abandoned the quantitative

---

1 Amy B. M. Tsui. *Pursuing Excellence: Case Studies in Teacher Professional Development*[M]. Translated by Chen Jing & Li Zhongru. Beijing: People's Education Press, 2003.

research method and adopted the descriptive method. By providing teachers with materials, such as some classroom recordings or videos of themselves or others, and asking teachers to describe the thinking process at that time, these studies often combined the comparison between novice teachers and expert teachers to examine how teachers understood, attributed, thought, judged and evaluated. The results showed that there were differences in thoughts, feelings and behaviors between novice teachers and expert teachers. Expert teachers could identify typical situations and classify students in the thinking process. Therefore, researchers firmly believed that "obviously, cognition can change behavior. Classroom decision-making research describes teaching behaviors at the cognitive level. Teachers can analyze, compare and model their teaching based on this. Studying classroom decision-making with psychological methods will undoubtedly help teachers' teaching effectively."[1]

3. Teachers' Growth in Groups

With the shift in perspectives on knowledge and the gradual deepening of people's understanding of the complexity of educational practice, the focus is no longer on summarizing a set of established knowledge system and technical rule for teachers. Supporting teacher development means revealing hidden factors such as teachers' beliefs, emotions, and practical knowledge, and these studies adopt the phenomenological research method to represent the complexity of teachers' work in the description of the life world. In addition, after the 1990s, researchers began to focus on the group factors that affect teachers' growth. What affects teachers' curriculum decision-making and curriculum actions? Besides stable individual factors, there are also group factors and situational factors. A dual analysis of individual and group learning among teachers is conducted, "taking the learning community as the analysis unit to examine how

---

1 Calderhead, J. A Psychological Approach to Research on Teachers' Classroom Decision-making[J]. *British Educational Research Journal*, 1981(1).

the professional community facilitates teacher learning"[1]. Teachers grow in the interpersonal communication relationship, learning as individuals in the mutual construction of groups and situations.

II. Forms and Characteristics of Teachers' Collective Curriculum Decision-making

Teachers' collective curriculum decision-making is the process in which a team of teachers collectively identifies feasible options and evaluates possible results, including the "automated and routine decisions" that are collectively recognized. In China, much of teachers' collective curriculum decision-making occurs in the process of collective lesson preparation. Although not all teachers are currently involved, its existence is an indisputable fact. In recent years, as a form of teacher communication, collective lesson preparation has attracted widespread attention in China, with mixed opinions on it. In fact, debaters hold sharply opposing views on "collective lesson preparation" because it is not a single form, and even for a certain form, the actual situations in operation can vary. Therefore, before discussing its significance and limitations, it is important to clarify the various forms of teachers' collective curriculum decision-making in educational practice.

(1) Forms of Teachers' Collective Curriculum Decision-making

1. Form of Overall Interpretation

It generally occurs in collective lesson preparation at the district or city level, where teaching and research personnel in charge of relevant subjects deliver lectures and make an overall interpretation of the teaching aims and contents of this subject during the current academic year. After the

---

1 Liu Xuehui & Shen Jiliang. Revision of and Reflections on Teacher Cognition Research and Its Implications for Teacher Education[J]. *Theory and Practice of Education*, 2006(6):46-49.

implementation of the new curriculum, this kind of interpretation also focuses on the level of curriculum standard, elaborates on the nature and task of the subject, and emphasizes the need to focus on students in the teaching process. However, due to the large number of participating teachers and the managerial, training-oriented nature of this interpretation, the information in such curriculum decision-making flows in one direction and defines the "operational space" for each teacher.

2. Form of Process Agreement

This form occurs in an academic year group or a subject group within a school, where most teachers can truly participate in curriculum decision-making. It is the most common and the most controversial form of teachers' curriculum decision-making at present. These decisions can be made at the beginning of the semester through discussion to make a unified plan for the textbook progress, and to formulate the allocation of class hours. Or they can also be made before each unit or even each class to formulate specific key points, difficulties, teaching processes, resources used, examination methods and scopes. At present, many schools adopt the method of "divided lesson preparation and sharing within the group", where one teacher focuses on preparing a specific part, makes a central speech in the lesson preparation meeting, while other teachers provide additions and suggestions to improve it.

3. Form of Case Study

Case study is a new form of teaching and research that has emerged in recent years as a result of curriculum reform, being regarded as the most effective form of curriculum discussion and decision-making by teachers. In the subject teaching and research group, participants focus on a specific unit or lesson to discuss and design the classroom content, organization form, resources used, presentation method and time allocation. One teacher makes the first teaching attempt, and other members conduct classroom observations. After that, all participating teachers reflect, discuss, modify and then try out the new plan in another class. In some schools, teachers share the lecture videos of famous teachers brought back from study tour or even classroom videos of foreign schools in the teaching and research group, and the teachers in the group jointly analyze and make comments. These discussions focus not only on teachers' own understanding of knowledge but also the consensus on pedagogical content knowledge. In other words, what is discussed and recognized is that how to design curriculum objective, content, and teaching method around students. This kind of decision-making is more professional for teachers and more challenging to wisdom.

4. Form of Problem-solving

This form occurs in formal lesson preparation meetings or informal discussions among teachers, in which teachers discuss and jointly design solutions to difficulties and differences in the understanding of subject knowledge, unexpected classroom situations, and challenging student issues.

5. Form of Curriculum Development

In the implementation of the new curriculum, many schools have independently developed school-based curricula with school characteristics and advantages. As a result, the school curriculum system needs to be reconstructed, and some school-based curricula even use self-compiled textbooks by schools. Although not all teachers have attempted to participate in this form at present, it can be affirmed that in this form of curriculum decision-making, teachers have a deeper understanding of the curriculum. After being given more "space" on decision-making, teachers began to consider issues in greater depth. They re-understand the curriculum from multiple perspectives such as the cultivation objective, curriculum function, knowledge system, students' interests, school resources, and teachers' characteristics, and rethink their own roles.

6. Form of Feedback and Adjustment

The feedback and adjustment form is a collective curriculum decision-making approach spontaneously formed by teachers in informal settings. In the forms of teacher decision-making like case study and problem-solving, there are often numerous issues that are difficult to reach a consensus on. In the end, teachers may just draw up a tentative decision, or several teachers conduct classroom practice according to their respective different plans. For the unresolved issues in the previous decision-making, after the attempts, teachers timely communicate about the situations, weigh the pros and cons, and make appropriate adjustments.

(2) Characteristics of Teachers' Collective Curriculum Decision-making

1. The Quality of Teachers' Cooperation Determines the Effect of Teachers' Collective Curriculum Decision-making

Teachers' collective curriculum decision-making is based on teachers' cooperation. In fact, much of the criticism towards the collective lesson preparation system in recent years have been triggered by the lack of sincere and high-quality cooperation in the collective situations they have experienced. Collective curriculum decision-making is by no means merely a technical issue; it is also a matter of culture, interpersonal relationship and psychology. Firstly, the cultural atmosphere of the school influences teachers' curriculum decision-making. If the interpersonal relationships among teachers in the school are more competitive than cooperative, and teachers are more concerned about the enrollment rate ranking and the stack ranking in their professional lives, it is naturally difficult for them to contribute their wisdom in cooperation. To encourage teachers to focus on their professional issues, it is necessary to provide them with a relatively stable space for development. Secondly, leadership style is also an important influencing factor. Teachers' collective curriculum decision-making is a process of curriculum deliberation, a process of stimulating personal wisdom, and a process of demonstrating everyone's subjectivity while removing authority. Many teachers complain about situations such as "one person dominates the conversation" and "the group leader or the authority speaks while others can only agree" in collective lesson preparation. The most decisive factor lies in how the group leader or the "authority" positions his or her own role, how to organize, stimulate and respect the thoughts of each member, and even depends on each teacher's trust in the leader's personality. Finally, curriculum decision-making is also related to the achievement motivation and work ability of each member teacher. If a teacher doesn't care about how to improve the curriculum, he or she will naturally "directly use the fruits of others' labor". Of course, we should also distinguish between such complaints among teachers, that is, distinguishing the difference between "being lazy" and "learning from others". We should allow and even encourage teachers to imitate good experiences and practices, as the purpose of teachers' collective curriculum decision-making is to share wisdom. After all, the primary nature of a teacher's job is to serve, to serve all students. Of course, if a teacher lacks a sense of responsibility and often "learns from others'" curriculum designs, it will make those teachers who always "contribute" feel uncomfortable.

2. Teachers' Collective Curriculum Decision-making Has a Hierarchical Nature in Terms of Objects

The object of teachers' curriculum decision-making is naturally the curriculum issue. As mentioned earlier, Klein divided the issues in curriculum decision-making into nine levels. Generally speaking, Chinese teachers' decision-making primarily focuses on textbook-level, subject-knowledge, pedagogical-content, and curriculum-development levels. At the textbook level, curriculum decision-making mainly revolves around the understanding of textbook content and the regulation of progress, providing more specific interpretations of textbook content and even stipulating the difficulty and progress. This work is also named as "the allocation of teaching tasks"[1] by Chinese scholars, which is a decision on affairs rather than a professional decision. In the decision-making at the subject knowledge level, teachers'

1 Chen Guisheng. Analysis on "Collective Lesson Preparation"[J]. *Journal of the Chinese Society of Education*, 2006(9):40-41.

discussions on issues trace back from subject curriculum to subject knowledge itself, hoping to form a deeper understanding and grasp of the curriculum and textbooks through in-depth inquiries and discussions on subject issues. The curriculum decision-making at the pedagogical content knowledge level is considered the most effective and is the most reasonable reason for the existence of the form of teachers' collective curriculum decision-making as the classroom teaching needs the pedagogical content knowledge. Shulman has a widely recognized definition of pedagogical content knowledge, which refers to teachers' ability to effectively organize content knowledge, supplemented with examples and illustrations, as well as involving selecting materials, expressing key points, and choosing appropriate modes of teaching.[1] Pedagogical content knowledge (not a simple and fixed knowledge system) is teachers' practical knowledge and the core of knowledge that distinguishes teachers from other professions. Curriculum decision-making at the pedagogical content knowledge level requires teachers to connect subject knowledge, textbook content with students' characteristics, combine curriculum resource with their own teaching style, and choose the best presentation and operation method. In the decision-making at the curriculum development level, teachers can determine the concepts of school-based curriculum at the academic level as mentioned by Klein, design textbooks at the formal level, and plan the curriculum structure and program at the institution level, participating in multiple aspects and directions. However, at present, this form of teachers' collective curriculum decision-making is not yet widespread in China.

3. Teachers' Collective Curriculum Decision-making Has Differences in Terms of Individual Needs

The "empowerment" of teachers' curriculum decision-making at different

---

1 Shulman, L. S. Theory, Practice, and the Education of Professionals[J]. *International and Comparative Education*, 1999(3):36-40.

levels has different meanings for "empowering" teachers' professional development. Meanwhile, the reliance on and demand for collective curriculum decision-making differ among teachers of various types. Teachers can be divided into novice teachers, experienced teachers, and expert teachers according to the stages of their career development. Novice teachers benefit from all forms of collective decision-making, as they lack practical curriculum knowledge. The reason is that novice teachers are seriously lacking in curriculum practical knowledge (including pedagogical content knowledge). Despite their rich subject knowledge, they don't know how to transform it into a curriculum operation system. Discussions on pedagogical content knowledge are instructive for them, and even the stipulation of key content serves as a prompt for teaching design. For experienced teachers, they have already grasped the general procedures of teaching and hope to conduct more in-depth discussions on subject teaching. They welcome case studies and also hope to improve themselves through discussions and addressing challenging issues. For expert teachers, they hope to play a role in collective curriculum decision-making to train and guide young teachers, to have more creativity in their classrooms and are therefore keen on finding a basis for their attempts. They value effective curriculum interpretation at the school or higher levels and welcome discussions on curriculum at the conceptual level, which novice teachers and experienced teachers may not have the time to focus on.

4. Teachers' Collective Curriculum Decision-making and Individual Curriculum Decision-making Extend to Each Other

The characteristics of teachers' work determine that collective curriculum decision-making cannot be extended to the classroom operation level of teachers. As the specific curriculum implementation is carried out by individual teachers, the results of teachers' collective curriculum decision-making come from the individual understanding of the curriculum by participating teachers. Collective decision-making plays a role in regulating, guiding and supporting teachers, who then internalize the collective decision-making into their own actions. Overly detailed and absolute collective curriculum decision-making is a restriction on the display of teachers' teaching styles, while overly rough collective decision-making only brings teaching tasks to teachers without providing any thinking, guidance or improvement. Therefore, in specific teaching practice, making suggestive decisions on the teaching process and conducting in-depth analysis of critical issues are key to formulating teachers' collective curriculum decision-making.

III. Limitations to Overcome in Teachers' Collective Curriculum Decision-making

(1) Overcome the Limitation on the Display of Individuality in Collective Curriculum Decision-making

Before an ideal culture is established, the significance of the system lies in guidance. There is nothing inherently wrong with the agreement on key points and difficulties in teachers' collective curriculum decision-making. Knowledge itself does not inherently contain key points or difficulties; these are defined by students' perspectives. This should be a reasonable starting point for teachers' curriculum decision-making. Difficulties are determined from the perspective of students' knowledge structure and cognitive characteristics, and key points are those knowledge, skills and methods that are of important value to students' future learning and life, which require teachers to have an overview of the origin and development of knowledge and a "bird's-eye view". However, if all member teachers are limited to the design of these key points, difficulties and general procedures, and all classrooms are the same without any differences, then the agreement will become a restraint and constraint. Teachers' collective curriculum decision-making determines the general issues related to the curriculum, and teachers' individualized curriculum decision-making based on collective decision-making is also a key step to ensure the quality of curriculum implementation. Therefore, the way of agreement also needs to be agreed upon. For example, some schools require teachers to prepare two lesson plans: the first for collective lesson preparation, and the second to add their own unique content in the blank spaces of the first one, encouraging teachers to try and innovate on the basis of reaching the general level of curriculum implementation.

(2) Overcome the Limitation of the Function of Various Decision-making Approaches

The form of process agreement helps teachers to have an overall impression of the curriculum. However, since the issues discussed are based on past experiences and presuppositions about the classroom rather than the real classroom, the rigid process is likely to erode teachers' enthusiasm for discussion. Especially for experienced teachers who have already mastered the general procedures of teaching, they will find it boring and overly formulaic. In contrast, the form of case study targets the real classroom, but it has a long cycle and cannot cover all curriculum contents. The form of curriculum development is most conducive to teachers' transcending the limitation of habitual thinking, expanding their horizons and changing their roles. However, at present, not all teachers have the opportunity to participate and experience it. Any system can hardly meet the needs of everyone, or in other words, it is impossible for everyone to benefit equally from all forms of curriculum decision-making. Even in the form of case study and curriculum development, it may become a mere formality due to the slackness and passivity of the participants. The key issue lies in how to create a positive cultural background for these forms of collective decision-making. In this regard, the participation of school leaders in the process and the inspection of results are crucial. In addition to participating in the discussion process and supervision, leaders or professional backbones should also raise transcendent and reflective questions to improve the quality of topics and deepen the understanding of the curriculum. Moreover, the quality of curriculum decision-making should be reflected in curriculum implementation, and regular and routine classroom observation itself is a test of the curriculum decision-making quality.

(3) Overcome the Limitation of Unbalanced Information Flow in

Communication

Teachers are inseparable from dialogue in teaching, including dialogue with texts, dialogue with students, dialogue with peers, and dialogue with their own past experiences. Curriculum decision-making is also a process of dialogue. However, the emergence of dominant discourse in communication is inevitable, which will appear in group deliberation and discussion and is affected by the breadth of knowledge, the level of understanding, personality and even status as these discussions are for solutions rather than free imagination. However, the problem is that for experienced teachers and even expert teachers, collective curriculum seminars are also necessary as what is familiar may not be truly known. Many concepts and behaviors that have been repeated many times in experience may be collective unconscious illusions. Young teachers, on the other hand, are not bound by fixed patterns and are more receptive to new ideas, it is therefore necessary to establish special mechanism in seminars to encourage their expressions.

[Originally published in *Curriculum, Teaching Material and Method* 2008(12) (Lv Lijie & Chen Jianhong)]

16. Motivations for the Transformation of Teachers' Curriculum Actions —A Curriculum Narrative of a *Morality and Life* Teacher

Morality and Life is a comprehensive subject in the new curriculum system of basic education, offered in the first and second grades of the primary school. This curriculum mainly targets children whose school and family lives have changed after entering school, helping them adapt to the school environment, develop healthy lifestyles, and cultivate civic virtues. Based on children's lives, it conducts moral education within the context of real-life experiences and constructs the meaning of the curriculum through activities and experiences, which should be a significant highlight of this curriculum in terms of its concept. Due to reasons such as the availability of teaching staff, in many schools, *Morality and Life* is concurrently taught by the homeroom teacher. So, what is the teachers' attitude towards the curriculum? Can they implement it seriously and demonstrate its significance? The following is the curriculum narrative of Teacher Shi, a *Morality and Life* teacher at a primary school in Nanguan District, Changchun City, as shared during a seminar after peer observation. From it, we can see the implementation status of this curriculum by the teacher.

Ⅰ. Teacher Shi's Story with *Morality and Life*

Actually, I didn't teach the *Morality and Life* very well before, and many teachers might have done the same as I did. Since I teach *Chinese Language* and also serve as the homeroom teacher, I would occasionally take advantage of the principal's absence to secretly give Chinese character dictation exercises during *Morality and Life* classes. Occasionally, I would lead the children to do exercise books or assign homework.

Since I have been working as a homeroom teacher for lower grades for a long time, and this semester I am also the homeroom teacher for the second grade, I felt that the work of a homeroom teacher was particularly tedious and exhausting. In the early days of the new semester, many children came to me to complain. When writing, two children would fight with each other, saying things like "Teacher, he drew on my book" or "He pushed me". Then, the next day, parents would call me and say: "Teacher, could you please change the seat? His deskmate always bullies him." When lining up, they would also push and shove each other, and the lack of unity in the class becomes more and more apparent. At that time, I had the idea of quitting the work of a homeroom teacher as it was just too tiring every day. Why was it so tedious? There were endless issues to deal with. Whenever a problem emerged, it had to be solved immediately. In the eyes of teachers, these were very small things, but for the children, they were very important and must be addressed.

Just when I was at a loss and didn't know how to solve these problems, I accidentally flipped to the second unit in the *Morality and Life* textbook titled *There Are Many Stories in Our Class*. Many small illustrations in this unit caught my attention, and I found that many of the scenes depicted in these illustrations were similar to those in my class, such as these things about children complaining. Then I thought that I might as well take this opportunity to properly educate the children in my class.

I compiled a series of short stories based on the things that children in my class complained about. Of course, the protagonists in these stories didn't use the real names of the children, and they listened with great interest. As their homeroom teacher, I knew the children in my class very well, so I specifically asked several of them to answer questions. I asked: "Which character in the story do you like? Which one don't you like? Why do you like or dislike him?" They answered very well, and it seemed that they had found their own shortcomings. A few days later, I found that the phenomenon of children complaining had decreased a little, although it still existed occasionally.

Then, I wanted to continue this curriculum by using the *Morality and Life* textbook, so I organized another activity in the second week's class. I took the children to the playground and prepared two games for them. One was the game of three-legged race, and the other was a relay race where two children carried a ball on their backs. These two games were designed to train the children's abilities of unity, cooperation and mutual coordination. Of course, some children played these games very well, while some children dropped the ball when carrying it, and some children even fell down. Some children didn't reflect on their own actions but blamed their partners, saying things like: "It's all your fault. Would the ball have fallen to the ground if it weren't for you? Would I have fallen if it weren't for you?" However, I knew that it was quite normal for such occurrences. Then I took these children back to the classroom and continued the class. I first asked those who played the games very well to answer questions: "How did you cooperate so well? How did you play the games?", and the children shared their experiences. Then I turned to those who didn't play well and asked: "Can you find the reasons why you didn't play well?" The children nodded and said they understood. Finally, I told them a story to illustrate the truth that "a single chopstick is easy to break, but ten chopsticks are hard to bend". Upon hearing this, the children had a moment of sudden realization.

The children in our class asked me after class: "Teacher, are we going to have a test on new characters in the next *Morality and Life* class? Does the *Chinese Language* class representative need to hand out notebooks?" When I heard this, my face suddenly turned red. I felt that I had been really sorry to these children in the previous period. It turned out that they liked the *Morality and Life* class so much in their hearts, but I had deprived them of this right. I even felt sorry to the principal...

Seeing that this activity was going quite well, I gave each child a piece of colored cardboard before the class in the third week and asked them to write a love card and a thank-you card on it, writing down whom they had bullied or with whom they had had some minor conflicts. The children were asked to exchange these cards, and each child keep the cards they received. Some parents gave me feedback, saying: "Teacher, my child didn't even allow me to throw away this card. He cherished it more than those musical cards I bought for him at Christmas." Now I think that the *Morality and Life* class has achieved twice the result with half the effort. Teachers in our grade who also teach the *Morality and Life* cooperate very well, and it can be said that our grade group is full of talents. For example, Teacher Li is particularly good at using his mind and is an intelligent type, just like a director who can direct us on what to do. Teacher Zhou is a computer expert, very skilled at operating computers and can search for information online. Then there is me. I am particularly willing to make some small teaching aids, draw pictures and cut things. We have a very good division of labor. For example, when we are going to teach a certain unit, Teacher Zhou will go online to search for information, Teacher Li will offer advice, and I will take action to make the teaching aids...

II. Analysis of the Case Story

(1) The Mental Process in Teacher Shi's Curriculum Behavior

People's behaviors are always closely linked to purposes and effects, and teachers are no exception. Teachers usually focus their teaching on those curriculum contents that are easy to show effects. In the current educational culture, it is not uncommon for the school and teacher to use the examination result as an important indicator to measure the educational effect. Naturally, the homeroom teacher Shi would "secretly" use the power to "give dictation of new characters" and "do exercise books" in the *Morality and Life* class as it is difficult to measure students' academic achievements and teachers' curriculum implementation levels in *Morality and Life* through examinations. Although Teacher Shi knows that such practice is "not good at all", it is "very similar to that of many colleagues". At this time, problems arise in Teacher Shi's work as a homeroom teacher. The second-grade children "complain" every day, often "fight", and "bully at their desk mates", making her feel "tiring" and "so tedious". Teacher Shi encounters many difficulties in her pursuit of goals, but one thing is clear to her: these "tedious" things are not only obstacles to her work but also "very important things" in children's growth. That is to say, she believes that correcting and educating the problems that trouble students' growth is also her responsibility and the purpose of her educational behavior, although this purpose is only realized when problems arise. In other words, when students had growth problems, the purpose and effect requirements of Teacher Shi's potential educational behavior changed. Under such circumstances, she "accidentally" "flips to" the *Morality and Life* textbook and is immediately "attracted" because "many of the scenes depicted in the small illustrations" are very similar to the educational dilemmas she has encountered, that is, the characteristics and functions of the textbook matches Teacher Shi's educational needs very well. Consequently, Teacher Shi begins to try to use the *Morality and Life* curriculum and solve the problems in students' growth and the troubles in her own work according to the activity mode provided by the *Morality and Life* textbook. After the attempt, she finds that the problems have "decreased a little". Next, Teacher Shi takes the initiative to develop and "continue" the *Morality and Life* class as she discovers the effects and significance produced by this new curriculum and in turn, feels "sorry" to the children and the principal for her previous neglect of the new curriculum. After the change in her attitude towards the curriculum and successful attempts, Teacher Shi continues to develop and extend it. At this time, she has received high praise from parents' feedback and believes that it has a "twice the result with half the effort" effect, which is both Teacher Shi's evaluation of this curriculum and her evaluation of her curriculum implementation level.

(2) Teacher Shi's Curriculum Behavior and Focus Have Undergone Three Transitions

In the story, Teacher Shi's curriculum behavior has undergone several transitions: from not implementing the curriculum to using the curriculum to passively address the troubles and contradictions in students' lives, to actively creating situations to stimulate students' thinking, and then to guiding children to conduct constructive self-reflection and create positive interpersonal relationships in the class. These several transitions have formed a relatively complete thematic unit about There Are Many Stories in Our Class, with the teaching content elements derived from students' real lives. For students, these three classes represent three leaps in the development of their cognitive abilities about class life. Although Teacher Shi's initial behavior of "compiling what students complained into short stories " attracts the interest of many students, from the perspective of the changes in students' psychological levels, students only learn what behaviors are right and what are wrong. In the design of the "three-legged race" game, students have a cognitive understanding regarding issues such as humility, cooperation and helping others. After experiencing the activity process and undergoing in-depth thinking, students achieved an sublimation in their emotions and attitudes when creating love cards. For Teacher Shi, these three classes are also three leaps in educational effectiveness. The initial behavior of compiling stories and telling them to students is a persuasive education aimed at the past, in which Teacher Shi focuses on solving the problems in her own work. When organizing the "three-legged race" game, Teacher Shi begins to design scenarios with a clear purpose. At this time, she begins to consider how to most effectively demonstrate the effects of the curriculum, focusing on sowing the seeds of friendship for students and directing activities toward their future development, and the teaching is designed with students' horizons being the core starting point. In these several transitions, the creation and development of the curriculum originates from Teacher Shi's familiarity with class work and students, as well as her educational wisdom and inspiration.

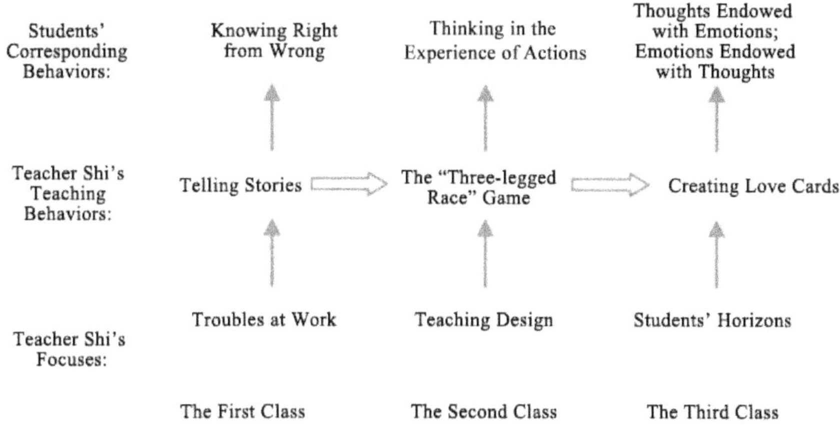

Figure 4-1

(3) Teacher Shi's Curriculum Implementation Presents Different Stages

Teacher Shi's curriculum implementation process is quite typical, and many teachers share "similar experiences", starting from resisting and not implementing the curriculum, to applying and attempting the new curriculum, and then to implementing the new curriculum independently, effectively and even creatively. This level of curriculum implementation is basically consistent with the eight level stage of curriculum implementation summarized by Hall and Hord, namely "non-use, orientation, preparation, mechanical use, routine, refinement, integration, and renewal"[1]. However, their theoretical system does not give the key point on how teachers can transition from not using the new curriculum to the initial attempt and mechanical use. In other words, a teacher who has never used the new curriculum will not necessarily make "orientation", "preparation", and "mechanical use" for using the new curriculum. Hall's eight levels of curriculum implementation are idealized and theoretical in nature.

1 Hall, G. E,, & Hord, S. M. Change in Schools: Facilitating the Process[R]. New York: State University of New York Press, 1987:60.

What motivates teachers to abandon established routines and adopt untested practices? After teachers mechanically use the new curriculum, what motivates them to continue using it, constantly improve it, and reach the levels of routine and refinement? We can see from Teacher Shi's curriculum story that this motivation lies mainly in the practical function of the curriculum itself. This function is manifested in whether it can solve the problems in work and those in students' growth, whether it can bring educational achievements, and of course, whether it can satisfy the principal, because Teacher Shi feels "sorry to the principal" when reflecting on her failure to use the new curriculum before. Once teachers understand and confirm this function, they will use and improve the new curriculum independently, even reaching a level of "refinement, integration and renewal". There are also relevant theories discussing the autonomy of teachers' implementation brought about by the practical function of the curriculum.

III. Discussion on the Key Points of the Transformation of Teachers' Curriculum Actions

(1) Teachers' Perception of the Curriculum Change Cost Is the Core of Teachers' Identification with the New Curriculum

The cost is the price that must be paid to obtain benefits. Teachers' estimation of the costs paid and the returns gained from curriculum change constitute their cost perception, which is related to teachers' attitudes towards the curriculum and their sense of identification with the curriculum. In a study on "Teacher Receptivity to the Unit Curriculum System" conducted by Waugh and Godfrey in Australia in 1993, they used seven related variables for the survey: (1) non-monetary cost benefit; (2) the practicality in the classroom; (3) alleviation of fears and concerns(through school support); (4) concerns about important issues of change; (5) other support for the change; (6) participation in the change decisions relating to the school and the classroom; (7) feelings towards the previous system compared to the old one. After questionnaire surveys and quantitative analysis, Waugh and Godfrey concluded that the most important variable affecting teachers' identification was cost benefit, followed by the degree of participation in the reform, the supporting factors for the reform, and the experience of previous reforms. In a 1998 comparative study on teachers' identification with the local curriculum and the general studies curriculum conducted by John Chi-Kin Lee, a scholar from Hong Kong, China, "teachers' evaluation of the non-monetary cost benefit of curriculum reform" was also listed as the top of the five variables. Cost perception affects teachers' identification with the new curriculum, and this identification, in turn, affects whether teachers can substantially adopt and implement the new curriculum. Then, what exactly are the costs and benefits in teachers' perception? Some scholars have summarized[1] (as shown in Table 4-1).

Table 4-1 Costs and Benefits in Teachers' Perception

Costs	Benefits
The additional learning time and preparation required for innovation	An increase of teacher stimulation and satisfaction
Abandon existing skills and learn unfamiliar skills and new knowledge	The improvement of classroom atmosphere
Prepare new teaching materials and resources	The improvement of classroom discipline
The time it takes to cover the new syllabus	Promotion
Changes in teacher-student relationships (e.g. increased teacher-student interaction in the classroom)	Higher status of teachers involved in innovation
Students may not do well in public examinations.	More opportunities to participate in decision-making
Changing relationships between principals and teachers, and between teachers and teachers	The improvement of teacher-student and teacher-teacher relationship
Teacher autonomy has been weakened.	An increase of salary
It may be a threat to the authority of the teacher's subject.	An increase of resource
	Increased participation in professional development and support activities

In this table, among the ten items of teachers' perception of benefits, nine

1 Morris, P. Curriculum Innovation and Implementation: A Cautionary Note[J]. *Educational Research Journal,* 1987(2):49-54.

are non-monetary costs and six are related to teachers' sense of educational efficacy. Some scholars even directly define the cost benefit return expected by teachers as "students' positive responses and the improvement of their learning quality"[1].

In Teacher Shi's story, she used to give dictation of Chinese characters in the *Morality and Life* class, which in fact reflects her perceived educational cost return - the improvement of students' academic performance by not implementing the new curriculum. Subsequently, the factor that leads to the transformation of her curriculum identification is her discovery of students' educational needs. After trying to use the new curriculum, she obtains changes in students' behaviors. Her attempt receives new returns, and she finds the new benefits implied by this curriculum. Thus, Teacher Shi's cost perception of the new curriculum of *Morality and Life* has changed. In the subsequent "continuation", she keeps getting returns, so that when she shares the story, she has formed a relatively good curriculum identification. Therefore, in this case, we can see that whether work efficiency can be obtained is the core factor affecting teachers' identification with and implementation of the new curriculum.

(2) Teachers' Curriculum Attitudes and Trial Behaviors Verify Each Other

Alex Fung (Fung, 1995)[2] proposed the 'Six-A' innovation process model from a school change perspective. The characteristic of the whole process is that the innovation is a non-linear one and consists of re-cycling loops channelling through six broad stages: awareness, attitude formation, adoption, adaptation,

---

1 John Chi-Kin Lee. *Curriculum, Teaching and School Reform*[M]. Hong Kong: The Chinese University of Hong Kong Press, 2002:100.

2 Fung, A. *Management of Educational Innovations: The 'Six-A' Process Model* in Wong, K. C and Cheng, K. M *Educational Leadership and Change - An International Perspective*[M]. Hong Kong: Hong Kong University Press, 1995:69-85.

action and application. Although this process generally follows a sequential order, in fact, each attempt may lead to the restart of the cycle. That is to say, each adoption and trial will bring the level of awareness and understanding about the innovation to a different level. This new attitude then determines whether the actor identifies with the innovation, adopts it and tries again. (As shown in Figure 4-2)

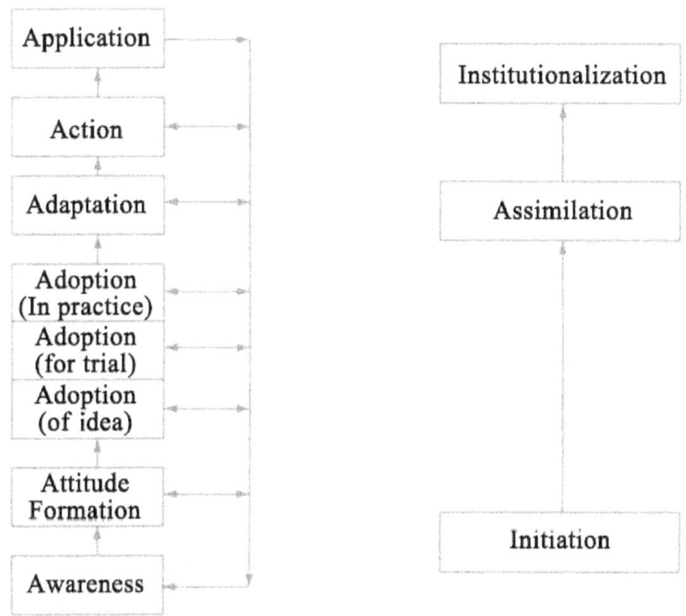

Figure 4-2 Alex Fung's Innovation Process Model

Guskey's research comes to a similar conclusion. He believes that in general, significant changes in teachers' beliefs and attitudes occur when they carry out successful practices and observe actual changes in their students. His model of teacher professional development begins with changes in teaching practices, which leads to changes in student achievement, and then leads to changes in teachers' beliefs and attitudes[1].

In Teacher Shi's story, when she notices that the illustrations in the *Morality and Life* textbook "mirrored my class", she has already formed an attitude towards this new curriculum. After successfully adopting and trying it, she further confirms her understanding and attitude, so that she puts more enthusiasm and energy into designing more effective thematic unit activities. However, if Teacher Shi's attempt fails, as the process in the figure shown above, the result of the attempt will also give feedback to the attitude and understanding, and influence the further adoption and attempt. In this way, teachers' curriculum attitude and curriculum change action develop and mature in the process of constant mutual correction. Therefore, when teachers initially adopt and implement the new curriculum with a tentative attitude, timely help, guidance, cooperation, or giving them technology and skills to promote success influence teachers' attitude towards acceptance of change and the continuous effectiveness of change behavior.

(3) The Role of Autonomy, Practice and Communication in Teachers' Professional Development

The process of teachers' professional development is also the process of teachers' autonomy learning, a characteristic it shares with many other highly independent and practice-oriented professions. For the elements and modes of autonomy learning in practice, European scholars Fei ao and Bomaisen have proposed a "learning cube model"[2] (as shown in Figure 4-3), with the X-axis representing the practicality of the learning content, the Y-axis representing the communicative nature of the learning process, and the Z-axis representing the

---

1 Guskey, T. R. Professional Development and Teacher Change[J]. *Teacher and Teacher Education*, 2002:8.

2 Yu Kaicheng. *Human Resource Management*[M]. Dalian: Dalian University of Technology Press, 2001:205.

autonomy of learning. Together, these three axes form the core fulcrum of the professional learning process.

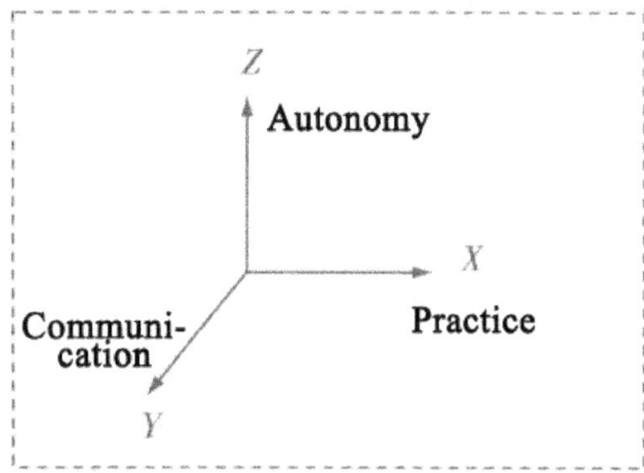

Figure 4-3 The Learning Cube Model

This model well explains the elements and patterns of teachers' professional development. That is to say, the desire for self-development, practical exercises, and communication and cooperation with peer experts can form the three elements of teachers' professional development, whose relationship is interrelated and mutually constructed. In other words, self-development motivation influences how teachers engage in reflective practice, how much self-observation and reflection can be integrated into practice, and whether they can keenly absorb and adopt theories and others' experiences. Practice is an inevitable working state for teachers, and the practice that permeates autonomy, learning, assistance and cooperation is the one with wisdom. Only the practice with an increasing quality and with effectiveness can give feedback to the desire for autonomous development. Filtering for interaction effectiveness leads to the natural generation of needs in practice. The premise of interaction is the willingness to cooperate and communicate, that is to say, only with the desire for self-development can communication be formed. In Teacher Shi's story, her initial practical attempts are made with a trial-and-error attitude. The success in practice strengthens her autonomous desire to develop the curriculum function, and the enthusiasm and desire for success support friendly, positive and complementary cooperation and communication among teachers. During this period, whether it is out of a sense of responsibility for students or the motivation for her own professional development, the autonomy in pursuing the educational efficacy runs through her educational actions.

[Originally published in *Global Education* 2007(3) (Lv Lijie)]

17. The Survey of the Principal's Curriculum Leadership Competency Based on Situational Judgement Test

The school is the basic unit of curriculum reform. The loyalty to curriculum implementation and the innovation level of curriculum development in schools determine the success or failure of the reform and even determine the quality of educating people in schools. The situation of school curriculum development is a complex issue. To examine school curriculum development, it is necessary to enter schools to conduct individual observation and understanding for curriculum setting, curriculum implementation process, and even the curriculum resource environment. Therefore, it is rather difficult to understand the situation of school curriculum development with large samples. For this reason, we have chosen the alternative indicator of principal's curriculum leadership competency, hoping to judge the necessary conditions or possibilities of school curriculum development by measuring the degree of principal's curriculum specialization. That is to say, we believe that school curriculum development and construction must rely on principals having good curriculum leadership competency, which is a necessary but not sufficient prerequisite for school curriculum development.

I. The Principal's Curriculum Leadership Competency and Its Theoretical Hypotheses

(1) Connotation of the Principal's Curriculum Leadership Competency

Since the 1980s, curriculum leadership has become a focal topic in curriculum research. Bradley, Glatthorn, and Brubaker were early scholars who systematically theorized about curriculum leadership. Since the late 1990s, numerous scholars in Taiwan, Hong Kong of China, and the mainland have also begun to pay attention to the issue of curriculum leadership. The common ground in the definitions and understandings of curriculum leadership by Chinese and foreign scholars is that they all take curriculum reform as the background and explain the meaning of curriculum leadership from the perspective of the role and function of the curriculum leader. For example, Bradley believes that curriculum leadership emphasizes curriculum development, provides necessary resources for curriculum development and the philosophical direction for curriculum development, allows the continuity of curriculum development, and serves as a bridge for the communication between curriculum development theory and practice.[1] That is to say, scholars pay more attention to the professional work tasks done by curriculum leaders in curriculum reform and curriculum leaders' professional value for curriculum development, rather than just general administrative leadership behaviors regarding personnel, finance, and materials. Therefore, curriculum leadership is a kind of professional leadership. The principal's curriculum leadership emphasizes that the principal should perform professional leadership function, not just enhance morale, handle interpersonal relationship, or stimulate employees' motivation, but focus on the professional work of school curriculum construction, lead and promote the establishment, optimization and innovation of school curriculum.

Some researchers believe that competency is a potential personal trait which will affect an individual's ability performance, behavioral decision-making, and relevant reference standard generated in complex working context.[2] Others define competency more directly as the specific application and actual behavior performance of knowledge, skills and motivation in particular

---

1 Bradley, L. H. *Curriculum Leadership and Development Handbook*[M]. New Jersey: Prentice-Hall, 1985:23-24.

2 Spencer, L. M., *et al. Competence at Work: Models for Superior Performance*[M]. Translated by Wei Meijin. Shantou: Shantou University Press, 2003.

situation.[1] That is to say, competency is some personal traits that affect work behaviors. These traits are in a comprehensive form of knowledge, skills, motivation, attitude and values, which affect people's behaviors and activities such as judgment, decision-making, and problem-solving in a subtle way. The principal's curriculum leadership competency refers to the personal traits including knowledge, skills, thinking model, and behavioral pattern displayed by principals in planning, developing, guiding, and supervising school curriculum construction work to promote school curriculum development.

(2) Theoretical Hypotheses of the Principal's Curriculum Leadership Competency

As curriculum leaders, principals need to lead and guide school curriculum construction and curriculum innovation with professional influence in school curriculum construction. Meanwhile, principals also need to use their job identities to motivate, coordinate interpersonal interactions, and establish mechanisms to create a sound environment for curriculum development. Therefore, we believe that the principal's curriculum leadership is mainly task-oriented, and at the same time, the general interpersonal-oriented function will also have a great impact on the principal's curriculum leadership.

What curriculum tasks do principals need to complete? Glatthorn divides curriculum leadership into four levels including national, local, school, and classroom from the decision-making level in curriculum reform. Different decision-making levels determine different roles and rights and responsibilities in curriculum reform. From the perspective of job analysis, school-level curriculum leadership should perform functions as follows: develop a high-quality school curriculum vision according to the local curriculum vision; supplement local education goals; develop its own learning program; develop a

---

1 Woodruffe, C. Competent by Any Other Name[J]. *Personnel Management*, 1991(9):30-33.

learning-centered class schedule; determine the nature and scope of curriculum integration; make the proposed, written, taught, tested and learned curriculum consistent; supervise and assist in the curriculum implementation.[1] In China, the *Professional Standards for Principals of Compulsory Education Schools* promulgated by the Ministry of Education in 2013 lists the principal's leadership in curriculum teaching as one of their professional responsibilities and makes clear provisions. On the basis of corresponding concepts, knowledge and policies, they should coordinate the national, local and school-based curriculum, implement the national curriculum standard, develop school-based curriculum, provide curriculum resources, and actively carry out teaching and research and teaching reform activities. From this, we believe that principals' curriculum leadership tasks at the school level include establishing the school's educational philosophy, planning the school curriculum according to the educational policy and educational philosophy, conducting school-based processing of the national curriculum, developing school-based curriculum, utilizing curriculum resources, establishing the curriculum management mechanism, and managing curriculum implementation.

Referring to the competency test model and combining with the functional requirement of principals' curriculum leadership, we construct a measurement model for the principal's curriculum leadership (as shown in Figure 4-4). The principal's curriculum leadership mainly aims to complete the function and tasks of their roles. Among them, mastering curriculum theories, having advanced curriculum concepts, and understanding national curriculum policies are the prerequisites for principals to perform their duties and complete tasks. These theories, concepts and policies are manifested in the form of implicit knowledge in practical situations, forming unique individual behavioral patterns and

---

1 Glatthorn, A. A. *The Principal as Curriculum Leader*[M]. Translated by Shan Wenjing, *et al*. Shanghai: East China Normal University Press, 2003.

affecting the effectiveness of curriculum development.

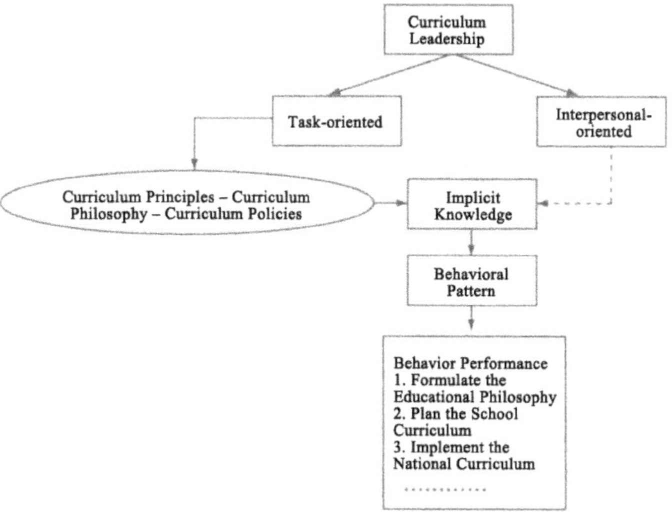

Figure 4-4 Theoretical Hypothesis of the Principal's Curriculum Leadership Competency

II. Measurement Design of the Principal's Curriculum Leadership Competency

(1) The Measurement Instrument Selection: Situational Judgment Tests

In the traditional measurement of teacher efficacy and principal competence, the target content of measurement is directly stated, and the measured objectives are asked to make their own judgments. For example, statements like "I can master the knowledge about curriculum design" and "I can make rational use of curriculum resources" are too general and broad, and directly use the conceptual terms that need to be measured. Unless the measured objective has a deep understanding of concepts such as curriculum design knowledge and curriculum resources, it is difficult for them to make a professional judgment. On the other hand, if the right of judgment is completely handed over to the measured objective, there will inevitably be doubts in terms of social desirability. Therefore, this study adopts the method of Situational Judgment Tests, which are designed as work simulations or work samples with low-to-medium fidelity for evaluating the appropriate behavioral tendencies in a certain work situation.[1] This method is more conducive to measuring the real attitude and implicit knowledge of the measured objective. The principal's curriculum leadership competency stems from his cognition for curriculum policies, mastery of curriculum theories, and grasp of educational concepts. These cognition, theories, and concepts need to be manifested through curriculum practice. The adoption of the method of Situational Judgment Tests aims to compile practical situations of typicality, authenticity and multi-dimensions, collect and measure the real behavioral response of the principal in curriculum practice, so as to judge the actual situation of his cognition and attitude.

(2) Measurement Instrument Development for Situational Judgment Tests

Step One: Curriculum Event Interview and Situation Setting

Based on the seven competency examination dimensions formed by the job analysis for the principal's curriculum leadership, we developed interview protocols for principals and curriculum experts, interviewing 10 principals and 4 experts as key informants. The ten principals are all leaders who actively attempt school curriculum innovation, and the four experts are curriculum experts who have presided over or participated in collaborative projects between institutions and have experiences in helping schools develop the curriculum. These fourteen experts, as subject matter experts, share the most effective or the most principle-violating curriculum events in their experiences around the

---

1 Weekley, J. A. & Ployhart, R. E. *Situational Judgement Tests: Theory, Measurement and Application*[M]. Translated by Liu Hengchao, Luo Fengying & Li Tingyu, *et al*. Shanghai: Fudan University Press, 2013.

interview topics. From the more than 30 curriculum stories and curriculum phenomena obtained from the interview, we conducted value-based screening guided by two principles: 1) whether the situational stories reflect the key points to be evaluated; 2) whether the situational stories have practical universality to ensure the construct validity of the questionnaire. Finally, nine curriculum phenomena or curriculum stories of complexity and typicality that can reflect the evaluation points are selected, processed and retained.

Step Two: Collect Corresponding Situation Reaction

Since only more than ten principals or experts are interviewed when collecting problem situations, and the curriculum stories they experienced and shared are also independent, the reaction term for each situation has not been tested and the problem of insufficiency exists. Therefore, we compile the 9 retained problem situations into a completely open-ended questionnaire and select a total of 54 rural principals, outstanding principals in Beijing, and principals in Changchun to give qualitative answers. Then, three doctoral students read and code each collected questionnaire, sort out the situational reaction terms corresponding to each situational question, remove the reaction terms that are irrelevant to the situation and have obvious tendency, merge similar reaction terms, and finally list 4-8 possible situation reactions under each situation. A 0-5 point scoring method is used for each reaction.

Step Three: Determine the Scoring Method and Optimal Option

After determining the situational questions and all reaction terms, we organize two senior curriculum experts and three provincial outstanding principals to give the optimal options for each reaction term. For questions with disagreements, collective consultation is adopted to finally reach a consensus. The optimal option is scored as 5 points, and other options are assigned 1-4 points according to their degrees of dispersion from the best answer. Finally, the differences between the scores of the reaction terms in the principals' questionnaires and the scores assigned by the experts are calculated. The smaller the difference is, the closer the surveyed principals are to the expert standard, that is, the higher the principal's curriculum leadership competency is. On the contrary, the larger the difference is, the farther the surveyed principals are from the expert standard, that is, the lower the level of the principals' curriculum competency is.

III. Results and Analysis of the Evaluation of the Principal's Curriculum Leadership Competency

A total of 482 questionnaires are distributed in this survey, among which 461 are valid, covering 24 provinces, municipalities directly under the Central Government, and autonomous regions in China. The specific situation is shown as Table 4-2.

Table 4-2 Statistical Table of the Basic Information of Sample Principals

Basic Information	Category	Number	Percentage
Gender	Male	305	66.16%
	Female	156	33.84%
Age	Aged 40 and below	56	12.15%
	Between 41~50	314	68.11%
	Aged 51 and above	91	19.74%
The First Degree	Degree in Secondary Normal School	202	43.82%
	Degree in Teachers College	137	29.72%
	Bachelor's Degree in Teacher Education	93	20.17%
	Bachelor's Degree in Non-Teacher Education	11	2.39%
	Others	18	3.90%
The Highest Degree	Junior College	33	7.16%
	Bachelor's Degree	386	83.73%
	Master's Degree	41	8.89%
	Doctoral Degree	1	0.22%

Basic Information	Category	Number	Percentage
School-running Level	Nine-year Compulsory Education	73	15.84%
	Junior High School	247	53.58%
	Primary school	141	30.59%

For numerical values in the reliability test, validity test, correlation analysis and significant difference analysis of this scale, IBM SPSS Statistics 21.0 is used to conduct statistical analysis on the collected data. The reliability test mainly examines the homogeneity reliability and split-half reliability of the scale. The homogeneity reliability is represented by Cronbach's Alpha coefficient (i.e., the α coefficient), and the split-half reliability is calculated by using the Spearman-Brown split-half correlation coefficient method. The α coefficient of this scale is 0.784 and the split-half coefficient is 0.756. Both values are greater than 0.7[1], indicating good reliability of the principal's curriculum leadership competency scale developed by our research group. The validity analysis is carried out in two ways including content validity and discriminant validity. The content validity is judged by the rationality of the item distribution. Based on theoretical and policy analysis, the principal's curriculum leadership competency scale in this study is composed of nine evaluation points, namely "explore the educational philosophy", "plan the school curriculum", "understand national curriculum policies", "school-based adaptation of national curriculum", "school-based curriculum design", "school-based curriculum implementation", "curriculum resource utilization", "establish curriculum management mechanism" and "monitor and supervise curriculum implementation". Five experts in this study analyze the consistency between the evaluation points and the purpose of the measurement items. All of them believe that the nine evaluation points of the scale have completely and detailedly evaluated the principal's curriculum

---

1 Henson, R. K. Understanding Internal Consistency Reliability Estimates: A Conceptual Primer on Coefficient Alpha[J]. *Measurement & Evaluation in Counseling & Development*, 2001(3):177-189.

leadership competency, and the evaluation situation is real and comprehensive. The Kendall (Kendall rank) concordance coefficient for the consistency of the measurement purpose is 0.317, and its P value is 0.027 ($P < 0.05$), which prove that the judgments of the experts are significantly consistent, indicating good content validity of the scale.

In the discriminant validity test, it can be seen from Table 4-3 that the correlation coefficients between different dimensions of this scale range from -0.125 to 0.466, indicating low to moderate correlations. The result indicates that the dimensions of the scale are highly independent and mutually non-interfering. The correlation coefficients between different dimensions of the scale and the total score range from 0.503 to 0.779 with moderate to high correlations, indicating that all dimensions can reflect the content to be measured by the total scale with good discriminant validity.

Table 4-3 Correlation Coefficient Matrix between Each Dimension and the Total Score

	Explore the Educational Philosophy	Plan the School Curriculum	Understand National Curriculum Policies	School-based Adaptation of National Curriculum	School-based Curriculum Design	School-based Curriculum Implementation	Curriculum Resource Utilization	Establish Curriculum Management Mechanism	Monitor and Supervise Curriculum Implementation	Total Score
Explore the Educational Philosophy	1									
Plan the School Curriculum	0.026	1								
Understand National Curriculum Policies	0.001	0.183**	1							
School-based Adaptation of National Curriculum	-0.125**	0.173**	0.236**	1						
School-based Curriculum Design	-0.045	0.205**	0.233**	0.343**	1					
School-based Curriculum Implementation	-0.090	0.312**	0.202**	0.223**	0.194**	1				
Curriculum Resource Utilization	-0.005	0.067	0.076	0.053	-0.060	0.094*	1			
Establish Curriculum Management Mechanism	-0.064	0.257**	0.291**	0.445**	0.466**	0.225**	-0.037	1		
Monitor and Supervise Curriculum Implementation	0.086	0. 134**	0.069	0.109*	0.226**	0.108*	-0.003	0.244**	1	
Total Score	0.590**	0.503**	0.660**	0.665**	0.751**	0.642**	0.630**	0.779**	0.669**	1

Note: ** indicates P<0.01, * indicates P<0.05.

(1) Overall Situation of the Principal's Curriculum Leadership Competency

1. Overall Situation of the Principal's Curriculum Leadership Competency

The score for each evaluation point of the principal's curriculum leadership competency is uniformly set at 20, so the total score of the scale is 180. Among the 461 principals, the highest score is 160.2 and the lowest is 86.9. Only 1 participant scores above 160, 159 participants score in the range of 140 - 159, 263 participants score in the range of 120 - 139, 35 participants score in the range of 100 - 119, and the remaining 3 participants score in the range of 80 - 99.

Statistics are made on the mean and standard deviation of each evaluation point of the principal's curriculum leadership competency (specific situations are shown in Table 4-4). Among them, the highest overall score is "school-based curriculum implementation", with an average score of 16.53, and the degree of dispersion (standard deviation) of individual data is only 1.44, which is also the smallest among all dimensions. The next is "understand national curriculum policies", with an average score of 16.37. However, there are relatively large differences among different individuals, and the standard deviation is 2.77, the second largest dimension in terms of individual dispersion value among the nine dimensions. Among the nine dimensions, "school-based adaptation of national curriculum" is the lowest dimension in terms of the principal's curriculum leadership competency in China, with an average score of 13.97. Among the nine dimensions, the individual differences among principals on "school-based curriculum design" dimension is the most obvious, with a standard deviation value of 3.07.

Table 4-4 Overall Mean and Standard Deviation of Each Examination Point and Total Score of Principals' Curriculum Leadership Competency

Statistics	Explore the Educational Philosophy	Plan the School Curriculum	Understand National Curriculum Policies	School-based Adaptation of National Curriculum	School-based Curriculum Design	School-based Curriculum Implementation	Curriculum Resource Utilization	Establish Curriculum Management Mechanism	Monitor and Supervise Curriculum Implementation	Total Score
Mean	14.21	15.93	16.37	13.97	13.18	16.53	15.04	15.59	14.39	135.23
Standard Deviation	2.39	2.00	2.77	2.20	3.07	1.44	2.05	2.53	2.43	10.22

In order to more intuitively and specifically see the score distribution levels of principals in each dimension, and analyze whether individual differences are caused by bipolar distribution or multi-layer dispersion of data, we draw the specific situation of different principal scores in the nine dimensions into a "rose garland diagram" according to the number distribution in intervals (as illustrated in Figure 4-5). In this diagram, the color depth represents the score interval, and the size of the sector area represents the distribution of population numbers. From the overall observation of this diagram, it can be found that most principals are distributed in the score range of 10-18, indicating that the scores in all dimensions are generally good. From the perspective of the number distribution in intervals, because the scores of most principals are distributed in the score range of 14-18, the dimension of " school-based curriculum implementation" has the best score situation, which is consistent with the situation of possessing the highest average score and the smallest standard deviation. There are relatively large differences regarding the "school-based curriculum design" dimension due to the multi-layer discrete distribution of data. In addition, regarding the dimension of "understand national curriculum policies", its standard deviation value is caused by the polarization among principals.

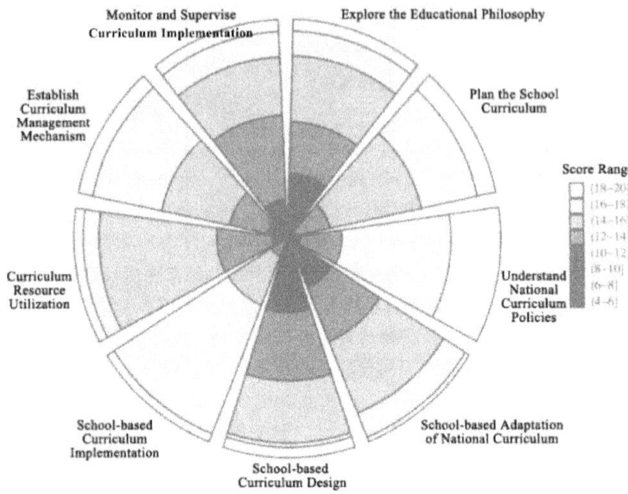

Figure 4-5 Score Distribution Ranges for Each Evaluation Point of the Principal's Curriculum Leadership Competency

2. Cluster Analysis of the Principal's Curriculum Leadership Competency

All principals' scores across the nine evaluation points are clustered based on their deviation from the mean, with clustering results illustrated in Figure 4-6. The clustering of this heatmap adopts the K-means average distance algorithm. Every grid cell represents each principal's score relative to the dimensional mean, with darker color intensity indicating higher scores while lighter shades correspond to lower values. Each line represents the score of the same principal in different dimensions, and the tree diagram on the left represents the clustering results of each principal.

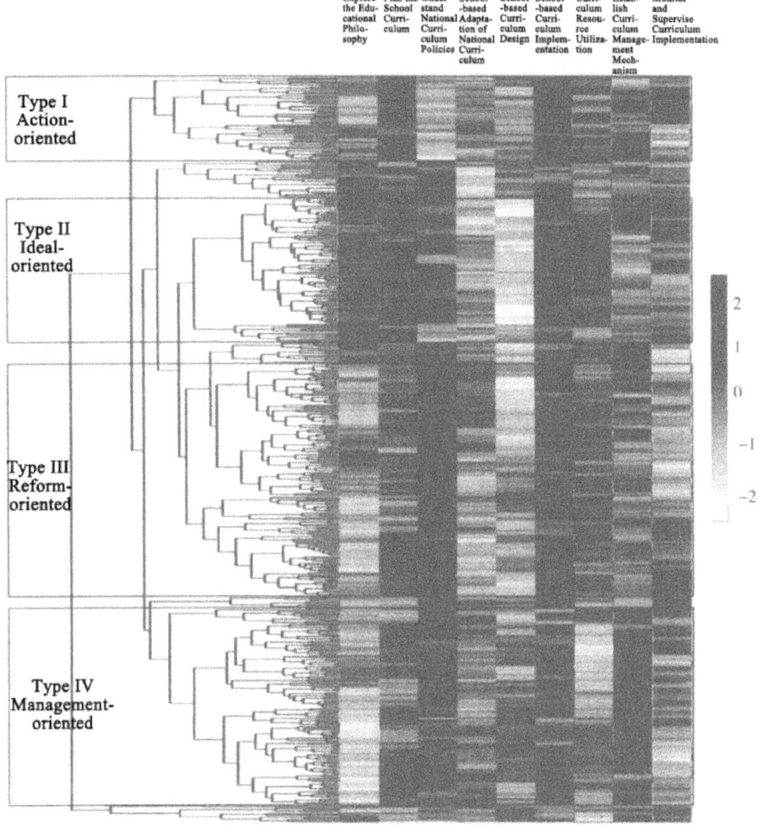

Figure 4-6 Cluster Heatmap of the Principal's Curriculum Leadership Competency

Principals of Type I, II, III and IV classified in this study have some identical performances in certain dimensions, thus becoming principals with four different characteristics. For the 461 principals surveyed, they can generally be classified into four types of principals with different curriculum leadership competency characteristics. Principals of Type I are action-oriented, who perform poorly in "understand national curriculum policies", but have excellent performances in "plan the school curriculum" and "school-based curriculum implementation". Principals of this type have experience in leading the curriculum reform, but their reform ideas mainly come from directly learning from other schools with insufficient understanding of policy basis. This type accounts for about 18% of the total number of principals. Principals of Type II are ideal-oriented, who have extremely excellent performances in "explore the educational philosophy", but perform poorly in some aspects such as "school-based curriculum design" and "school-based adaptation of national curriculum". This type accounts for about 15% of the total number. In practice, principals of this type are good at grasping the macro development direction of schools but lack experience in handling curriculum affairs. Principals of Type III are reform-oriented. Principals of this type score very high in "understand national curriculum policies" and also have good performances in aspects such as "plan the school curriculum" and "school-based adaptation of national curriculum", but perform poorly in "explore the educational philosophy" and "school-based curriculum design". They account for about 30% of the total number of principals. Principals of this type have experience in curriculum reform and have implemented curriculum reform in schools, but they have certain deficiencies in curriculum development theories and professional techniques. Principals of Type IV are management-oriented. They have excellent performances in "establish curriculum management mechanism", but are slightly insufficient in the two dimensions of "curriculum resource utilization" and "explore the educational philosophy". Principals of this type are also good at planning the operation mechanism and institution of schools and have little experience in handling professional curriculum affairs. Principals of this type account for 20%-25% of the number surveyed in this study.

(2) Differences in the Principal's Curriculum Leadership Competency

1. Gender Differences in the Principal's Curriculum Leadership Competency

In this study, a total number of 305 male principals and 156 female principals are surveyed. According to the significance analysis of SPSS, it can be found that significant differences have emerged between male principals and female principals in both the overall scores and the scores of multiple dimensions. The average score of male principals' total scores is 134.15, with a standard deviation of 10.80, and the average score of female principals' total scores is 137.33, with a standard deviation of 8.66. The difference in total scores is extremely significant at the level of $P < 0.01$, indicating that female principals' curriculum leadership is significantly higher than that of male principals. And the analysis of the violin plot of the data distribution (as illustrated in Figure 4-7) indicates that the scores of female principals are significantly higher than those of male principals because there are no individuals with lower scores among the female principals, while male principals exhibit greater score dispersion.

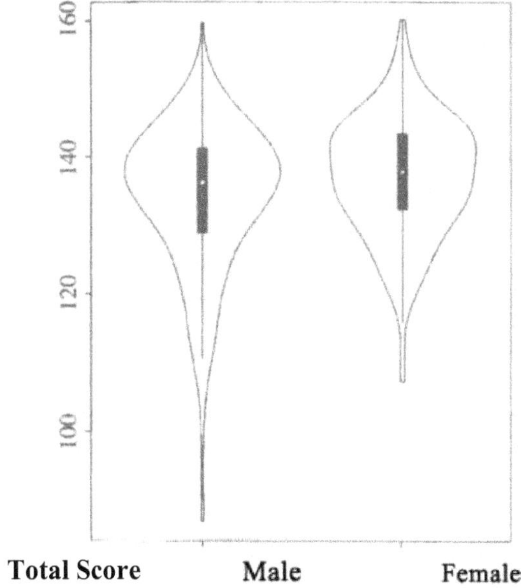

Figure 4-7 Violin Plot of the Curriculum Leadership Competency Scores for Male and Female Principals

In addition, we use SPSS to conduct a significant difference analysis on the gender differences in each dimension. The dimensions at the level of $P < 0.05$ are presented by the violin plot (as illustrated in Figure 4-8). It can be found that male principals are significantly higher than female principals in the item of "explore the educational philosophy", and both their upper quartile and median are higher than those of female principals. However, in terms of the four evaluation points of "plan the school curriculum", "understand national curriculum policies", "school-based adaptation of national curriculum" and "establish curriculum management mechanism", the curriculum leadership competency of female principals is significantly higher than that of male principals. This is particularly evident in the item of "understand national curriculum policies", where the lower quartile of female principals is higher than the upper quartile of male principals. This indicates male principals prioritize macro-level strategic vision and concept innovation, while female principals have more experience in personally leading curriculum practice and have better understanding of national policies.

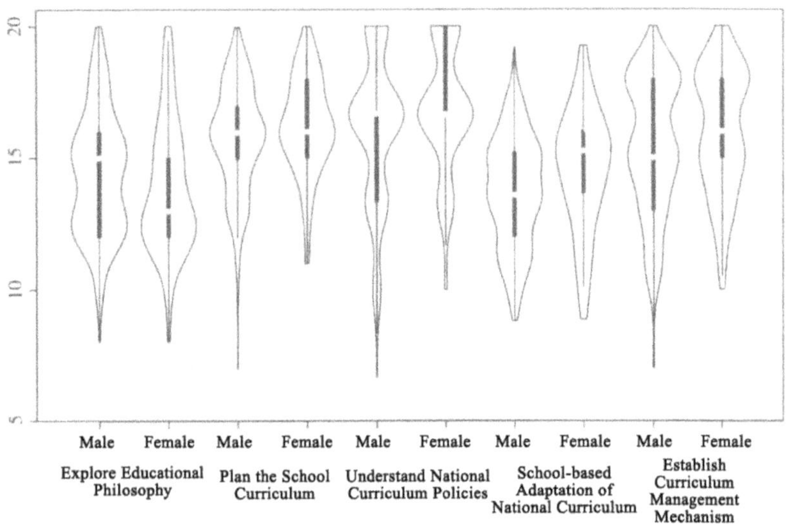

Figure 4-8 Violin Plot of Dimensions with Significant Differences in Curriculum Leadership Competency between Male and Female Principals

2. Differences with Different Educational Background

The first degree of the principals surveyed in this study are secondary normal school, teachers college, bachelor's degree in teacher education, bachelor's degree in non-teacher education and others, with the numbers being 202, 137, 93, 11 and 18 respectively. The highest degree are junior college, bachelor's degree, master's degree and doctoral degree, with the numbers being 33, 386, 41 and 1 respectively. There is no difference shown in the significance statistics of the total scores among principals with different educational background. A special case is the only doctor in the surveyed sample, whose total score of 160.2 is the highest. However, due to the extremely small sample size of this kind, the score does not have statistical significance. In the significant difference analysis of all content dimensions, only in the item of "plan the school curriculum" does master's degree holders score significantly higher than undergraduates and junior college students, with the mean value differences being 1.45 (P=0.008) and 0.86 (P=0.031) respectively. Generally speaking, the difference in educational background has limited impact on the principal's curriculum competency.

3. Differences in Different Educational Stages

The survey includes 73 principals from nine-year compulsory education schools, 247 junior high school principals, and 141 primary school principals. From the perspective of the significant difference in total scores, the curriculum leadership competency of primary school principals is significantly better than that of principals of nine-year compulsory education schools and junior high school principals, with the mean value differences being 4.34 (P=0.011) and 4.773 ($P < 0.001$) respectively. It can be found from the data structure diagram (as illustrated in Figure 4-9) that the reason why primary school principals have high scores is that there are no individual in the low score range. There are quite a number of junior high school principals in the low score range, and the degree of dispersion is also large. However, the highest score also appears in junior high school. From the perspective of all content dimensions (as illustrated in Table 4-5), primary school principals are significantly better than junior high school principals regarding "understand national curriculum policies", "school-based adaptation of national curriculum", "curriculum resource utilization" and "establish curriculum management mechanism", and are significantly better than principals of nine-year compulsory education schools regarding "understand national curriculum policies" and "establish curriculum management mechanism". The above indicates that primary school principals have more space to practice curriculum reform and more experiences in leading curriculum construction, thus improving their level of curriculum leadership competency.

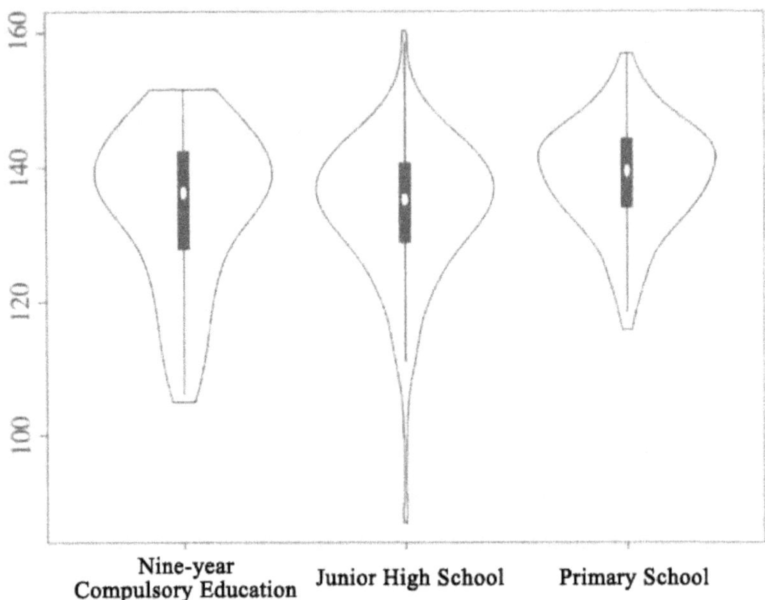

Figure 4-9 Violin Plot of the Overall Curriculum Leadership Competency of Principals at Different School-running Levels

Table 4-5 Significant Differences Analysis in Each Evaluation Point of the Principal's Curriculum Leadership Competency at Different School-running Levels

Dimensions	Nine-Year Compulsory Education (M/SD)	Junior High School (M/SD)	Primary School (M/SD)	F-value	Post hoc Multiple Comparison
Explore Educational Philosophy	14.08/2.14	14.40/2.52	13.96/2.25	1.608	n.s.

Dimensions	Nine-Year Compulsory Education (M/SD)	Junior High School (M/SD)	Primary School (M/SD)	F-value	Post hoc Multiple Comparison
Plan the School Curriculum	15.89/2.16	15.85/2.04	16.09/1.84	0.694	n.s.
Understand National Curriculum Policies	15.84/3.03	16.03/2.93	17.23/2.11	10.358**	Primary School >Nine-Year** Primary School> Junior High School**
School-based Adaptation of National Curriculum	14.05/2.37	13.51/2.04	14.74/2.17	14.993**	Primary School> Junior High School**
School-based Curriculum Design	13.27/3.27	12.93/3.14	13.58/2.81	2.060	n.s.
School-based Curriculum Implementation	16.29/1.44	16.52/1.50	16.68/1.32	1.820	n.s.
Curriculum Resource Utilization	15.05/1.89	14.81/2.21	15.43/1.80	4.128*	Primary School> Junior High School*
Establish Curriculum Management Mechanism	15.37/2.74	15.23/2.54	16.33/2.25	8.991**	Primary School >Nine-Year* Primary School> Junior High School**
Monitor and Supervise Curriculum Implementation	14.27/2.49	14.42/2.48	14.42/2.33	0.106	n.s.

Note: ** indicates P<0.01, * indicates P<0.05.

4. Difference Analysis of Training Factors

This study investigates whether principals have received principal leadership training for more than one month and curriculum construction training for more than one month. Among them, 344 participants have received principal leadership training for more than one month and 117 participants have not, and 244 participants have received curriculum construction training for more than one month and 217 participants have not. As illustrated in Table 4-6, there is no significant relationship between principal leadership training and the total score of principal's curriculum leadership competency. However, the leadership training has a significant impact on "explore educational philosophy" for principals. Whether principals have received curriculum construction training for more than one month is significantly related to the total score of their curriculum leadership competency, and it is very significantly related to the dimension of "school-based curriculum design". Obviously, different training contents have different impacts on principals. A systematic one-month specialized curriculum training has an impact on principals' curriculum leadership competency. Among them, curriculum design is the most professional and technical content, at which principals are different to be competent only with general management experience. So specialized training really plays a significant role.

Table 4-6 Significant Differences Analysis in Dimensions and Total Scores of the Principal's Curriculum Leadership Competency across Different Training Programs

	Explore the Educational Philosophy	Plan the School Curriculum	Understand National Curriculum Policies	School-based Adaptation of National Curriculum	School-based Curriculum Design	School-based Curriculum Implementation	Curriculum Resource Utilization	Establish Curriculum Management Mechanism	Monitor and Supervise Curriculum Implementation	Total Score
Principal Leadership Training	2.123*	1.968	1.089	1.183	-0.085	1.289	0.590	1.537	-1.437	0.737
Curriculum Development Training	-0.023	-0.162	1.042	1.889	2.635**	0.576	-0.359	1.861	1.827	2.342*

Note: ** indicates P<0.01, * indicates P<0.05

IV. Reflections on the Development and Application of the Measurement Instrument

1. The Measurement Instrument Possesses both Fidelity and Limitations

Situational tests offer moderate fidelity but cannot fully replicate real-world contexts. The measurement instrument developed this time also has such characteristics. The test can examine whether the subjects can identify the theoretical logic and action principles behind the situations. However, the ability to describe and reflect situations is limited after all, and cannot fully reproduce the complexity of educational practice, so the completely authentic examination of educational behaviors can only be completed in real situations. The competency evaluation in this test is more task-oriented, while the factors "below the iceberg" such as motivation, traits, self-concept, and attitude within the competency are not sufficiently addressed.

2. The Typicality of Situational Test Questions Determines Their Non-sustainability in Use

The situational questions developed this time are compiled based on typical problems in school curriculum construction against the background of the current curriculum reform. These problems reflect the phased misunderstandings, confusions, and issues in the process of curriculum reform. However, with the development of curriculum reform and the deepening of the principal's practical experience with curriculum, the currently prevalent issues will gradually improve. At the same time, the curriculum reform will also face new challenges, and new typical problems will emerge in school curriculum. Therefore, these situational test questions have a time limit in application and need to be continuously revised with the development of the change.

3. Attempts at Multi-level Data Analysis

This study initially attempts to use various R language programs in the field of artificial intelligence for graphical display. For example, violin plots and rose garland diagrams are used to show the multi-dimensional distribution patterns of data. This can not only help understand basic data information such as the average and standard deviation of the principal's competency but also clearly and intuitively explain the direct reasons for a series of numerical differences, so as to facilitate educational researchers to conduct cause analysis or summary of laws from a more concrete level[1], thus making the data more presentable and describing reality more accurately.

[Originally published in *Curriculum, Teaching Material and Method* 2019(9) (Lv Lijie, Ding Yiran & Yang Man)]

---

1 Chapman, C., & Feit, M. D. *R for Marketing Research and Analytics*[M], Springer International Publishing, 2015.

18. Curriculum Action Research Inquiry: A Study from the Perspective of Methodology

Fullan posits that educational change is a process, not an event.[1] This is especially true of curriculum change. We say that this process is a process of cultural turn and must also be a process of research. As the new curriculum reform advances and the “teacher-as-researcher” paradigm gains traction, teachers’ curriculum research has become the focus for initiating and promoting curriculum change and an effective way to enhance the professionalization of the teaching profession. Curriculum action research is an important and unavoidable form of teachers’ curriculum research. Therefore, it is necessary for us to take the curriculum action research as an issue to conduct theoretical analysis and reflection.

I. Grasp the Meaning of “Curriculum Action Research”

(1) The Emergence of the Curriculum Action Research Concept

Action research, as an intuitive concept - using information to evaluate and make decisions on how to improve practice, may be as old as teaching behavior itself. As a research method, action research emerged after the 20th century and was reflected in the activities of some progressive educators. For example, they hoped to find a method to analyze the work of talented teachers so as to obtain something that others could learn from their work. In the 1940s, John Collier and Kurt Lewin systematically summarized and applied the action research method in their own research work and had a great impact. Collier applied the action research method in applied anthropology research. In the study on the methods to ensure democracy in ethnic minority areas, he adopted methods such as the participation of Indians and non-directive consultation by experts,

---

1 Fullan, M. *The Meaning of Educational Change*[M]. New York: Teachers College Press, 1982:41.

emphasizing that actions were caused by community needs and that the community directly benefited from the research. Lewin adopted the action research method in social psychological research and described his research process in his article *Action Research and Minority Problems* in 1946, standardizing it into three steps: planning - executing - reconnaissance. He pointed out that in order to understand and change a certain social practice, social scientists must consider those real social practitioners at each step. Lewin's constructed action research theory made action research an acceptable and operable research method. The research of Collier and Lewin was carried out under the social background of the Great Depression, World War II, and the emergence of ethnic minority issues and was closely related to the progressive movement. In the 1950s, with the decline of progressive education and the change of the social background, people's interest in action research decreased. In the 1960s and early 1970s, action research became consultants providing advice to practitioners. In the mid-1970s, action research began to revive. With the needs of educational change, action research has been widely used in educational research in the United Kingdom, the United States, Australia and other countries. For example, the Humanities Curriculum Project directed by Stenhouse in the United Kingdom, the Ford Teaching Project hosted by Elliot, and the research carried out by Kemmis and others in Deakin University in Australia, all strongly advocated the approach of action research. At the end of the 1980s, Mckernan first officially used the term "curriculum action research" in his article and published the monograph Curriculum Action Research in 1991. In the book, he explored the history and philosophical basis of the action research movement, the standards of ethical rules for teachers as researchers and professionals, the handling of observation, narration, self-study, reporting techniques, conversation analysis methods in the implementation of action research, the problem-solving techniques for teaching problems in teaching and learning situations, as well as strategies for solving teaching problems (brainstorming, group discussion), various procedures and techniques for critical reflection, evaluation and analysis of action research materials, the establishment of action research network organizations and associations, and case studies of action research.

(2) The Concept of Curriculum Action Research: Commonality Amid Complexity

Concepts are both descriptions of reality and historical interpretations embedded in practice. For action research, what people see and pursue are not exactly the same. For example, Elliot[1] defined action research as the study of a social situation with a view to improving the quality of action within it. Its purpose is not to write research reports or publish works but to understand events, situations and problems, thereby increasing their effectiveness in solving practical problems. Kolb[2] extended the concept of the action research system. As a learning process, people learn and create knowledge by criticizing and reflecting on their own behavior and experience, forming abstract concepts and testing the application of these concepts in new situations. Practitioners can create their own knowledge, understand situations and behaviors, and improve practical development knowledge in this field. Wilfred Carr[3] conceptualized action research through a critical-emancipatory lens as a form of self-reflective inquiry, in which practitioners improve teaching practices and their understanding of these practices in social situations and explain the fairness and rationality of these practices. In fact, action research also has some other names: cooperative inquiry, participatory action research, action inquiry, appreciative inquiry, research partnerships, etc. Action research seems to be a big family. It is not a single method but an approach that combines research and action.

---

1 Elliot, J. *Action Research for Educational Change*[M]. Bristol, Pennsylvania: Open University Press, 1991.

2 Kolb, D. A. *Experiential Learning: Experience as the Source of Learning and Development*[M]. Englewood Cliffs, New Jersey: Prentice-Hall, 1984.

3 Carr, W., & Kemmis, S. *Becoming Critical: Education, Knowledge, and Action Research*[M]. Philadelphia, PA: The Falmer Press, Taylor&-Francis Inc, 1986.

No matter from which angle the definition of action research is described, it must contain certain common beliefs that gather people under the banner of curriculum research. Among the various forms of curriculum action research, we think that four elements are very crucial: power sharing, participation and cooperation, knowledge acquisition, and social change. Curriculum action research must be an activity process that combines research and action to solve the practical problems encountered by teachers in the curriculum field. Researchers, including teachers, cooperate to jointly explore the nature and scope of the problems, understand the causes of their occurrence, seek solutions, and put them into practice. This process includes five necessary characteristics: (1) The research topic comes from the specific curriculum implementation situation in schools. (2) The purpose of the research is to solve practical curriculum problems, rather than or not mainly to establish theories or universal problem-solving solutions. (3) The process of curriculum implementation is the process of curriculum research. (4) Teachers participate in the research and negotiate equally with other researchers to jointly interpret and explore curriculum problems. (5) The research process requires continuous evaluation and repeated implementation. McKernan[1] has also summarized the three basic principles of curriculum action research: "Teachers as Researchers". He believes that people experiencing real situations are the best people to conduct research and exploration, and teachers are one of the main bodies of curriculum research. "Naturalistic and Practical Orientation". He believes that human behaviors are deeply influenced by the real situations in which they occur, and behaviors are behaviors in situations. "Priority of Field Study and Qualitative Methods". Field study seeks to understand and describe rather than measure and predict results. Qualitative research emphasizes the subjective feelings of participant observers, the narration of the environment, and personal subjective values, and interprets

---

1 McKernan, J. *Curriculum Action Research: A Handbook of Methods and Resources for the Reflective Practitioner*[M]. New York: St. Martin's Press Inc, 1991.

the observed phenomena empathically.

(3) Types of Curriculum Action Research

According to the premises and assumptions of curriculum action researchers in their research, curriculum action research can be divided into three types: technical, practical, and emancipatory.[1]

1. Technical action research. It is assumed that there are universal and objective curriculum plans, and the research is to test the rationality of the assumptions. The characteristics of researchers and collaborators are technical and facilitating. Researchers dictate problem definition and implementation, while practitioners comply and agrees to the method implementation. The communication in this research form is mainly between the facilitator and the group. The research is directed by one or more experts, and the purpose of the research is to obtain a more effective implementation method. The research activities are centered on achievements and are carried out within the existing conditions and limitations.

2. Practical action research. In this type, the research assumptions are often open, and the research problems are generated in the research process. The research plan is a potentially problematic issue jointly determined by the researcher and the participants, as well as their next goals and possible implementation methods. The purpose of action research is to develop new implementation methods, and the problems are defined after the researcher and the practitioner have a dialogue and understand each other. This type is called practical or pedagogical because this kind of action research attempts to improve practice by applying the wisdom of the participants. In this kind of action research, the communication between group members and helpers cannot cause mutual harm. The research activities focus on the process and rely on personal

---

1 Grundy, S. Three Modes of Action Research[J]. *Curriculum Perspectives*, 1982(3):23-24.

wisdom to guide actions.

3. Emancipatory action research. This type of action research is an exercise to enhance the emancipatory consciousness among participating practitioners, that is, to enhance the critical consciousness, which is manifested in political and change-promoting practices. Researchers using this method have two purposes. One is to improve the closeness of the connection between practitioners in a specific situation when facing practical problems and the theories used to explain and solve these problems. The second purpose is to help practitioners identify and elaborate on the basic principles of the problems by enhancing their cooperative consciousness. In the research, the research process is arranged by the group members themselves, and the purpose is to develop new implementation methods or break through the existing ideological or institutional limitations. This type of action research requires a radical reform consciousness. Therefore, some people think that this type of action research is very rare and requires a group of participants with strong judgment and radical reform consciousness to work together for a long time.

II. Research on the Methods and Methodologies of Curriculum Action Research

(1) General Procedures of Curriculum Action Research

There is broad consensus on the procedural stages of action research, which is also an important reason why people recognize the existence of the concept of curriculum action research. Borrowing Altrichter's statement, we believe that educational action research can be divided into four stages: finding a starting point, clarifying the situation, developing action strategies and putting them into practice, and making knowledge accessible to others. Carr and Kemmis also think that action research is a continuous cyclic process, including the identification of problems, action planning, implementation, evaluation and reflection. These understandings are obtained from the initial cycle to the planning of the second cycle, during which the action plan will be revised and the research will be repeated.

Therefore, we can precisely define curriculum action research as such a continuous cyclic process: First, identify the problem. The problem comes from the difficulties encountered in practice and is also the starting point of the research. For example, the research on the effect of classroom group discussions. This topic comes from the confusion of teachers in curriculum implementation and is a problem that teachers urgently need to solve in teaching. Second, collect and analyze data. This stage includes research behaviors such as observation, reflection, and communication by actors and researchers. For example, teachers reflect on the reasons for designing group discussions, the classroom situation at that time, observe the discussion status and students' achievements, and understand students' perceptions of group discussions. The data should be described in detail, and at this time, researchers should not give too much value guidance. Third, formulate specific action plans. Assumptions are made about the factors affecting group discussions, such as the appropriateness of curriculum content, the form of organization, or students' interests, and simultaneously formulate action plans and strategies. Fourth, implement, reflect and derive meaning. These three links should occur intertwined, and the implementation process is constantly monitored and reflected upon, leading either to strategy adjustment or to definite explanations for behaviors and results. The conclusions of observation and reflection are presented in the form of group discussions, written reports or thesis.

(2) Methodological Interpretation of Curriculum Action Research

The resurgence of curriculum action research coincided with the 20th-century paradigm shift in curriculum studies.[1] It was premised and based on the shift in human thinking and had sufficient methodological impetus to compete with traditional positivism. Therefore, it is necessary to reflect on the methodology of curriculum action research to improve the selection, application, and value assessment of different methods in practice.

Curriculum action research is a rebellion against the doctrines of rationalism, especially instrumental rationality. Since the Enlightenment, the core idea of Western social thought has been to break away from divinity, and the rationality represents truth and progress. If Galileo's experimental method is regarded as the symbol of the positivization of natural science, Descartes and Bacon has rationalized and ideologized this research attitude. "I think, therefore I am" and "Knowledge is power" can be said to be the declarations of the modern rationalist movement. The 16th and 17th centuries were a period of great development of natural science, which was distinguished from other forms of knowledge by its methodology. In the 1820s, the French philosopher Comte introduced this positivist spirit into social science. He believed that society could also be studied logically and rationally, and sociology should become a science like biology and physics. With the booming of the Industrial Revolution, the will to power and the desire for control in humans became the turn of the rational spirit, and the opposition between the mathematical tradition and the experimental tradition converged into "instrumental rationality" here. At the beginning of the 20th century, rationality was not only used for the analysis of social phenomena but also served for the management of social activities and the research of educational science. Thorndike is claimed to have said that "everything that exists must exist in some quantity and can therefore be measured". The creed of quantification and experimentation makes educational

1 Ma Yunpeng & Lv Lijie. The Evolution and Reflection of Modern Curriculum Research Paradigm[J]. *Educational Research*, 2002(9).

research, including curriculum research, follow a completely different trajectory from practice. Undoubtedly, the progress of science and technology in the 20th century has brought earth-shaking changes to human life, but at the same time threw humans into environmental pollution, energy crises and world wars.... The deification of rationality also plunged humans into crises, and the rebellion and turn of human thought were bound to come. First, in the field of natural science research, quantum mechanics, cosmology, especially the publication of Einstein's theory of relativity (and its verification in the solar eclipse observation four years later) completely shook the foundation of the scientific rational edifice - Newtonian mechanics. Driven by this major scientific event, Popper's falsification theory and Kuhn's historiography science began to challenge rationality in the form of rationality. In fact, in the field of sociological research, doubts about Comte's positivist sociology emerged at the end of the 19th century. Human differences, plasticity, and difficulty in verification have intuitively told us that human society has characteristics different from those of the natural world. Therefore, we cannot assert the whole society by observing a person just as natural scientists infer all the properties of a substance by observing molecules. The German sociologist and philosopher Dilthey is a representative of this view. He believes that due to human free will, human behavior is irregular and unpredictable, and historical events are unique and accidental, and there are no universal historical laws. Therefore, the study of humans and society can only use subjective methods to interpret and explain individuals and events. At the beginning of the 20th century, facing people's belief in rationalism in educational research, Dewey once reminded: "The science of education cannot be established solely by using the experimental and measurement techniques in physics." We should seek "methods to analyze the work of talented teachers so as to obtain something that others can learn from their work."[1] Therefore, it is not difficult to explain the fact that doctrines such as action research were fully promoted after rationalism was deconstructed in the middle of the 20th century.

Specifically, curriculum action research is based on several important ideological sources:

1. Humans Are the Subjects of Self-selection

After Kant and Hegel, rationalism seems to have completed its mission of exploring human thought. In fact, as early as the middle of the 19th century, philosophers had already shouted for the liberation of rationality, which converged into a trend of humanistic thought and deeply influenced the 20th century. For example, Nietzsche believed that excessive emphasis on rationality withered the tree of life and made people lose themselves. He said: "God is dead, and now we hope for the birth of the Superman." Bergson said that God is unceasing life, action, freedom. The universe is not created by God but is constantly generated by the impulse of life in duration. "Each of us can live but one life, a choice must perforce be made." Kierkegaard, starting from the "single individual", directly pointed to Hegel's rationalism. "Only the emotional experience of the spiritual self is the most authentic existence of the individual."... This trend of humanistic thought has a common tendency, which is to call for human individuality and freedom, trying to liberate people from the new "divinity" - the shackles of rationality and laws, and realize the freedom of human choice and creation and the right to exist. Researchers who believe in rationalism objectify the research objects. The research objects not only have no decision-making power but are even isolated from the research process. The research activities are "deified". Although this kind of research seems objective,

---

1 Noffke, S. *Themes and Tensions of Action Research*[C]//Hollingsworth, S. *International Action Research: A Casebook for Educational Reform*. Translated by Huang Yu. Beijing: China Light Industry Press Ltd., 2000.

it may not reflect the integrity, authenticity and fluidity of the research objects, so its conclusions may not be effective for the research objects. Action research restores human power. Humans are the authors of their own actions, and the reasons for behaviors are their own judgments and choices. Since it studies human behaviors and experiences, and how to behave, the research objects should also be one of the decision-makers. Conversely, all personnel who restrict and influence the problems, orientations, processes, and conclusions of the research, whether they are action implementers or interveners, should also be research objects.

2. All Human Knowledge Is Value-laden

Scientists themselves have long doubted the objectivity of human knowledge: what a person sees depends not only on the object he sees but also on the guidance of previous visual-conceptual experiences (Kuhn). Theory determines what you can observe (Einstein). Observation is permeated with theory (Hanson). Theory precedes observation (Popper). Observation depends on theory (Chalmers).[1] The phenomenological movement originating from Husserl completely inherits this doubt, and the core idea of the phenomenological method is "going back to the things themselves". From Heidegger's ontology to Gadamer's hermeneutics, this cognitive method has been elevated to the height of philosophical ontology. In their view, people are "thrown" into this world and are destined to have "preconceptions". "Pre-understanding" and "pre-interpretation" doom our understanding to be unable to be neutral. It must be historical. "Understanding has never been a subjective act towards a given object, but belongs to the effective history of the understood thing. That is to say, understanding belongs to the existence of the understood thing." This kind of "effective history" understanding is legitimate because

---

1 Popper, K. *Unended Quest: An Intellectual Autobiography*[M]. Translated by Zhao Yuese. Shanghai: Shanghai Translation Publishing House, 1988.

"what people need is not to persevere in pursuing ultimate questions, but to know what works, what is possible, and what is correct here and now."[1] In action research, neither actors nor researchers can truly be value-neutral. They all enter the research site with their own educational beliefs and judgment standards. What matters is that the collaborators can truly understand each other and have a fusion of horizons. Of course, there is also a shift towards subjectivity as a prerequisite, that is, the shift from the singularity of the subject to intersubjectivity, recognizing the pluralization of the subject and the consistency and commonality among multiple parallel subjects, that is, the possibility of different subjects having the same understanding of a certain object. Facing common curriculum problems, different subjects influence each other with their different horizons, which may be subjective but not necessarily negative.

3. Human Activities Have an Interest in Liberation

Critical theory is an important branch of modern philosophy. The Frankfurt School, represented by Habermas and Horkheimer, is deeply influenced by Marxist philosophy and at the same time accepts the hermeneutic methodology. With its unique social critical perspective, it stood out in the ideological camp of the 20th century. Habermas believes that human cognitive interests determine human scientific activities, and each scientific activity has its own special cognitive interests. He divided interests into three types: technical interest, practical interest, and emancipatory interest. Among them, the emancipatory interest is human interest in freedom, independence and the subject, which is "to liberate the subject from the forces attached to objectification". Habermas believes that only the critical social science guided by the emancipatory interest can solve the dilemma of tense human social relations. "The self-reflective

---

1 Gadamer, H. *Wahrheit und Methode: Second Edition*[M]// Hong Handing. Classic Hermeneutics Anthology. Beijing: The Oriental Press, 2001:182.

activity of changing life is an emancipatory activity."[1] The emancipatory interest is based on the subject reflection, and is manifested in the action research as suspicion, suspension, examination and criticism of existing theories, conclusions, and concepts, and exploring the deep social, historical and cultural meanings behind behaviors.

According to Western Marxist critics, action researchers often neglect to explain the historical, social, political and cultural forces that lead to students' silence and defensive states. The way to transcend this accused approach is to link teacher researchers with the emancipatory pedagogy. For example, Paulo Freire advocates teacher-student cooperation, with problems coming from real-life situations, and seeking solutions through questioning and reflection. Even if their actions are not successful, students will gain new knowledge and viewpoints and learn to criticize in thinking and actions.

III. Defense of the Rationality of Curriculum Action Research

(1) Curriculum Action Research Is a Pursuit of Goodness

The reemergence of curriculum action research mirrored the 20th-century epistemological shift in human thought. In contrast to the experimental and quantitative positivist orientations of curriculum research, the logical purpose of curriculum research exploration has shifted from exploring the external standards of the curriculum to focusing on the inherent scale of human beings, interpreting experiences, recognizing interactions, and presenting the whole. What it cares about is no longer the laws of the phenomenal world but an ontological pursuit and interest. Here, the ontology is no longer an entity, nor even just the ultimate existence itself, but an intentional pursuit, a commitment

---

1 Habermas, J. *Erkenntnis und Interesse*[M]. Translated by Guo Guanyi & Li Li. Shanghai: Xuelin Press, 1999.

to the ideal. It is based on the supremacy of human thinking, and always presupposing an ideal goal that is rooted in reality and transcends reality. It pursues idealistic realities through practical certainty, sustaining human activities in a state of virtuous tension, vitality, and the tension of self-criticism and self-transcendence. The justice of curriculum research lies in the fact that the process of this research is always a process of pursuing ontology and the ideal state, a unity of presupposition and generation, and a dialectical negation of the rationality of the existing curriculum state. Curriculum action research abandons the absolute certainty and absolute reasoning of positivism, corrects misinterpretations, breaks down assumptions, and dispels deification from a practice-oriented way of thinking. With an activity-oriented and generative viewpoint and taking problem-solving as the fundamental, it reserves necessary choices for itself among different methods and instantaneously reconstructs its own thinking. In action research, there is no absolute right or wrong in methods, only refined or clumsy usage. Researchers are neither captives of established method programs nor need to reject any method programs a priori. What matters is to make choices among complementarity and diversity.

(2) Curriculum Characteristics Determine the Practical Value of Curriculum Action Research

Curriculum reform is not merely a policy or instrumental (textbooks, facilities) shift but a cultural transformation at its core. It is rooted in all schools, all teachers, and all classrooms. Many Western curriculum scholars admit that many previous curriculum reforms have failed before they are truly implemented. Teachers hold the direction of curriculum reform. As a strategy for curriculum cultural change, curriculum action research is an effective intermediary between national curriculum and teacher curriculum. Elliot (1991) argues that action research bridges top-down policy mandates and bottom-up teacher-led curriculum development.[1] Because on the one hand, the curriculum development and change at the national level need pilot experiments and can be continuously reviewed and revised through curriculum action research. On the other hand, school curriculum and teacher curriculum development can also improve their theoretical basis and educational efficacy through curriculum action research. In addition, curriculum action research is of great significance for promoting the improvement of teachers' professional abilities and the formation of collective professional confidence. Most general educational research is mainly led by researchers. Even if teachers participate in research groups, they mostly play the role of assistants. However, action research is jointly constructed and shared by everyone. Teachers have decision-making power, which will make the research more in line with their own curriculum practice, and they can experience and understand in close combination with practice to achieve the improvement of professional abilities. In addition, when teachers communicate their tacit knowledge with others, they must undergo in-depth reflection on experience, thereby establishing professional thinking habits such as examination, criticism and construction. In generally, teachers' action research will basically lead to three aspects of results: the improvement of theoretical level and professional skills; the improvement of one's understanding of the meaning behind curriculum implementation behaviors; and the improvement of the actual effect of curriculum implementation.

(3) Explanation of the Rationality of the Conclusions of Curriculum Action Research

Curriculum action research comes from specific implementation situations, including specific curriculum content, curriculum resources, teacher conditions and student characteristics. The research process is also a process of subjective

1 Huang Kuang-Hsiung & Tsai Ching-Tien. *Curriculum Design*[M]. Taipei: Wu-Nan Book Inc., 1999.

decision-making. Therefore, the research conclusions are highly subjective, individual and holistic for individuals. Compared with quantitative research, its conclusions do not have the ability to provide universal explanations or be widely promoted, so they are also questioned by some people. In this regard, the qualitative researcher's understanding is the most convincing. They believe that the problem is not whether the research cases are representative, but which category they represent. When readers with similar experiences resonate with the research results, it indicates both the broader dissemination of the ideas and the validation of the study's credibility. In addition, not all research needs to have a direct effect on decision making. Research results can be part of the information for decision-makers and interact with other research in the decision-making information network. Regarding the results of curriculum action research, the presentation of curriculum action research should attach importance to describing the mental process of researchers in the research. Chinese scholar Fang Zhihua's suggestion based on the Ethics of Care is worth noting. He believes that researchers inject subjective feelings into educational works, so that readers can be inspired and get courage from them. In addition to understanding the techniques of solving problems, readers should also feel the intentions and creative spirit of practitioners. Therefore, the research report should not only present the research results, but also the learning derived from the researchers' feelings and actions during the research process.[1]

[Originally published in *Studies in Foreign Education* 2003(3) (Lv Lijie & Ma Yunpeng)]

---

1 National Institute for Educational Policy Research of the Ministry of Education, Culture, Sports, Science and Technology. Survey on the Implementation of the National Curriculum in Elementary, Lower Secondary and Upper Secondary Schools [EB/OL] [2015-11-01]. http://www.Mext.go.jp/b_menu/shingi/chukyo/chukyo3/004siryo/06080913/010/012.htm.

19. Reflection on Teacher Practical Knowledge Study and Its Enlightenment

Since the 1980s, inspired by Elbaz, Connelly, Clandinin, Schön, and others, teacher practical knowledge (TPK) has emerged as a pivotal area in teacher research. People no longer solely focus on compiling a set of established knowledge systems for qualified teachers. Instead, they focus on what knowledge teachers actually have or how teachers generate knowledge. The advocacy of teacher practical knowledge regards teachers' classroom practical life as the foundation and clarifies the fundamental purpose of knowledge production in teachers' professional lives. However, emphasizing practical knowledge does not mean that simply reversing the status and order of theoretical knowledge and practical knowledge will lead to a reasonable solution for teachers' professional development. What are the core characteristics of TPK? How does it influence teachers' practice?

I. Reflection on Practical Knowledge Study

(1) Practical Knowledge Needs Relative Corroboration

Gary D Fenstrmacher (1993), an educational philosophy scholar, believes that practical knowledge does not necessarily arise from teachers' practical activities. In other words, since it is called knowledge, it should still have relative stability. He critiques Connelly & Clandinin's exclusive focus on TPK while overlooking its epistemological validation, but they pay limited attention to the issue that knowledge should be tested. They strive to reveal what teachers actually know, but only examine it from the perspective of researchers, ignoring that teachers' knowledge should be verified, which is not beneficial to teachers' professional development. He believes that "some studies by Schön and

Clandinin are too hasty"[1]. Fenstrmacher's concern is reasonable. At least the research tendency of practical knowledge is likely to cause misunderstandings in practice. The emergence of teacher practical knowledge lies in the fact that people have discovered the paradoxes and difficulties in carrying out practical activities in a theoretical way of thinking. However, if we simply turn the problem upside down and record and believe in the conclusions obtained in practice as knowledge, there will also be problems. It doesn't mean that knowledge cannot be generated in practice, but the generation of knowledge in practice is a historical process. Reflection on accidental events can form experience, but it may not necessarily be knowledge or theory. Even if it is knowledge or theory that can guide oneself, Fenstrmacher's reminder is worthy of attention. "There are many studies on teacher practical knowledge that clearly show teachers' beliefs, intuitions, feelings, and reflective knowledge. However, the epistemological problem here is that these mental activities do not necessarily bring about real knowledge. These mental activity contents inferred and expressed must undergo the test of cognitive value. Without cognitive value, no matter what kind of teachers' understanding, beliefs or awareness, they cannot be defined as knowledge, or at least not as knowledge with cognitive value. Only when it has epistemological value can it be determined as knowledge. The use of practical knowledge should be cautious, and what is generated in practice also needs to be tested"[2].

(2) Practical Knowledge Is Relatively Individual

Practical knowledge requires corroboration, but "the question is whether there is a testing method for practical knowledge like the one for testing theoretical knowledge?" If the basis in practice is completely individual and

---

1 Fenstermacher, G. D. The Knower and the Known: The Nature of Knowledge in Research on Teaching[J]. *Review of Research in Education*, 1994(20):3-59.

2 Fenstermacher, G. D. The Knower and the Known: The Nature of Knowledge in Research on Teaching[J]. *Review of Research in Education*, 1994(20):3-59.

absolutely relative, it is obviously difficult to establish such a testing standard. The question is whether human practical activity is an absolutely individual operation process. Chinese philosopher Wang Nanshi posits that while practice objects are individually unique, but from the perspective of the subject's practice methods, it is impossible to use individual methods for each object"[1]. He believes that treating each individual thing individually can only be an aesthetic ideal. Even in aesthetic activities, it is very difficult for us to treat each individual thing individually, and we can only pursue this as much as possible. Denying the absolute individuality of the practical activity method does not mean admitting that abstract universal laws can be used in practice as in theoretical activities. Instead, it is to envisage establishing a method between the universal method of theory and the completely individual method, a "finite individual" or quasi-individual method, that is, to classify the objects into various categories, large or small, and practice according to the categories of things. "In essence, treating each individual uniquely is a divine capability, not a human one." In this way, "this practical world can only be a world constructed by human practice, a world that is somewhat categorized, a world composed of quasi-individual things"[2]. Practical knowledge is relatively individual knowledge. It can be analogized, imitated, felt and evaluated.

(3) Deliberation as a Way to Test Practical Knowledge

It is indeed difficult to find fixed rules and systems for testing practical knowledge. However, Western scholars Cochran-Smith & Lytle[3] and Fenstermacher endorse the use of teacher deliberation as a test of practical

---

1 Wang Nanshi. Rethinking the Relationship Between Theory and Practice[J]. *Zhejiang Academic Journal*, 2005(6):5-14.

2 Wang Nanshi. Rethinking the Relationship Between Theory and Practice[J]. *Zhejiang Academic Journal*, 2005(6):5-14..

3 Cochran-Smith, M., & Lytle, S. L. Relationships of Knowledge and Practice: Teacher Learning in Communities[J]. *American Education Research Association*, 1999(24):249-296.

knowledge. Smith and Lytle are very concerned about the cooperation topic between teachers and university researchers. In fact, their idea is a development of Schön's teacher reflection, combining teachers' personal reflection with theoretical explanations and combining the research among teachers' peers with that of professional researchers. Because in such deliberations, theoretical knowledge and discourse are understood and developed, forming new judgment patterns that are more adapted to practical discourse. In addition, the deliberation also satisfies the value characteristics of practical knowledge and can consider moral issues in practice.

(4) Distinguish the Practical Knowledge Nature and the Practical Cognition Types

Fenstrmacher believes that in the research on teacher knowledge, it should first be made clear that the type of knowledge and the way of cognition are different. The former refers to what the essence of knowledge is, while the latter refers to how people acquire knowledge. "When two persons examine according to different cognitive ways, the conclusions they obtain are different, and the things they see are different. However, the epistemological type of knowledge may not change"[1]. For this reason, the working methods of teachers and university researchers should be distinguished.

There are two main cognitive ways in educational research. One is the cognitive way frequently used by the teaching profession, and the other is the one often used by theoretical researchers. The purposes of their research are different, but they both engage in the acquisition of practical knowledge. Theoretical research is a thinking process that connects attributes into principles, and thinking relies on intuitive insights and rational analysis. This kind of research will also enter practical situations, but it is to extract the attributes and

---

1 Fenstermacher, G. D. The Knower and the Known: The Nature of Knowledge in Research on Teaching[J]. *Review of Research in Education*, 1994(20):3-59.

relationships in entities and “acquire knowledge”. It is precisely because theoretical research reveals various attributes of practical situations in a categorized manner that the understanding of practical situations will not be empty. However, after all, the pursuit of non-contradiction is the nature of theoretical thinking. The orientation of the research process will be more concerned with summarizing universal principles, that is, the focus of the research is on the universal principles and common essence of the attributes and relationships of the research objects. Teachers’ practical research, on the other hand, uses intuitive judgment to analyze and study the real structure of the research objects and the characteristics of elements. In such research, it is to examine as much as possible, rationally describe and reveal the non-essential attributes and overall characteristics of various elements in the curriculum situation. Of course, such a holistic approach can neither - nor need to - exhaustively cover every aspect of the subject. Like all value-driven selection centered on research questions, this study provides a basis for assimilating theoretical rules and models into the real-world structure, for further decision-making and value judgment, and for weighing the rationality of practice. The unity in the nature of knowledge does not mean that teachers’ practical activities can produce results in the same way as theoretical activities do. In research, practitioners and teachers employ distinct modes of thinking, and even utilize different research tools and methods. Teachers’ research is directed at problem-solving, specific operation methods, and obtaining conclusions on problems in situations.

II. Application Characteristics of Teacher Practical Knowledge

Teaching is inherently a practice-driven profession. In this process, theoretical knowledge and practical knowledge penetrate each other and are unified in practice, and are manifested in the forms of judgment, decision-making and action.

(1) The Judgment in Teacher Situation Has Modular and Simulated Characteristics

This is a matter of degree that needs to be handled carefully. Our criticism of traditional classrooms lies in their being mechanical, rigid and procedural. Teachers regard all the students they face as the same type of people and simplify all classrooms into one type of situation. Therefore, we call for classrooms to be dynamic, ecological and generative. However, as epistemology scholars have pointed out, the classification of various things in human practice cannot be pushed to the extreme. Teachers navigate practical problems through situational interpretation and cognitive structuring, with the characteristics of using block thinking and simulating thinking. They will classify the current situation and the students they face into certain types of judgments of their own or others'. And it is precisely because of such simulation and classification that it becomes possible for humans to understand things. Absolute individuality can represent the actual situation of things, but this kind of understanding is beyond human reach. For this reason, understanding in practice is a process of subjective construction. When teachers deal with individual things, they will also classify the individual things into certain categories or patterns in the structure of practical knowledge and strive to adapt and balance within the original structure. Therefore, the original practical knowledge structure plays a shaping role in teachers' new judgments.

(2) Teachers' Decision-making Is a Game of Various Factors

This critique of TPK research does not undermine its practical legitimacy but highlights its context-bound nature. It should be said that since people began to pay attention to teacher practical knowledge, they have already recognized and adapted to the characteristics of the non-systematic, diverse, and multi-level use of knowledge in teachers' work, that is, their thinking process does not rely on a consistent theory or logic but is a selection process in situations. Based on the needs of the situation, they extract elements from numerous principles, conventions, cognition and experiences and instantaneously combine them to form judgments. As for what elements are chosen and why these elements are chosen, it is a vague process. What can be determined is that it is not only influenced by teachers' cognitive experiences but also includes complex factors such as teachers' beliefs, emotions, needs, life experiences, personalities, and motivations. Ultimately, the adopted strategy is a process of the game among various factors.

(3) Teachers' Verification of Practical Knowledge Depends on the Effectiveness of Problem-solving

Theoretical knowledge's reflection on and guidance of teachers' original knowledge, as well as the conclusions obtained by teachers themselves or their peers in practice, will all impact teachers' knowledge structures. Whether it can finally become the practical knowledge that teachers believe in depends on the effectiveness of solving practical problems seen by teachers after applying knowledge and experience. However, in the process of applying knowledge and experience, if teachers misunderstand the theory itself and believe that the theory can provide absolute and comprehensive guidance in all situations, for all people and things, or if they set the standard of effectiveness to immediate and narrow interests, it will be difficult to form appropriate verification conclusions. Precisely because of this, practical knowledge needs to be tested, revised and disseminated in deliberations and instant conversations.

III. Examine the Construction Paths of Teacher Practical Knowledge

(1) Practical Knowledge Begins with Occasional Reflection

That is to say, we need to have in-depth reflections on the issues teachers have reflected upon. Some teachers said: "In recent years, our school has also advocated that teachers do reflections. We are required to submit a reflection diary every week. But actually, most of us don't really know how to reflect. In fact, I just think about whether my work is done correctly and how it should be improved." Teachers can make two kinds of judgments obtained through observation: one is a normative judgment, and the other is a descriptive judgment. The significance of teachers' reflection should lie in elevating descriptive judgments to normative judgments or using relevant normative judgments to measure and explain descriptive judgments, so as to form the "value" of reflection. Although the description of facts is vivid, it should not be the end point of teachers' reflection activities. Western scholar Clarke once reminded: In the past, the advocacy for teachers' reflection only called on teachers to do more reflections or required teachers to think carefully about what they were doing and why they were doing it. He believed that although this slogan-like advocacy reminded teachers to think hard, it was not necessarily conducive to teachers' professional development. More in-depth research requires teachers to answer such questions as "How does a person think hard? What to think about? What is the purpose of thinking?"[1] Human actions are necessarily accompanied by thinking. Not all activities that can be called reflections are predictable, as reflection activities are incidental and thematic. "Arnot (1994) also believes that Schön's distinction between 'reflection-in-action' and 'reflection-on-action' is theoretical rather than real. When examining real examples, it is very difficult to draw a clear line between the two"[2]. Teachers' reflection is not a requirement in terms of time and quantity. When "accidental" events occur, it needs to rely on some procedures, platforms or activity methods to deepen or extend thinking. Teachers' reflection must be connected with verification actions and must be connected with dialogues with others or theories. And the occurrence of accidental events is indeed unexpected.

---

1 Clarke, A. Born of Incidents but Thematic in Nature: Knowledge Construction in Practicum Settings[J]. *Canadian Journal of Education*, 1998(1):47-62.

2 Amy B. M. Tsui. *Pursuing Excellence: Case Studies in Teacher Professional Development*[M]. Translated by Chen Jing & Li Zhongru. Beijing: People's Education Press, 2003:50.

(2) Cooperation Requires Certain Prerequisites

Shulman's concept of "mediating theories" bridges theoretical frameworks and practical contexts, that is, to directly predict and control educational practical behaviors without taking theory as an inevitable rule. However, theory must serve as an element that provides teachers with reflection, monitoring and constraints. "Even if they are limited in scope and lifespan, they can make a critical contribution to practical thinking in education and increase the understanding of observed phenomena"[1]. In this way, on the one hand, theory does not have absolute guiding power, and on the other hand, practice cannot move towards absolute relativity without any constraints. In practice, the relationship between theory and practice is sometimes specifically manifested as the relationship between researchers and teachers. Currently, it has become a consensus that it is naturally inappropriate to simply use the authoritative judgment of knowledge to evaluate teachers' actions in situations. Meanwhile, there is another aspect to this problem. In communication, some teachers are used to passively waiting for researchers to announce the "correct answer", and even their expectation of the correct answer is that it can directly solve the problem rather than explain the problem. Communication between researchers and teachers is necessary, but the prerequisite for communication is the presence of teachers' subjectivity, accepting the adjustment or even "destruction" of their practical knowledge structures by theory. On the other hand, researchers also need to disassemble their theoretical knowledge structures of their own systematic logic, and learn to adapt, extract, criticize and create in changing, complex and chaotic situational problems.

---

1 Shulman, L. S. Theory, Practice and the Education of Professionals[J]. *International and Comparative Education*, 1999(3):36-40.

(3) Teacher Practical Knowledge Does Not Necessarily Have Universality

Teachers are the owners of knowledge, and they are also the creators of knowledge. The role positioning of teachers as researchers should be affirmed. However, this knowledge, creation and research should be properly defined and understood. Teachers' research is practical research, aiming at solving problems rather than constructing theories. Teachers' theoretical knowledge is manifested in the form of interpretation and application in specific situations and in the process of solving individual problems. In the process of application, teachers may enrich, develop, limit and revise theoretical understandings, but these creative understandings do not necessarily have universality. Of course, many teachers have the ability to verify practical knowledge and sublimate it into theory, but this only shows that they are playing two roles of knowledge holders and researchers. For most teachers, it is very difficult to do so. However, the practical knowledge of excellent teachers is only spread among their surrounding peers, which is limited after all. Moreover, as teachers retire, this practical knowledge will naturally disappear. Therefore, more theoretical workers are needed to take practical knowledge as the object of thinking, enter teachers' working situations, and use cognitive forms such as induction, generalization and refinement to process, sort out, sublimate and disseminate it, and finally complete the cycle of the reconstruction of theoretical knowledge through practical knowledge.

[Originally published in *Research in Educational Development* 2007(22) (Lv Lijie)]

20. The Structure and Approaches of Teacher Cooperative Teams

Chinese K-12 teachers have long maintained a tradition of collaborative practice. Since the 1950s, there has been a system of collective lesson preparation or collective meetings among teachers of the same subject or the same grade group. The new curriculum reform has changed China's curriculum policy. The state only provides macro curriculum standards, and teachers have the right and must redesign the curriculum. Some new curriculum types, such as comprehensive curriculum and comprehensive practical activities, also require teachers to implement them in a cooperative manner. The development of school-based curriculum requires teachers to explore in cooperation and mutual assistance. Teacher cooperation, as a way to promote curriculum development and ensure the effective implementation of the new curriculum, has been put forward again and received attention. The significance of teacher cooperation on school culture and the quality of school education has become a consensus. However, in reality, the advocacy of new social behaviors relies on school culture and school systems with strong inertia, and cooperation inevitably encounters problems.

I. Current Problems in Teacher Cooperation

(1) Some Cooperative Approaches Are Too Standardized, Making Some Teachers Passive in Cooperation

Since cooperation has been emphasized as an approach to teacher professional development after the new curriculum reform, cooperation has also become a symbol indicating the implementation degree of the new curriculum. Therefore, regularly held teacher seminar salons and new curriculum forums have become standardized cooperative modes for many school teachers. The operation of formal organizations requires unified action norms and coercive force. However, the true meaning of teacher cooperation is not the aggregation of overt behaviors but a kind of "fusion" of ideas accompanied by emotional integration. Mandating fixed timelines, venues, and agendas undermines professional autonomy and independence of each individual's thoughts and forcing teachers to think about problems that they do not discover or care about. Cooperation is the symbol of the implementation of the superior spirit in schools, and naturally it becomes the behavioral obligation of teachers to perform passively.

(2) In Some Cases, Administrative Power Oversteps Its Boundaries, Making Some Teachers Silent in Cooperation

Peer observation and assessment are approaches for teachers to expand their ideas and promote self-reflection. Meanwhile, while peer observation can foster reflection, when administrators participate as supervisors, it blurs the line between research and management and work quality. In the same two ways, the realization path is the same, but the purpose and meaning are different. When the team of observation and assessment includes school leaders and grade leaders, and these members with supervision and management rights do not properly change their roles, the line between research and management become blurred. Administrative power exceeds professional thinking, and teachers' recognition of managers' attitude has become a survival mode for self-preservation.

(3) The Alienation of Individual Performance Assessment Makes Some Teachers Resistant in Cooperation

The dehumanized examination culture has antagonized the relationship between colleagues in schools. When teachers face 'bottom-ranking elimination' due to poor class performance on final exams, who would like to share their experiences with colleagues? In management science, people are divided into "eagle" and "dove" types according to their competitive consciousness. People who are competitive and have more competitive consciousness than cooperative consciousness are "eagles". On the contrary, "dove" type people who like stability and do not require themselves to have outstanding achievements are easy to get along with colleagues. The alienated teacher assessment standards are strongly linked to teachers' welfare, status and even survival, turning all teachers into "eagles".

II. The First Effective Strategy for Teacher Cooperation: Create Structures

How can teachers cooperate effectively? Forming a teacher research team is considered one of the effective approach to teacher cooperation. Then, the structural characteristics of this community or this team should ensure the effectiveness of team cooperation.

Drawing from management science literature on high-performance teams in the workplace, work teams or high-performance teams often have the following characteristics. First, high-performance teams are usually relatively small in size. Second, in the process of cooperation, members have formed complementary skills - including technical skills, problem-solving and decision-making skills and interpersonal skills. Third, team members have formed a common and meaningful understanding of the team purpose that inspires pride and a sense of responsibility. Fourth, the team has a series of common, unquestionable goals directly related to the team's purpose. Fifth, team members invest time to understand how they will cooperate to achieve their purposes and goals and how to enhance the level of constructive conflict necessary for mutual trust and success. Sixth, the team has enough dedication and trust to shoulder the responsibilities of a team.[1]

Teacher education researchers MacLean and Mohr have also made quite detailed descriptions of the composition and characteristics of teacher cooperation teams in schools. They believe that a research team can have 3 to 5 members. They cooperate, question and promote each other regarding relevant

---

1 Katzenbach, J. R., & Smith, D. K. *The Wisdom of Teams*[M]. New York: Harper, 1993. Cited from: L.A.Baloche. *The Cooperative Classroom*[M]. Translated by Zeng Shouchui, *et al*. Shanghai: East China Normal University Press, 2005.

classroom practice problems and share the joy of cooperation. Such a team should have discussions twice a month during the school year. In the discussions, each member talks about his or her research situation in this stage, and other members listen carefully. At least one member in the team should have experience in teacher research. In the meetings of the research team, everyone shares what they have seen and heard, discusses and analyzes the data in the research logs, and makes the initial findings clear. Teachers forming a cooperation team can reduce the isolated state of teachers' work, share experiences, and solve problems. In order to make the team work more effective, the research group should include three elements: Members in the teacher cooperation organization have a common learning goal; Around this common learning goal, teachers work together, cooperate, and are actively interdependent, and work together to practice and achieve this goal; In the activities to achieve the goal, each individual teacher achieves professional growth on the original basis.[1] Our conclusion to related statements suggests that the effectiveness of teacher cooperative teams is related to the following necessary components.

(1) Stable and Appropriately Sized Membership

The number of team members is related to team cohesion. In a small-sized team, each person is an important pivot in forming the team, so that there will be rights and responsibilities belonging to each individual. Of course, staff turnover will also have a serious impact on the team. There also needs to be someone in the team who plays the role of a leader. The leader in this team may not necessarily hold an administrative position, but should be good at communication, have organizational skills, possess research experience, and have considerable professional judgment ability. His or her main responsibilities

---

1 MacLean, M, S. & Mohr, M. M. *Teacher-researchers at Work*[M]. Berkeley, California: National Writing Project, 1999.

are: reminding everyone to organize group meetings on schedule, mastering public contact information such as email addresses and phone numbers, selecting appropriate meeting venues, coordinating relationships to maintain team vitality, establishing team functions, establishing connections between teaching and research through team discussions when there are differences of opinion among team members, providing research methodologies, and providing guidance for team members, etc.[1]

(2) Common and Clear Work Goals

The formation of a team relies on the "common will" of a group. A clear goal is one of the most stable factors for the existence of a research team and is the driving force for teachers to cooperate, continue to cooperate, and focus on research issues. For example, jointly developing a curriculum, solving similar problems encountered in the classroom, etc. This "common will" is the core issue. When forming the team, if members do not have urgent problems to solve, or the team's goals are too macroscopic and cannot be achieved in the near future, cooperative research will become passive with additional work that has to be fulfilled, naking it inherently meaningless and inefficient.

(3) Team Identity

Team identity includes two aspects: one is the identity of members towards the team, and the other is the identity among members. A shared identity fosters adherence to norms and constructive dialogue during disagreements and communicate and tolerate fully when there are differences in opinions or even interests. Identity determines the formation of team culture.

(4) Members' Sense of Autonomy

The sense of autonomy seems to contradict the sense of identity. In fact,

---

1 MacLean, M. S. & Mohr, M. M. *Teacher-researchers at Work*[M]. Berkeley, California: National Writing Project, 1999.

the former should be the premise of the latter. The key is that team members have a sense of autonomy and pursue the same results. The sense of autonomy means the subjective presence of researchers and is a prerequisite for researchers to gain something, that is, discussions should have voices that truly come from their own thinking. This interpretation and judgment of problems based on one's own thinking may lead to disputes, but it is precisely in disputes or even stubbornness that the significance of ideas is revealed. The value of the subject and the development of the individual are both manifested in such confrontations.

(5) Research Problems Originate from Practices

Theory extracts certain attributes in entities and specific situations among entity objects and reveals them in a categorized manner, so that theoretical understanding can be deepened and developed. However, these already categorized attributes and theories necessarily cannot explain all the meanings of a new practical situation. Or rather, each practical situation is complex, mixed with subject laws, the individual characteristics of students, and the potential driving forces of social culture, etc. These factors are intertwined and sometimes even manifested in a mutually opposing and exclusive manner. Teachers need to make a relatively appropriate judgment and take actions in real and complex practical situations. Therefore, teachers' research problems must come from practice. Taking out these confusing and controversial problems from situations and exploring the reasons, attributes and rules behind them is a process of reflection and also a process of obtaining inspiration for actions. Although situations are unique and cannot be completely repeated, the constituent factors of the situations that teachers face are the same and interlinked. They can be felt, evaluated and shared through the commonality of thinking. The research on such situational problems is not simply "dealing with things as they are", nor deliberately pursuing the systematic nature of experience and theory, but reflecting and deliberating as much as possible the experiences and theories relavant to situational problems, carefully weighing and clarifying them to arrive at an appropriate decision for further action.

III. The Second Effective Strategy for Teacher Cooperation: Focus on Approaches

Once a teacher cooperation team has reasonable elements, how these elements are composed, that is, what the working approaches of these elements are, determines the cooperation effectiveness. Clatthorn believes that there are at least five ways for teacher groups to work together[1]: (1) Professional discussion; (2) Curriculum development; (3) Peer observation; (4) Peer coaching; (5) Action research. The collaborative teacher group activities that Johnson and others focused on are centered around classroom teaching activities. It can be a cycle of joint design, separate teaching and joint processing and analysis.[2] In this cycle, their work content can be summarized into six items: (1) Regular professional discussion of cooperative learning; (2) Members share the work of finding curriculum resources and methods by joint planning and design; (3) Teach cooperative curriculum separately or jointly, and deal with the results jointly; (4) Jointly evaluate whether the collaborative lesson is successful; (5) Jointly plan to revise, refine and improve the new curriculum; (6) Teach new curriculum separately or jointly. The existing cooperative research forms in school-based teaching and research in our country include: collective lesson preparation, peer observation, salon forum, mentoring system, project research and so on. We can categorize them into three major categories:

Conventional cooperation. Centered on practical challenges, grade-level or subject-based teachers engage in spontaneous reflection, argue, inspire and accept each other. This is a relatively loose team, which can appear in the daily

---

1 Good, T. L. & Brophy, J. E. *Looking in Classroom*[M]. Translated by Tao Zhiqiong, Wang Feng & Deng Xiaofang. Beijing: China Light Industry Press Ltd., 2002:1.

2 Johnson, D. W. *Leading the Cooperative School*[M]. Translated by Tang Zongqing, *et al.* Shanghai: Shanghai Educational Publishing House, 2003:198.

work of teaching and research groups, or in collective lesson preparation or teacher discussion meetings. The premise for this behavior to be called team cooperation is the spontaneity of problem raising, the unpredictability of conclusions, and even accompanied by continuous re-action and re-discussion.

Task-based cooperation. School-based curriculum in China's new curriculum can be brand-new curriculum independently developed by teachers, or they can be the editing and adaptation of national curriculum. In order to develop school-based curriculum, teachers of the same grade and the same subject, or teachers of different subjects under the same theme gather together. Their cooperation has specific goals and time limits. They jointly conduct curriculum design, cooperate in implementation, reflect and exchange experiences and gains and losses. The products of cooperation are not only the newly developed curriculum but also their self-development in mutual inspiration.

Developmental cooperation. Cooperating with universities to conduct project research can also have clear research purposes. If the project itself comes from real problems in classrooms and curriculum situations, teachers can obtain the motivation for continuous research in the harvest of the research. Teachers need to conduct research in teams to obtain motivation, strength and encouragement in interpersonal interdependence, and to obtain new information and new perspectives. Ultimately, teachers need to establish teams and conduct research to achieve development without administrative management, supervision, or even the guidance of theoretical researchers on the content.

[Originally published in *Teaching & Administration* 2007(15) (Lijie & Yu Cong)]

21. Effective Reflection of Classroom Assessment and Its Function Transition on Research
— A Section Which Contribute to the Research of Lesson Study and Its Enlightenment to Teachers' Professional Development

Classroom assessment denotes the evaluative judgment of instructional practices through methods like classroom observation. It can refer to teachers' assessment of students' academic achievements or classroom performance, or the assessment of teachers' teaching level and quality. This article refers to the latter. Classroom teaching assessment in China has experienced a process from disorder to order, and from managerialism to promoting teacher development.

I. Changes in Classroom Assessment and the Paradox of Effectiveness

Promoting teacher development is our current understanding of the classroom assessment function. Therefore, many studies focus on how to improve assessment methods: updating scales, adopting multiple assessment methods, and using multi-subject assessment methods, etc. However, in reality, assessment schemes are either not used or become barriers that restrict teachers' classroom performance.

(1) The Evolution of the Focus in Contemporary Classroom Assessment

Before the mid-1980s, classroom teaching assessment in China mainly relied on peer observation and assessment to judge teachers' teaching levels based on experience and guide teachers' teaching improvement, with problems such as being dominated by the will of superiors, subjectivity and arbitrariness. With the introduction of Western educational measurement and assessment techniques, some quantitative assessment methods, such as formulating the index system of classroom assessment, scale measurement, and quantitative processing and analysis techniques began to be used. Of course, these techniques did not completely replace the subjective assessment of observers, but rather served as a convincing evidence and a means of verification. Different from before, classroom assessment in this stage began to focus on clarifying the ideal goals of classroom teaching and used them as the basis for quantitative or subjective assessment. After the 1990s, with the change and development of educational and teaching concepts, people's expectations for the ideal classroom became increasingly rich and diverse. Consequently, the focus of classroom assessment also became increasingly diversified. However, the problem that emerged in classroom assessment was that although the scales were made more and more complete and the focuses of peer observation and teaching assessment became richer and richer, the differences between the assessed classrooms and regular classrooms became larger and larger, and even a special "course type" of "performance class" appeared. This stems from classroom assessment standards deriving from idealized classroom conceptions rather than authentic practice. For schools, such teacher assessment methods are only used in various forms of classroom assessment activities, semester inspections and master teacher competitions. In the atmosphere of exam-oriented culture, students' academic achievements are the real hidden yardstick for schools to assess teachers' work performance. What teachers really care about is how to improve students' exam scores. It is not surprising that such carefully crafted performance class, which are different from daily teaching, have emerged. In performance class, teachers try their best to meet the various goals of the assessor, organize student discussions, cultivate students' emotions, and encourage students to play their subjectivity. As a result, open classes become lively and full of variety, and once the open classes are over, everything returns to "normal". Such assessment can neither contribute to the improvement of teachers' work ability nor diagnose the root causes of their educational and teaching attitudes.

(2) Theoretical Limitations of Improving Classroom Assessment

Techniques

Paying attention to students, recognizing their subjectivity in the classroom, focusing on their activities and experiences in class, and concerning about the multiple value goals that classroom teaching brings to students are all the due pursuits of modern teaching concepts and should reasonably serve as the basis for classroom teaching assessment. However, these teaching concepts are pursuits at the conceptual level and are the standards that classroom teaching should achieve within a certain educational stage. Although this kind of expression has clear hierarchies and systems, and is easy to quantify, compare and manage, the problem is that these systems summarize and extract the commonalities from countless specific classrooms. When using these common standards to judge each specific classroom again, classrooms are all specific situations. Variations in lesson types (e.g., new content, review, practice) create context-specific complexities. They may also stem from differences in content - some content is suitable for teachers' clear presentation, while some content requires students' constructive experiences. Moreover, factors such as different subjects, different age groups, different teaching styles of teachers, students' original foundations and habits, and the established tacit understanding between teachers and students, may all play a role. Assessment rubrics embody idealized classroom attributes, often divorced from contextual realities. In fact, it is almost impossible to find a classroom that can meet all the requirements of the index system, and the attribute structure cannot be restored to each individual class. Therefore, the decomposition of the classroom assessment index system as a pursuit at the conceptual level in a technical way is to express a diachronic problem in a synchronic manner. After clarifying the ontological characteristics of the classroom assessment index system, let's examine how this index system is used. It is not surprising that the classroom assessment index system is used as a yardstick to measure teachers' classroom teaching levels and attitudes. The problem lies in how it is used. Due to its clear organization and ease of quantification, it has the qualities of being simple and easy to operate and objectively measurable. School administrators directly link the test results of the index system with teachers' professional titles, bonuses and honors, etc., and use it to perform management and reduce losses caused by differences in opinions. And the basis for this inspection or the index system is a certain teaching inspection class, open class, observation class, or competition class. This is equivalent to requiring teachers to display the tasks that need to be completed in a certain stage in a single class. The paradox suggests that the improvement of classroom assessment not only requires enriching and adjusting the focus and content orientation of assessment with modern teaching concepts but also needs to adjust its usage mode.

(3) Functional Limitations of Improving Classroom Assessment Techniques

The ultimate significance of assessment lies in promoting the improvement of education and teaching quality and the development of students through changes in teachers' behaviors. For a comprehensive examination of a certain cross-section of the teaching process, some functional negative effects are manifested as follows. Firstly, in terms of the management effect, such assessment can hardly bring about fundamental changes in teachers' teaching attitudes and behaviors. Such assessment is separated from the teaching process. Its occurrence is intermittent and accidental, while the real teaching process is difficult to predict, diagnose and examine. Secondly, during the assessment process, teachers undergo subtle psychological shifts that may influence assessment outcomes, and even affect their feelings about profession as individuals. A survey on teachers' psychological reactions in teaching assessment[1] shows that before the assessment, teachers will have psychological states such as suspicion, nervousness, and being on trial. During the assessment, there will be psychological states such as catering, resistance, perfunctory

1 Cai Min & Feng Ying. Investigation on Teachers' Psychological Reaction in Teaching Assessment[J]. *Journal of the Chinese Society of Education*, 2006(1):65-68.

attitude and defense. After the assessment, there will be adverse psychological states such as sensitivity, embellishment and argumentation. The reason is that during the assessment process, the assessment subject and the teaching subject are completely separated or in a relatively opposing relationship of scrutinizing and being scrutinized. In a passive psychological state, it is difficult for teachers to sincerely reflect and effectively improve. Finally, even if teachers adopt a positive attitude in the assessment and are ready to obtain inspection and verification from the assessment to promote the improvement of their behaviors, the information that such assessment can provide to teachers is incomplete and limited, just some conclusions about good or bad. Moreover, these conclusions about good or bad are only based on some fragmentary facts and do not necessarily have statistical significance, or they do not deeply examine the reasons, situations and experiences behind these fragments. It is even more difficult for teachers to distinguish exactly what is good and bad, and how to grasp the degree of good or bad and so on. In reality, due to the limitations of the assessment function, "these assessment standards and indexes are rarely used for real classroom teaching assessment, or it can be said that there are hardly any research reports on the application of a certain assessment standard and index to classroom teaching. The classroom teaching assessment system, which was originally designed with strong applicability has become a purely theoretical concept, lacking practical application. Therefore, although researchers have continuously introduced one assessment system after another, they ultimately prove to be nothing more than passing clouds. In practice, educational administrators or teachers still rely on their own experiences to create an assessment system respectively"[1].

---

1 Ding Chaopeng. Overview, Problems and Ideas of Classroom Teaching Assessment Research in China[J]. *Educational Science Research*, 2006(12):10.

Ⅱ. Developmental Classroom Assessment: Proposals and Research Functions

In recent years, more and more scholars believe that the function of classroom assessment does not lie in managing and supervising teachers' work. More importantly, it is to promote teachers' professional development through classroom assessment and finally achieve the purpose of improving the quality of education and teaching. When summarizing the assessment reform in the new basic education experiment, Professor Ye Lan describes developmental teacher assessment like this: "Our purpose is not only to assess the results (whether phased or final), nor is it just to understand and explain the facts. Instead, it aims to discover the problems and experiences in the reform process and the different levels reached by teachers through assessment, and form an abstraction of the new classroom teaching process structure. Our purpose is not only to stay at the formation and improvement of process understanding but also to promote teachers' self-reflection and our own reflection on research through assessment. This is a kind of assessment that combines researchers, practitioners and evaluators. It is a very comprehensive and complex assessment facing the practice of reform. What it needs to form is not just an assessment tool but a series of assessment systems that serve the realization of the above goals. It can only be gradually explored and created by us in the process of reform."[1] Whether the function of promoting teachers' professional development can be realized, the key to the problem lies not only in the rationalization of the assessment content and structure but also in in what way this function is used, through identification or research. The characteristics of teachers' professional development determine that the assessment of teachers also needs process and humanity. Classroom assessment needs to be combined with the research model

---

1 Ye Lan. & Wu Yaping. Reform of Classroom Teaching and Reform of Classroom Teaching Evaluation[J]. *Educational Research*, 2003(8).

that guides teachers' development to be truly a classroom assessment that is beneficial to teachers' professional development. The integration of research, teaching, and assessment lies at the core of developmental teacher assessment. In such a model system, the following can be provided for teachers:

1. Research ideas and methods. In the mechanism of integrating research, teaching and assessment, both assessor and assessee play the role of researchers at the same time. Joint research activities can start as early as the preparation stage of classroom teaching. They jointly research students, curriculum content, and teaching plans. In this process, teachers obtain a research idea and an expanded vision, while assessors can truly understand the background of the classroom, teachers' foundations, abilities, advantages and deficiencies.

2. Contextualized comments and reflections. The core of technical classroom assessment lies not in the assessment technology itself, but in the fact that users rely on the objectivity and scientificity of the technology and use a general standard or scale to measure each specific classroom. In the integrated assessment, assessors do not determine the right or wrong, good or bad of teachers' classroom performance by referring to certain standards. Instead, they try their best to collect information in the classroom as a basis for joint discussion and reflection with teachers. Teachers' choices in the classroom are the results of the game among various situational elements. The rationality of choice is specific, and it is difficult to have absolute standards. Only in the interaction between assessors' comments and teachers' reflective activities can there be profound ideological activities and cognitive transitions.

3. Individualized and continuous information for teachers' development. In the process of combining assessment with research and teaching, long-term cooperation between assessors and assessed teachers is required. Assessors obtain information on teachers' growth process. Assessment can be formative or intra-individual difference-based. Only this assessment process that is not based on management purposes can truly produce management effects.

III. Research-oriented Assessment in the Research of Lesson Study Model: Functions and Implications

(1) The Research of Lesson Study: A Teacher Professional Development Model Integrating Research, Teaching and Assessment

The research of lesson study refers to the professional development process of teachers, which involves collective lesson preparation, teaching observation, collaborative work and systematic reflection for a lesson's teaching content to achieve more effective teaching and learning. Its ultimate purpose is to enable students to learn more effectively. It is a form of action research. Teachers are both educators and researchers, reflecting through actions and conducting more effective teaching through reflection. It is also a way of collaborative learning. Through teachers' collective lesson preparation, pre-class and post-class meeting exchanges, peer observation and assessment and other collaborative work, the goal of common improvement is achieved. The research of lesson study has different manifestations in different countries and regions. For example, in Japan, such activities are called "Lesson Study", with a history of more than 50 years. It "is a cooperative research within the scope of classroom activities"[1]. In Japan, teachers regard professional development and the progress of teaching skills as a lifelong pursuit. They believe that personal experience, self-study, colleagues' criticism and self-reflection are important components of the professionalization process. Teachers are divided into different groups according to subjects and grades to prepare a "research lesson". Each group holds regular meetings, carefully discusses the learning content of the research lesson, determines its key points, and analyzes whether these key points can reflect students' learning difficulties. Then, teaching is designed according to the difficulties, and one of the teachers will teach the lesson. The whole process

---

1 Matoba, M. *Lesson Study: International Perspective on Policy and Practice*[M]. Beijing: Educational Science Publishing House, 2006:1-2.

lasts about one month to one year. Finally, teachers share the results of the seminar with teachers from other schools through seminars or publications. Many Japanese educational practices have been noticed by Western educators, and they have tried the possibility of applying them in the United States and other countries. Some American scholars have studied the teaching videos of teachers in Japan, Germany, and the United States[1], systematically introduce the role of Japanese lesson study research in teachers' professional development and the possibility of applying this model in the United States from different perspectives of teachers' professional development in the three countries. In recent years, many educational scholars in many states in the United States have joined action research plans similar to the research of lesson study. In Hong Kong, China, this research has emerged over the past decade. It originates from the practice and thinking of the basic education reform at the turn of the century in Hong Kong, referring to the "Lesson Study" model in Japan, borrowing from the teaching and research practices of China's mainland, and using the Theory of Variation as the theoretical framework for implementing the research of lesson study. After the practice of multiple research lessons, a model for systematically carrying out the research has been gradually formed.[2]

In the research of lesson study, the determination of research questions marks the beginning and provides direction for the study. The questions can be general ones - such as how to stimulate students' interest in learning mathematics, or specific ones - such as how to improve students' understanding of adding fractions with different denominators. They usually come from teachers' teaching practices and problems existing in students' learning. Collective lesson preparation is to verify certain viewpoints in specific

---

1 Stigler, J. W. & Hiebert, J. *The Teaching Gap*[M]. The Free Press, 1999:112-115.

2 Lu Minling, Pang Yongxin & Zhi Peimin. *Catering for Individual Differences through Learning Studies*[M]. Translated by Li Shuying & Guo Yongxian. Beijing: Educational Science Publishing House, 2006: VIII.

classroom situations on the basis of teachers' looking up relevant materials for this lesson after choosing learning goals. The goal of the research lesson is not only to design a good lesson but also to understand the reasons and ways in which classroom practice promotes students' understanding of learning content. After the initial teaching plan is determined, feedback is usually solicited at the school faculty meeting and then modifications are made to prepare for implementation. When the curriculum is implemented, except for the presenting teacher, other members of the research group put aside their own teaching work and go to the teaching site to observe the class. When students are required to think, discuss, research, and learn by themselves, the observing teachers should walk around, observe students' learning situations and make detailed records, and sometimes videotape them. After the teaching is completed, the teachers in the research group immediately organize a meeting. Usually, the presenting teacher speaks first, summarizing his or her teaching situation and existing problems. Then other teachers make assessments on the problems existing in each section of the teaching. The focus of such assessment is on classroom teaching, not on the presenting teacher. Because this lesson is the result of collective work, the process of teachers' assessment is that of their own work and a process of self-improvement of teaching activities. Based on observation and reflection, the teachers in the research group modify the curriculum plan according to the misunderstandings of students on a certain problem shown in the curriculum implementation process. This modification may involve changes in learning materials, changes in activities, and a refinement of questions asked, etc. Once the revised curriculum plan is determined, this lesson will be implemented in another different class. It can be the teacher of the previous lesson who continues to teach, but usually, another teacher in the research group will teach. The difference is that this time, all teachers in the school are invited to participate in the research lesson. After this lesson is completed, all teachers in the school are invited to participate in the exchange, and assess and reflect on the progress of the research lesson. Sometimes, external experts are also invited. Just like the previous procedure, the presenting teacher speaks first, elaborating on the goals that the research group tries to achieve, assessing the successful parts of this lesson and the parts that requires reconsideration. Other observing teachers analyze the research lesson and put forward suggestions. However, the assessment and analysis of the research lesson should respect students' learning achievements, as well as the value assumptions guiding the design of the research lesson and the research design under these assumptions. There are several different ways to share the final results. One is that the research group writes a research report, stating the stories in the work process of the research group. Sometimes, these reports are published in book form for school teachers, principals, and even policymakers in the education field to read. Another way to share the results is to invite teachers from other schools to observe the class during the implementation of the revised curriculum plan.

(2) Implications of the Research of Lesson Study for Assessment

The ultimate goal of assessment is to foster teacher professional growth. However, the exertion of this promoting function should be grounded in practical foundations, with questions being raised in a targeted manner. Since each teacher faces unique practical challenges, the initiation of the research of lesson study provides targeted solutions to this issue.

As a collaborative model for teacher development, the research of lesson study generally consists of the following steps: problem exploration, curriculum design, on-site teaching, effectiveness assessment, lesson plan rewriting, re-teaching, assessment and reflection, and finally outcomes sharing. Teachers remain actively engaged throughout this process. From the perspective of assessment, such a research process that lasts for a certain period of time can give us the following implications:

1. Keep a normal mindset and view assessment from a long-term perspective. All participants, whether they are researchers, practitioners, or assessors, should view the whole process of the activity with a normal mind. Each assessment has an indicative function and does not have a conclusive value. Each research process of lesson study adheres to such a value assumption: The

improvement of teaching quality is a continuous and gradual development process. The research on a lesson needs to go through several rounds of repeated discussions, designs and re-implementations. Therefore, the significance of assessment lies in its continuous correction of each link, guiding the development of the research of lesson study to move towards the ideal state.

2. The goal of assessment returns to students' development. The most critical dimension of assessment in the research of lesson study is the improvement of students' learning performance, instead of giving teachers an assessment of good, medium or bad. All participants focus on students' academic levels and classroom performances, and teachers' performances serve as the process and means to achieve students' development. Such assessment can avoid some formal and trifling issues as much as possible.

3. The focus of assessment is positioned on teaching work rather than teachers themselves. The classroom research process is a collaborative process of a group, and its effectiveness ultimately depends on the continuous efforts of all teachers in the group. Although each research lesson is finally implemented by a teacher and the individual ability of the teacher is important, the continuous improvement of the research of lesson study still depends on the long-term efforts of the research team and their reflective design on methodological issues, rather than on the individual strength of an excellent teacher. Teachers should analyze the factors involved in and underlying their teaching work, rather than turning the assessment process into an assessment of an individual teacher's personal abilities.

4. Assessment is targeted at specific classroom situations. Each research lesson occurs in a specific classroom situation, with specific students, specific teachers and specific curriculum. Therefore, the assessment should avoid one problem: "Borrowism" - using others' standards to measure one's own practice. Abstract standards are always cold, while specific classrooms are rich and colorful. In specific classroom learning environments, the assessment should make specific and detailed value judgments on the problems emerging in the

classroom.

5. Teachers become one of the main assessors. There are many factors that promote the development of the research of lesson study, such as students, parents and administrative managers. However, teachers are the main driving force for its development. In the process of conducting research lessons, teachers jointly identify the problem, design the curriculum, implement them together, observe each other and reflect together. They are firsthand participants and experiencers of classroom teaching, who best understand students' needs and the real-world problems. Their assessment of problems provides an important perspective.

(3) The Leading Value of the Research of Lesson Study for Teacher Professional Development

The research of lesson study, as a kind of teamwork, takes the goals of student development and teacher professional development as its working purposes. Within a certain period, through the collective efforts of group members in several aspects such as identifying research problems, designing the curriculum, conducting on-site teaching, assessing and reflecting, and redesigning, it continuously improves the design and implementation of each research lesson. The research of lesson study, as a form and part of teacher professional development, enables teachers participating in the research to achieve different degrees of professional development.

1. Expectations for the future. Every teacher has a wonderful expectation in his or her heart, which is to become an outstanding teacher. This aspiration is especially evident in the early stage of their career. Therefore, they always hope to develop their profession through various forms of training. The initiation of the research of lesson study can effectively preserve and continue this expectation. It incorporates teacher professional development into a standardized form and becomes the greatest motivation for teachers to participate in research.

2. The power of the collective. The research of lesson study is a kind of teamwork and also a way of collaborative learning. Driven by the common goal, each member of the team can divide the work, cooperate with each other, and pool their wisdom together, thus continuously improving the quality of the research of lesson study. For example, in the research lessons in Hong Kong, China, each lasts 3 to 4 months, which involves a large amount of work, including selecting learning content from a variety of curriculum resources, conducting pre-tests on students, using the Theory of Variation to identify the key attributes of learning content, designing the curriculum, implementing observations, collecting and analyzing data, etc. These tasks cannot be completed by one person alone. Therefore, the research of lesson study is an excellent way to achieve personal development with the help of the collective. It is through this way that teachers carry out their professional development.

3. The wisdom of reflection. Through the research of lesson study, teachers must break away from the state of simply repeating existing teaching behaviors based on experience, and begin to reflect on their own teaching and students' learning results. The feedback from other teachers on the problems emerging in practice and their observations of teaching behaviors can always touch teachers and make them think about the problems. Reflecting on the problems in their own practice enables teachers to gradually move from heteronomy to self-discipline, consciously recognize and adjust their teaching behaviors in practice, and form a strong sense of professional development. The role of reflection lies in its capacity to make teachers generate a process of cognitive reconstruction of their habitual practices, so as to construct more effective ways of thinking and problem-solving methods in the process of thinking and communication.

4. Communication and cooperation. The research of lesson study enables teachers to step out of their respective "castles" and conduct systematic reflections on collective work outcomes. In the process of communication, different views of teachers on the same issue will be of great benefit to expanding their horizons. Different depths of understanding of the same issue

by teachers will also bring different surprises to different teachers. It is through dialogues in a common context that teachers discuss, reflect on and correct cases that they have personally experienced, continuously improving their professional levels.

IV. Classroom Assessment: From Management to Research

The proposal of the concept of developmental assessment has shifted the focus of the assessment function back to the fundamental issue of teacher development. However, under the guidance of the developmental concept, there can be quite different approaches to establishing an assessment system, such as expanding the assessors to include teachers, peers, principals, and students in the assessment activities, increasing the frequency of assessment, or focusing on the generative elements in the classroom. In such an assessment reform, assessment still serves management, or rather, it is still used to distinguish the work level for the purpose of evaluating professional titles, increasing salaries, and awarding bonuses. It remains trapped in the paradox of technical classroom assessment. The traditional workflow of planning, organizing, implementing, and assessing embodies managerialism that were prevalent in the first half of the 20th century. Their main purpose was to maximize work efficiency through strengthened control, and their assumption about human nature was that human behavior could be changed through supervision, restraint or interest-driven. Since the middle of the 20th century, various social trends of thought have been criticizing and correcting this way of managing people from different perspectives. Teaching work requires wisdom and enthusiasm. Each teacher's work is a link in the chain of students' growth process, but each teacher's work is completed independently. Therefore, fundamental changes in teachers' work attitudes and abilities require more democratic, personalized, and professional leadership styles. Teachers need to grow in a culture where they are respected and make efforts to achieve greater achievements. If teachers' work quality is divided into good, medium, and bad or first, second, and third prizes based on a certain class, it will only create a highly sensitive or overly competitive mentality. As the core purpose of classroom assessment shifts to cultivating teacher professionalism and achieve high-quality classrooms, assessment needs to be operated in a new mechanism which does not aim at management but at research. The research off lesson study model provides us with a reference framework. Assessment activities are integrated into teaching and research through collaborative planning and implementation between assessors and teachers. This constitutes a framework for teacher professional development and classroom quality improvement, where assessment functions as one of the service steps. Of course, the normal and orderly operation of schools requires management activities. In fact, in a research-oriented assessment framework, the management function will also naturally emerge. The differences in teachers' abilities and levels will be more clearly demonstrated in the process of research, discussion, and teaching. However, this demonstration, accompanied by professional guidance and mutual communication, will make teachers more convinced of the assessment around them. Through leading rather than supervising, the ultimate significance of teacher professional development and classroom assessment can be truly realized.

[Originally published in *Journal of Northeast Normal University (Philosophy and Social Sciences)* 2007(2) (Lijie & Zhao Tongyou)]

www.ingramcontent.com/pod-product-compliance
Lightning Source LLC
LaVergne TN
LVHW010637110826
845149LV00014B/2863

* 9 7 8 1 9 6 7 2 7 7 4 0 7 *